Certified in Production and Inventory Management

Master Planning Reprints

Articles selected by the
Master Planning Committee
of the APICS Curricula and Certification Council

©1991 The American Production and Inventory Control Society, Inc.
International Standard Book Number: 1-55822-040-2
Library of Congress Number: 91-71923

Stock No. 05014, 6/91, 5,000

Please note that these reprints are a compilation of articles from various publications. Therefore, the quality of reproduction may vary.

Table of Contents

Preface

This compilation of master planning articles consists of materials published by the American Production and Inventory Control Society in its various journals, proceedings, and similar forums. The articles have been selected by the APICS Curricula and Certification Council's Master Planning Committee. Although the articles were chosen because they are of high quality and report on important topics, during the selection process some very good articles may have been overlooked and others may have been excluded because of subject matter.

The field of production and inventory management is dynamic. Personnel working in this field will continue to demand updated definitions as well as additions to the body of knowledge. This volume is a modest attempt to answer that demand, but clearly it is not the definitive work. On the issue of scope, the consensus was that the book should augment existing textbooks, training aids, etc. Article selection in this book has been made on key tips, how-to pieces, and case examples. The assumption is that the reader is knowledgeable about the basics and is looking for additional insights.

Some of the articles are preceded by an annotation page, written by Tom Vollmann, a former member of the committee. The primary purpose of the annotation is to point out the key contribution of each article and what the reader should gain by careful study.

We welcome recommendations for future inclusions from the APICS membership. The committee may be contacted through society headquarters.

Master Planning Committee

Roy Martins, CFPIM (Chairperson)
R. Leonard Allen, CFPIM
John J. Bruggeman, CFPIM
Steve Chapman, CPIM
Carol L. Davis, CPIM
Susan Haythornthwaite, CPIM
Mike Hunter, CFPIM
Ann Marucheck, CFPIM
Blair Williams, CPIM

Reprinted from the APICS *1975 Conference Proceedings.*

FORECASTING FOR INVENTORY CONTROL

By H. Lawrence Abbott
Crompton & Knowles Corporation

What is meant by forecasting?
  Why do we need a forecast?
    How do you implement a forecasting system?

Today, I will address these questions and show how the results of the forecasting model you chose can be applied in the control of inventories. I will cover some of the forecasting models and techniques which are more easily used, how to monitor the results and how to combine into the forecast, consideration of predictive or special knowledge information. Finally, I would like to mention some thoughts on getting started in implementing your forecasting and inventory system and some of the pitfalls to be recognized or avoided.

Forecasting is a subject that has been a constant and great concern to me. It is a subject that has consumed much of my time and one that involves all levels of management. For it is on forecasts that management, whether sales, finance, inventory control, or production control, bases it's planning. Without forecasting, no matter how simple or complicated, no one could plan for the tomorrows.

First, let me leave with you two very important thoughts; one, the forecast is an element of an Inventory Control System, and two, the forecast should seldom be used as a single value estimate, but should be accompanied by, at least, an estimate of its range - a high and low value or a frequency distribution. As a single value, the forecast is as useful as the statement that 'the average family has 1-1/2 children'. Then what is a system? A system is a set of elements joined together to perform specific tasks, to achieve a common goal. In our case, this common goal might be described as 'having the right product at the right place at the right time while balancing the economic factors of acquiring inventory versus holding inventory'. Our system should then determine:

1. How Much To Order
   Depends on:
   a. Future demand or forecast
   b. Costs - unit, order and holding
2. When To Order
   Depends on:
   a. Forecast of demand over the lead time
   b. Standard Deviation of forecast over lead time
   c. Service level desired
3. Reasonableness of The Forecast
   a. Monitors forecast vs demand
      to determine:
      (1) When demand out of the realm of the forecast or model
      (2) When forecast error calls for a change in smoothing constant
   b. Other statistical values which describe the error distribution of the forecast

WHAT IS MEANT BY FORECASTING? Webster says: "To calculate or predict (some future event or condition) usually as a result of rational study and analysis of available pertinent date". (1) Brown(2) however, prefers to divide the subject into two areas: 1. forecasting and 2. prediction. I will refer to these classes in the same way. The first type of estimate often uses 'time-series analysis' of the past in anticipating the future. So we may say that forecasting is the process of estimating events or value of events which may occur in the future. By using a series of these historical values, we can make or calculate a guess as to the next event or value. Later, when the value is known, we profit by the error and use this information as a correcting factor when arriving at the next value. Thus the forecast is never final, it is constantly being updated by the latest information. The future is uncertain and forecasts are seldom accurate, but any forecast with an estimate of it's range is usually better than no forecast. So we must constantly strive to find better ways to protect against this uncertainty. We do this by using scientific techniques for forecasting and by using the distribution of the errors of the forecast. Sherlock Holmes said, "One forms provisional theories and waits for time or fuller knowledge to explode them".

Prediction, on the other hand, can be thought of as an estimate based on what these values mean. It is a subjective process using intuition, indepth analysis and other known factors which can affect these future events. Factors such as experience, marketing plans, competition, economic conditions, political climate, and geography are often used. As a result, prediction is probably more accurate but takes longer to arrive at an answer, usually longer than we in PIC, can afford to wait.

Forecasting also can be either long range or short range. For our purposes of inventory and production control, short range forecasting is used. It usually encompasses less than a year, is frequently updated and is quite often a calculated forecast. On the other hand, long range forecasting extends over several years and is used in planning the future of the enterprise, manpower requirements, capital needs such as plant and equipment, etc. Figure 1 shows the flow of information for short and long range forecasts.

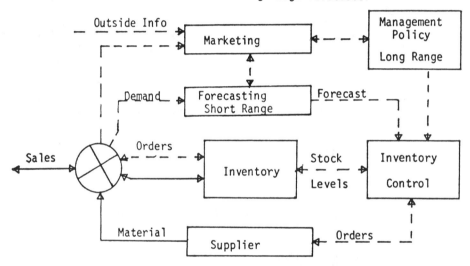

Figure 1. Information Flow

WHY DO WE NEED FORECASTS?
To plan for our customer's future needs since we cannot acquire raw material, manufacture and deliver these needs instantaneously. Since lead times are involved in the process of acquisition, manufacturing and delivering, we are not only concerned with the forecast for that future period when we receive the order, but must also know the forecast of sales over the lead time periods as well.

Once we have the forecast (a type of moving average) and the measure of its expected variability (standard deviation), we can calculate a safety stock that will protect us against repeated high sales over the lead time. This can be done and justified economically. But too often, we become preoccupied with the accuracy of forecasts, we blame the forecast or forecaster for shortages or excess when instead we should be looking at the system and improving it. For it is a fact of life that forecasts will seldom be accurate.

The basic and more familiar forms of the short-range forecast are:
- A. Forecasts prepared by individuals
- B. Moving Averages
- C. Least Squares
- D. Statistical Forecasts
  1. Exponential
  2. Discounted Multiple Regression
  3. Adaptive
  4. Period to Period

A. <u>Forecasts prepared by individuals</u> - These are usually recognized as lists of products with spaces that are to be filled in by someone with a 'guestimate' for the next week, month, quarter, etc. These forecasts are often biased. This bias will be affected by who completes the form. Sales personnel tend to be optimistic and forecast for inventory if supplies for a product have been tight, are less likely to reflect loss of business by a reduced forecast. Also, the forecast prepared by an individual is lacking in the continuity necessary for developing a measure of the error so that value can be used in developing safety stock levels since he does not include the range - high and low values.

B. <u>Moving Averages</u> - The unweighted moving average is a lagging value. A 12 month moving average has the mean centered after the 6th month, not at the more recent month. This approach was used extensively before the computer and prior to Brown's introduction to statistical forecasting in 1957.[3] An added disadvantage is the need to store the latest 12 monthly values.

C. <u>Least Squares</u> - is an arthmetial device for fitting a line to a set of data. It has the form

$$y = b + mx \qquad (1)$$

where the level component or y intercept (b) and the trend component (m) are calculated to form an equation for a straight line. From equation (1) a forecast can be extrapolated using (x) for the number of periods from the origin of data. But, this forecast is an extension of the total historical data used and is not weighted towards the present. It is a better model than the 12 month moving average since it provides a trend value. But, here again a lot of calculations are required to continually refit the line and you must retain 12 or more months of data. However, least squares is excellent for initializing the statistical forecasts described next.

D. <u>Statistical forecasts</u> are nothing more than the mathametical treatment of discrete time series. This is nothing new, but Brown[3] should be credited with the simplification, popularization and application of a special kind of weighted moving average which he dubbed, and we know as "exponential smoothing".[3,pp13] The earliest applications of this technique was developed by Brown for IBM's IMPACT[5] working with Bergen Drug[6] and Ralph's Grocery[7].

1. Exponential smoothing - to get a new estimate of the demand we take the old estimate and add (or subtract) a fraction of the error between the actual demand and the old estimate.

New Estimate = Old Estimate + H (Demand - Old Estimate)   (2)

Note: The letter H is used here as representing α, the Greek letter Alpha or the smoothing constant and is 0>H>1, but most often .05 to 0.5.

Expression (2) may be rearranged to give

New Estimate = H·Demand + (1-H) Old Estimate   (3)

This approach has a big advantage over the regular moving average in that only the value for the new estimate and α need be stored.

Note, that when H = .1 in (3), that the latest demand is weighted at 10% with exponentially lesser weights given to each preceding month such that 19 months of history is representative. Brown[3] relates the months of representative data 'N' to H by the following expressions:

$$H = 1 - B^2 \qquad (4)$$

$$B^2 = \frac{N - 1}{N + 1} \qquad (5)$$

then
$$H = 1 - \frac{N - 1}{N + 1} \qquad (6)$$

$$N = \frac{2 - H}{H} \qquad (7)$$

Equation (3) is a horizontal model without trend or seasonality. If trend is present, then Second Order or Third Order Exponential Smoothing can be used. The 1st three orders of expontential smoothing, where X is Demand, have the following equations:

$$S_t = H*X_t + (1 - H)S_{t-1} \qquad (8)$$

$$SS_t = H*S_t + (1 - H)SS_{t-1} \qquad (9)$$

$$SSS_t = H*SS_t + (1 - H)SSS_{t-1} \qquad (10)$$

Double smoothing is used more often than triple smoothing. With double, H should be one-half the value used for single smoothing in order to have the same time span represented. The double smoothed forecast consists of a Level and a Trend component after updating (8) & (9).

$$Level = 2*S_t - SS_t \qquad (11)$$

$$Trend = SS_t - SS_{t-1} \qquad (12)$$

$$Fcst_{t+1} = Level + Trend \qquad (13)$$

which may be written
$$FCST_{t+1} = 2*S_t - SS_{t-1} \qquad (14)$$

To extrapolate the forecast, use (13) and multiply the trend by the months away from t+1.

Seasonal data can be smoothed using 1st order and a seasonal or base index B1.

$$S_t = H \frac{X_t}{BI_t} + (1 - H)S_{t-1} \qquad (15)$$

$$FCST_{t+1} = S_t * BI_{t+1} \qquad (16)$$

Where the seasonal index is revised by smoothing by
$$BI_t = V * \frac{X_t}{S_t} + (1 - V)BI_t \qquad (17)$$

The index smoothing factor V should be chosen by experience, but is often 0.2 or 0.3

2. Discounted Multiple Regression - This is a class of exponential model proposed by Brown[9] which has the effect of moving the time axis origin to the most recent data point-that is to now.[8,pp8-21] The two models we will consider here are the linear with trend and the seasonal or sinusoid models.

a. The linear model resembles the lease squares formula (1) shown here as
$$F_{t+u} = A1 + A2*u \qquad (18)$$

To update the model we will first find the error (E) between the forecast for this month and the forecast.

$$E_t = X_t - F_t \qquad (19)$$

then move the time to now and smooth in the error

New Level $A1_t = A1_{t-1} + A2_{t-1} + H_{1t}(E_t)$ (20)

New Trend $A2_t = A2_{t-1} + H(E)$ (21)

where H_1 and H_2 are the smoothing constants. To initialize, we use the least squares calculation for the last 12-24 periods, set A1 to period 1 and A2 to the trend and smooth thru the initial data to settle the system. The smoothing constants H are chosen using the formulas (4) thru (7) plus an additional equation for H_2 of

$$H_2 = (1 - \sqrt{B^2})^2$$ (22)

If N = 19 then $H_1 = 0.1$ and $H_2 = 0.00263$

b. The Seasonal Model - It is expressed as a function of time T. Since we are limited in time and the initialization and update are involved, I will refer you to Brown[9] and [8,pp19-12] for a detailed discussion on the sinusoid model. IBM application program COGS[10], which you might wish to consider as your forecasting module, incorporates these discounted multiple regression models.

$$F_{t+T} = A1_t + A2_t*T + A3_t*Sin30*T + A4_t*COS30*T +$$

$$A5_t*Sin60*T + A6_t*Cos60*T + \ldots\ldots$$

$$A13_t*Sin180*T + A14_t*Cos180*T$$ (23)

Each coefficient A is updated using the error E and has its own smoothing constant. The use of this model is only possible on computers, but it will easily fit seasonal data such as Figure 2. A minimum of 24 periods with 36 periods preferred must be used to initialize using least squares. Because the coefficients are constantly being adapted to the changing requirements of the data, these two models are often referred to as Adaptive Smoothing.

3. Adaptive Models - The P&IC Handbook[8,PP8-23] refers to this group of models as those whose factors are being changed by the current performance of the model. In most cases, the forecasting models are those mentioned above, but algorithims for revising the smoothing constants based on the error have been devised. I divide these into two types; (a) where the monitoring system causes the constant to be changed to one to three pre-calculated constants, 'normal', 'fast' or 'panic' "Alpha" by use of a tracking signal, and (b) where the smoothing constant is continiously re-calculated such that an infinite number of values for 'Alpha' is possible. Three of these, "Trigg & Leach Modification", "Burgess Model" and "Dudman Model" are covered in the P&IC Handbook. A word of caution, be sure to thoroughly test this type of model, for there is a tendency for the model to use the trend for tracking and thus causing negative or high values to occur when extrapolating out 4-8 periods.

4. Period to Period - This is my name for a procedure to handle lumpy demand. I describe an item as having lumpy demand when, over a three month period, two of the months have demand less than 20% of the average for the three months. Whether this item should be forecast or estimated at all will depend on the industry and the value of the demand. More often it will be a 'C' product and not justify carrying safety stock, but still be required to service customer's needs.

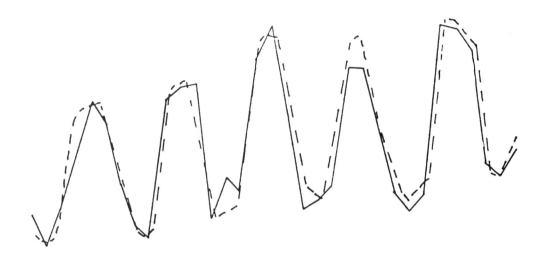

Figure 2. Seasonal Data and Forecast

In the dye business, we have many such items that are demanded only once a quarter. We usually handle these by projecting last quarter's demand into the same month of the next quarter. Another alternative is to use a simple three months moving average for the lumpy items. Whatever methodology you use, keep it simple, but be sure to include procedures which will recognize a significant change in demand and hence a change in forecasting model.

HOW DO WE HANDLE PREDICTATIVE OR SPECIAL KNOWLEDGE INFORMATION? Prior to the time of the forecast update by the computer, the product manager, marketing manager, salesmen and market research may be considering what quantitive effects their promotional plans, sales effort or business trends will have upon a particular product, family of products or the company as a whole. Once determined, these values should be reflected in the forecast at the time of the update.

Let us take equation (18) where A1 is the level component and A2 the trend with values of 1000 and 50 respectively. Then the forecast for the next 6 periods where u = 1-6 is

$$F = 1000 + 50*u$$

Month	1	2	3	4	5	6
Forecast	1000	1100	1150	1200	1250	1300

Table 1. Forecast Extrapolation

if we want to increase the level of business to include a new customer at 500 per month we set AA1 equal 500 for this update and equation (20) becomes

$$A1_t = A1_{t-1} + A2_{t-1} + H_1(E) + AA1_t \qquad (24)$$

This method can also be used for adjusting the coefficients for a change in demand pattern not forecast (Figure 3). If the trend needs changing, just replace A2 with a new value. Then of course we have promotions. If marketing sets a promotion for months 3, 4 & 5 of 3000, 5000, 2000, you can set up a matrix table for the month vs AA3 and tack on AA3 to (18) as follows

$$F_{t+u} = A1 + A2*u + AA3(u) \qquad (25)$$

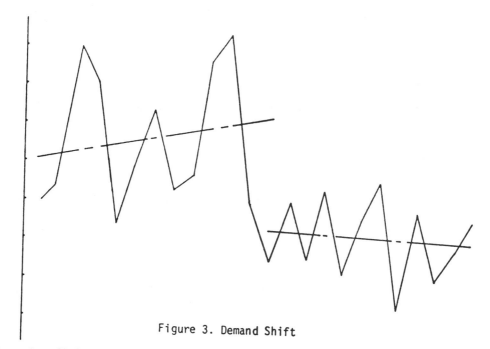

Figure 3. Demand Shift

Note that Al is not changed for the promotion, and only when u is for the proper month will it be added in. Of course, after each update, u is decremated by 1 as the promotion date nears.

Matrix:

Month	1	2	3	4	5	6
AA3	0	0	3000	5000	2000	0

Table 2 Promotion Matrix

Equation (25) will now amend the forecast of Table 1 as shown in Table 2

Month	1	2	3	4	5	6
Forecast	1050	1100	4150	6200	3250	1300

Table 3 Forecast Plus Promotion

Should the error, when you get to month 1 of the promotion, be larger than normal, the impact of the promotion should be evaluated and perhaps the error corrected for the large over or under estimate of the promotion. The forecast can then be rerun so the update error will reflect the normally expected error.

USE IN CONTROLLING INVENTORY - In smoothing or calculating a new forecast we have used the Error between demand and the forecast for that period to adjust the old forecast and give us a new forecast. In inventory control we want to use the distribution of these errors in establishing a safety stock to protect us against those random fluctuations of the demand from the mean. The Standard Deviations is used by statisticians to measure or describe this scatter of the demand around the average or mean, but we prefer to use the Mean Absolute Deviation (MAD) because of its ease of computation and updating. The MAD is the average value, without regard to sign, of the forecast error and is updated by smoothing. It has the relationship

$$\text{STD. DEV} = 1.25 \text{ MAD} \qquad (26)$$

In a normal distribution, we would expect half the errors to be plus and half to be minus and the sum (with sign) to be close to zero. This value is approximated by Smoothed Sum of Errors (SME).

To obtain and update the value of MAD we again use smoothing in the familiar form

$$\text{MAD}_t = (1. - H)\text{MAD}_{t-1} + H(\text{ERROR}_t) \qquad (27)$$

and at the same time we can update SME by
$$SME_t = (1. - H)SME_{t-1} + H(ERROR_t) \qquad (28)$$

Having the above information, we can proceed to calculate the Safety Stock (SS). SS is that stock required to protect against successive months of sales exceeding the forecast over the period needed to replenish stock. The forecast period and the lead time are not always equal; therefore, we must convert MAD for the forecast period to that for the Lead Time (LT). This is accomplished by

$$MAD_{LT} = MAD_F(LT)^B \qquad (9, pp30) \qquad (29)$$

However, Brown[3] has found that the formula below gives a very reasonable approximation for converting MAD for all but long lead times.

$$MAD (0.659 + 0.341 * LT) \qquad (30)$$
$$\text{and}$$
$$SS = k * 1.25 \, MAD (0.659 + 0.341 * LT) \qquad (31)$$

where 'k' is the safety stock factor having a value between 0.1 and 4.0. You can arbitrarily choose a value for k or you calculate it using the service function for each item or group of similar items as described in IMPACT[5pp134] or Brown[9]

Figure 4. WHAT MAKES A PRODUCT DIFFERENT

1. DEMAND
   - A. Level of Demand
     - 1) High volume
     - 2) Medium volume
     - 3) Low volume
   - B. Demand Pattern
     - 1) Horizontal
     - 2) Trend
     - 3) Seasonal
     - 4) Lumpy
     - 5) Trend seasonal
   - C. Variability of Demand

2. SENSITIVITY
   - A. Number of customers buying
   - B. Product Stability
     - 1) A fad or fashion item
     - 2) A basic item
     - 3) A commodity type item
   - C. Product Base at Customer
     - 1) Used in many processes
     - 2) Used in specialized process
     - 3) Used in many industries
     - 4) Used in few industries
   - D. Availability from other manufacturers
   - E. Product shelf life

3. OTHER FACTORS
   - A. Source
     - 1) Ordering constraints
     - 2) Lead time
   - B. Cost

Since each product or group of similar products is different, and each will have a different MAD, it is best to have different safety factors also. In practice the value of K should be fine-tuned to give the best results for that product. Some of the characteristics which make products different are shown in Figure 4. You can now understand why it is not a good policy to assign the same safety stock factor for all products, nor to use the age old approach of one month's supply etc.

I think Figure 5 gives you a good picture of the forecast (circles) for a particular set of demand data. In most cases, the forecast plus one Standard Deviation σ is greater than the demand. Thus, Safety Stock based on σ should be more than adequate.

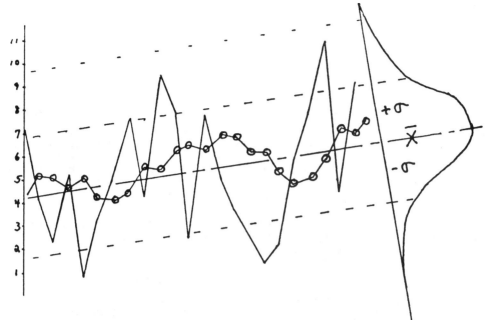

Figure 5.   Forecast showing data plus one
Standard Deviation around Mean.

MONITORING THE FORECAST - It is inevitable that the demand will not always be as expected and excessive demands will occur. For this reason, it is important to set up a means of monitoring the data and the results so you will know when the model or parameters need attention. First, you must be able to recognize when a particular period's demand is zero, minus, or the (demand-forecast) error exceeds the control limits you have set. This control limit is set in terms of so many MADS such as ±4.0*MAD. Many times you will have to use net sales information instead of actual demand and minus values will occur. When the demand is minus, set it to zero and then set up counters for zero demands and outliers over 4.0*MAD. Perhaps you will want to reject these abnormal demands and update in time only by setting the error to zero. However, if you find you are getting too many successive zeros on rejecting too many outliers, you will want to change either the model or the rejection level.

Sometimes it is nice to know when the trend has changed from (+) to (-) or vice versa and was confirmed over two periods, or perhaps that trend has changed by some percentage, etc. All of these bits of exception information can help you manage the forecast, provided the boundries allow only enough exceptions each period for you to check out the reason behind exception.

The most common of the monitor indicators is the Tracking Signal. This indicator is used to automatically switch the statistical forecast from Normal to Fast smoothing when it's control limit is broached. This ratio is calculated as an absolute value.

$$\text{Tracking Signal TKS} = \frac{\text{SME}}{\text{MAD}} \qquad (32)$$

When the Tracking Signal exceeds the break point TKSBPT, then the system is switched to fast smoothing. TKSBPT is calculated as

$$\text{TKSBPT} = K*0.55\sqrt{H_1} \qquad (33)$$

where K can be 2 to 4 for A items, 3 to 5 for B items and 5 to 7 for C items and H_1 is the smoothing constant used in smoothing MAD and SME.

The decision on how long to stay at 'Fast' smoothing is a matter of choice. Some references use 9 or 10 periods, however, I feel if the tracking signal TKS has settled down to half the TKSBPT, this should be sufficient to cause a change back to normal. Note that when the alpha (H_1) changes to Fast that the

TKSBPT will also change. If this second TKSBPT should be broken, it is time to look for the problem. Some things to consider are:

    a. Review choice of update period (weekly, monthly, quarterly, etc.)
    b. Is choice of model correct (Horizontal, trend, or seasonal)
    c. Are the Level or Trend component reasonable?
       Should the model be re-initialized with the more current data?
    d. Is the data too lumpy?
    e. Are the smoothing constants the best for this product or model?
       See Table 4.

Normal				Fast		
H_1	H_2	N		H_1	H_2	N
.05	.00263	39		.1	.00263	19
.1	.00263	19		.2	.011	9
.15	.00612	12.3		.3	.0267	5.7
.2	.011	9		.4	.0508	4

Table 4. Smoothing constants more commonly
used in (8), (20), (21).

There are additional statistical functions which are very useful in evaluating the forecast results or in choosing a model.

$$\text{Coefficient of Variation} = \frac{\text{STD. DEV.}}{\text{AVG. Demand}} \qquad (34)$$

$$\text{Standard Error} = \frac{\text{STD. DEV.}}{\sqrt{N}} \qquad (35)$$

Since the forecast is a weighted average of the demand over the last 'N' months, substitute the forecast for the average demand unless the latter is readily available. Acceptable values for the Coef. of Var. are less than 0.5, preferably less than .3. A higher ratio indicates an item with high variability and hence the large MAD would call for a large safety stock.

The Standard Error is calculated using the 'N' associated with the smoothing constant unless you are conducting a test where the specific number of periods of data are known. The smaller the Standard Error the better. Often this ratio is used in comparing the results of several models.

GETTING STARTED - As you can see, the forecasting subsystem is one of the more important elements of our inventory control system. Therefore, it is well to choose a forecasting model which is best suited to your product or industry. To do this means getting involved, conducting some simulations on the computer with various models and various update periods for the same data.

By getting involved, I don't mean calling in the Systems people, I mean learning to write your own programs using FORTRAN. In this way you can begin to understand the use of the computer while you test out various models. FORTRAN is not difficult to learn. Using an IBM programmed instruction course, you can begin writing your own programs after five night's work at home.

As you work with your models, you will have to make some decisions on how to handle problems with available data such as minus sales, zero sales and sales that give large forecast errors and, of course, the predictive and special knowledge information. Once you know how your test models should work, then call in the Systems and Programmers to implement YOUR Forecasting and Inventory Control System. But don't sit back and wait for the final product, stay involved, hold weekly progress meetings, approve input form layouts and make sure the reports are meaningful to you.

After the system is up and running, don't spend your time comparing forecasts to actual, but note whether the system is responding to your needs. With a new inventory control system, inventories will usually rise because you will build safety stocks for those products that needed larger protection, while it takes a little longer to reduce the excess safety stocks for those needing little or no protection. The monitor should be giving you exception reports on outliers and tracking signal breaks so you can determine when problems occur and can make adjustments as required. But in the end, the real test of your system is the results in managing inventory. Does it fulfill the desires of management in meeting customer service while keeping inventory at an acceptable level?

SUMMARY - In conclusion, I would like to enumerate the pitfalls which you must be wary of and understand in order to have a successful forecasting and inventory control system.

A. The forecast will be wrong most of the time, it is not the 'Gospel'
B. The forecast is an element of a system, it is not the system.
C. The forecast should seldom be used as a single value, but should include a measure of the (forecast-demand) error such as the Mean Absolute Deviation (MAD).
D. The MAD should be used in calculating Safety Stocks in the system.
E. Safety Stocks are used to compensate for the expected error in the forecast over the replenishment lead time.
F. The system must have a monitor to notify you when the demand is outside the boundry of the forecast or model.
G. The forecast vs demand must be analyzed to determine why these large differences occurred.
H. The forecast model must be able to accept adjustments, or the parameters changed, once these differences have been defined.
I. The forecast model must be able to accept specific known intelligence or predictive information.
J. The success of any system depends on the complete involvement of the user from design to implementation.

REFERENCES

1.   Webster's Seventh New Collegiate Dictionary, G. & C. Merrian Co. 1965.
2. Brown, R.G.,   "Less Risk in Inventory Estimates", Chapter XI, "New Decision Making Tools for Managers", Edited by Bursh & Chapman, Mentor Exec. Lab., New American Library, N.Y.C., 1965.
3. Brown, R.G.,   "Statistical Forecasting for Inventory Control", New York; McGraw-Hill Book Co., 1959
4. Brown, R.G.,   "Smoothing, Forecasting and Prediction", Englewood Cliffs, N.J. Prentice-Hall, Inc., 1963
5.   "Impact, Inventory Management Program and Control Techniques", I.B.M., (E20-8105).
6.   "Impact-The Bergen Drug Co.", I.B.M. (E20-0094).
7.   "Impact-Ralph's Grocery Company", I.B.M. (E20-0153)
8.   "Production & Inventory Control Handbook", McGraw-Hill Book Co. 1970.
9. Brown, R.G.,   "Decision Rules for Inventory Management", Holt, Rinehart & Winston, Inc., N.Y., 1967.

BIOGRAPHY

H. Lawrence Abbott, is Manager of the Computer Information Center, Chemical Group, Crompton & Knowles Corporation. He is responsible for data processing and systems, particularly in the area of inventory control and scientific forecasting. Prior to this assignment, he was Manager of Inventory Control and Distribution for the Dyestuffs Division for 5 years. Larry came to this organization after 12 years experience with Pfizer, Inc. in inventory control and systems. He is past-president, vice-president and secretary of the Northern New Jersey Chapter of APICS and now a member of the Schuylkill Valley Chapter of APICS and DPMA. He holds a B.S.E.E. degree from Lehigh University. He is also a member of the Forecasting Sub-Committee for Curriculm and Certification.

Reprinted from 1986 APICS Conference Proceedings.

A FRESH LOOK AT LINKING PLANS WITH SCHEDULES: TYING MASTER SCHEDULING TO PRODUCTION PLANNING

Lloyd Andreas, CFPIM
IBM Corporation

INTRODUCTION

Production planning and master scheduling are related activities performed by different levels within an organization. Production planning establishes aggregate production goals aligned to the marketing and distribution goals of the company, while utilizing production resources in an efficient and cost effective manner. Master scheduling is the redefinition of the production plan, broken down into buildable units with specific dates for completion.

Current approaches to the development of a master schedule from aggregate production plans present severe drawbacks. The objective of this paper is to define the relationships between production planning and master scheduling, and present a practical method of converting the plans for product families into schedules for the individual items within the families.

THE ROLE OF PRODUCTION PLANNING

Production plans generally cover a one to three year horizon, typically broken down by months in the near term and quarters in the later time frame. Demand forecasts, backlog, and inventory levels are the basic data elements used in the production planning process. These factors are treated in aggregate - grouped into product families. A product family usually consists of master scheduled items having common resource usage.

Decisions made in the production planning process affect the overall production levels, investments, manpower levels, and output for a company. The production plan is top management's "control lever" on the business, and a tool for communicating company goals and policies to all levels of the organization. Production planning is an iterative process, identifying goals and testing the resource implications until a plan is found that is acceptable to management. The production plan should:

° Support the business goals

° Follow company policy

° Meet all the demand

° Minimize inventory

° Optimize resource usage

° Be achievable

The production plan is an agreement between all areas of the company. It should represent a common "game plan" that is acceptable to the senior management representing each area.

THE ROLE OF MASTER SCHEDULING

The master schedule is the vehicle for implementing the production plan. The master schedule states what will be produced, when it will be produced, and the quantity which will be produced. The production plan deals with groups of items on an aggregate basis. The master schedule deals with specific items; usually finished goods or major assemblies. The production plan is stated in periods; months and quarters. The master schedule assigns specific dates to items within those periods.

The objective in developing the master production schedule is to create a schedule that:

° Supports the business goals (Production Plan)

° Follows company policy

° Meets all the demand

° Minimizes inventory

° Optimizes resource usage

° Is achievable

Look familiar ? It should. The objectives of master scheduling are the same as the objectives of production planning. If the master schedule is developed to support the production plan, and that is achieved, then the production plan will be met.

Different techniques have been used to assist the master scheduler in creating an overall schedule that is equivalent to the production plan. The following example will be used to illustrate one approach and its advantages over other methods currently in use.

DEVELOPING THE PRODUCTION PLAN

The product family 'MOTORS' consists of 3 electric motors, shown in Figure 1. The on-hand inventory and each month's total demand is also shown for each motor. To keep the example simple, safety stock, allocations, and other factors will not be considered.

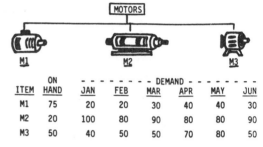

ITEM	ON HAND	JAN	FEB	MAR	APR	MAY	JUN
M1	75	20	20	30	40	40	30
M2	20	100	80	90	80	80	90
M3	50	40	50	50	70	80	50

Figure 1

The monthly demand for each motor (Fig. 1) is a total of what shipments are planned each month, and represents a consolidation of forecasts and backlog.

By aggregating, or adding together, the demand and inventory figures for all 3 motors in the production family, the basis for production planning is established (Figure 2).

PRODUCT FAMILY: MOTORS   MAX RATE: 180/MONTH

- FAMILY -		JAN	FEB	MAR	APR	MAY	JUN
DEMAND		160	150	170	190	200	170
PRODUCTION PLAN							
PROJECTED INV.	O/H 145						

Figure 2

Although a production plan would usually exist from the previous planning cycle, the example will assume that there is no plan in place. In this manner, the development and use of the production plan can be better illustrated. The numbers in Figure 2 represent units, but could also be stated in dollars.

The format of the production plan shown in Figure 2 is nothing more than a time-phased inventory record for the product family. The determination of the ending inventory level for any period is calculated as the previous period's ending inventory, plus the production plan, minus the demand. If any two of the factors (demand, production, or inventory) are known, the third element can be calculated. Top management, knowing the demand, can establish production targets and calculate the resulting inventories. Or, they may want to set target inventory levels and, based on the demand, calculate the production required to attain the desired inventory. In effect, the production plan format is a spreadsheet for "what-if" analysis by executives of the company.

Alternatives can now be tested against company objectives. The most likely objective will be meeting the demand. If a secondary objective is to minimize inventory, then the inventory currently on hand should be used to satisfy demand in the early periods while production is used to meet the period-by-period demand in the later time frame. A third objective may be to optimize the resource usage, avoiding big "swings" in the level of production. At this point, conflicts arise and compromises must be made. Figure 3 shows a solution that meets demand, reduces inventory, and does not exceed the maximum production rate. The compromise in this situation is an unstable production rate.

The production plan in Figure 3 appears to be valid, assuming that it serves the needs and follows the policy of the company. There is a severe problem, however, that is not exposed by the data shown in Figure 3. The problem is created by the "mix" of the aggregate on-hand inventory.

For example, if the demand of 160 units in January was all for motor 'M1', and the 145 units in inventory were all 'M2's, the production plan of 90 would not meet the demand, and the inventory at the end of January would still be 145!

PRODUCT FAMILY: MOTORS   MAX RATE: 180/MONTH

- FAMILY -		JAN	FEB	MAR	APR	MAY	JUN
DEMAND		160	150	170	190	200	170
PRODUCTION PLAN		90	100	180	180	180	180
PROJECTED INV	O/H 145	75	25	35	25	5	15

Figure 3

SOLVING THE "MIX" PROBLEM

The production plan, at a minimum, must meet the "net demand" of each item in the family. For production planning purposes, net demand is calculated as demand that exceeds currently available inventory. Using the demand and inventory data from Figure 1, the net demand for each motor and a total for the product family is displayed in Figure 4.

CALCULATING NET DEMAND

- M1 -		JAN	FEB	MAR	APR	MAY	JUN
DEMAND		20	20	30	40	40	30
INVENTORY	O/H: 75	55	35	5			
NET DEMAND					35	40	30

- M2 -		JAN	FEB	MAR	APR	MAY	JUN
DEMAND		100	80	90	80	80	90
INVENTORY	O/H: 20						
NET DEMAND		80	80	90	80	80	90

- M3 -		JAN	FEB	MAR	APR	MAY	JUN
DEMAND		40	50	50	70	80	50
INVENTORY	O/H: 50	10					
NET DEMAND			40	50	70	80	50

- FAMILY -	JAN	FEB	MAR	APR	MAY	JUN
NET DEMAND	80	120	140	185	200	170

Figure 4

The net demand for the family is the number of additional units that must be produced to meet the demand after considering the mix of current inventory. Figure 5 highlights the problem that may exist when the production plan for a period is less than the period's net demand. Even though the production plan in Figure 3 seemed to satisfy all the demand, a different picture emerges in Figure 5 when using net demand.

- FAMILY -	JAN	FEB	MAR	APR	MAY	JUN
PRODUCTION PLAN	90	100	180	180	180	180
NET DEMAND	80	120	140	185	200	170
PROD'N - NET DEMAND	+10	-20	+40	-5	-20	+10

Figure 5

The fact that production is less than net demand in one or more periods may not mean the plan is invalid. When demand patterns are seasonal, cyclical, or have random spikes, the net demand in a period may exceed the available capacity in that period. In these situations inventory must be built earlier, when capacity is available. Even though the negative numbers in the bottom line of Figure 5 do not necessarily invalidate the plan, a further test is needed. The production plan for the entire horizon exceeds the net demand by 15 units, but the timing of the production relative to the net demand may pose a problem. If production matches or exceeds the net demand throughout the horizon on a cumulative basis, then demand spikes in later periods can be met

by excess production from earlier periods (inventory!).

Taking a cumulative look at the "PROD'N - NET DEMAND" data from Figure 5 yields:

	JAN	FEB	MAR	APR	MAY	JUN
PROD'N - NET DEMAND	+10	-20	+40	-5	-20	+10
CUMULATIVE	+10	-10	+30	+25	+5	+15

Although an extra 10 units will be produced in January, it will not be enough to satisfy the net demand in February. The cumulative difference between the production plan and the net demand is the key to validating the plan. Demand will not be met in any period where the cumulative value is negative. Figure 6 represents a plan with leveled production, resulting in reduced inventory and meeting demand.

PRODUCT FAMILY: MOTORS   MAX RATE: 180/MONTH

- FAMILY -		JAN	FEB	MAR	APR	MAY	JUN
DEMAND		160	150	170	190	200	170
PRODUCTION PLAN		150	150	150	160	160	160
PROJECTED INV.	O/H 145	135	135	115	85	45	35

NET DEMAND	80	120	140	185	200	170
PROD'N - NET DEMAND	70	30	10	-25	-40	-10
CUMULATIVE	70	100	110	85	45	35

Figure 6

At this point, the production plans for all product families would be tested against the critical resource constraints to validate the feasibility of achieving the overall plan. Changes may have to be made to some product families if required resources are not available, or if capacity cannot be increased. When the plans are agreed to by top management, and considered achievable in terms of capacity, they must be translated into master schedules.

TRADITIONAL APPROACHES TO CREATING SCHEDULES

In many companies, a formal, documented production plan may not exist. The master scheduler operates with no idea of top management's goals or intended business direction other than periodic caveats to "reduce inventory", "increase customer service", or "stabilize the schedules". The master schedules for each end item can be grouped by production family and summed up to provide an aggregate picture of scheduled production. If management feels the numbers are too high or too low, the master scheduler must make changes at the item level to attempt to meet management's elusive goals. This hit-or-miss approach, if used at all, is inefficient and time-consuming. The benefits of formal production planning will not be realized in this environment.

Even in companies having a formal production plan, no linkage may exist between the plan and the master schedule. The master scheduler must also use the inefficient hit-or-miss approach in this situation, trying to establish schedules at the item level that when summed together by family are equivalent to the production plans.

Much of the literature available to-date has described an approach to creating master schedules from production plans commonly referred to as "disaggregation". Figure 7 is an illustration of this approach using the data from preceding examples.

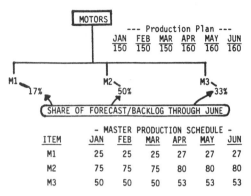

MOTORS

--- Production Plan ---

	JAN	FEB	MAR	APR	MAY	JUN
	150	150	150	160	160	160

M1 — 17%   M2 — 50%   M3 — 33%

SHARE OF FORECAST/BACKLOG THROUGH JUNE

- MASTER PRODUCTION SCHEDULE -

ITEM	JAN	FEB	MAR	APR	MAY	JUN
M1	25	25	25	27	27	27
M2	75	75	75	80	80	80
M3	50	50	50	53	53	53

Figure 7

This method is essentially an explosion technique which uses a planning bill of material. The production "family" is the parent, having each item in the family as its components. The "quantity per assembly" of each item is simply a percentage of the item's forecast or backlog relative to the entire family. The family production plan is exploded using these percentages to yield schedules for each item.

This disaggregation approach is straightforward and easy to use and understand. On the surface it appears to be a feasible method of linking the production plan to the master schedule. However, major obstacles exist in its operational use. The first drawback is the use of forecast or backlog, rather than net demand, to determine the explosion percentages. The master schedule in Figure 7 shows only 75 M2's being scheduled in each of the first 3 months. The net demand for M2 in each of those months is greater than 75, as shown in Figure 4. The use of forecast/backlog percentages does not consider current inventory mix, and resulting schedules may not meet the true demand.

Even when net demand percentages are used in disaggregation, a problem may still exist in the timing of production. Using the percentage of net demand for each item over the planning horizon may produce insufficient schedules in early periods if the net demand decreases through the horizon. Demand percentages based on the entire horizon are averages, thus making seasonal and trend demand patterns difficult to accomodate. New product introductions, phaseouts, or replacements also pose severe drawbacks in the use of an "average" percentage of demand.

The use of net demand percentages calculated on a period-by-period basis overcomes these problems, but creates new obstacles. Because net demand will change with the passage of every period, the resulting schedules will fluctuate with each planning cycle. This "nervousness", mainly in the early periods, needs to be avoided to achieve a stable schedule. In addition, period-by-period percentages provide no visibility into the future demand spikes that need to be addressed by earlier production.

The example being used here has only 3 items in the product family. Some families could easily consist of more than a hundred master scheduled items. Even 50 to 100 items can cause a problem in terms of the rounding errors, especially with low volume production quantities.

What at first seemed to be a simple, easy approach to linking production plans to master schedules has become a difficult, if not infeasible, method. A new approach is needed!

THE CONCEPT OF 'ITEM PRODUCTION PLANS'

Item production plans are the detailed breakdown of the aggregate production plan for the family, showing the planned production quantities, by period, for each item. The item production plans should:

° Meet the net demand

° Balance to the family production plan

° Allow for planned inventory build-up and depletion

° Recognize time fences to reduce nervousness in early periods

° Simplify the master scheduler's job

The starting point for creating item production plans is the family production plan. Figure 8 is the family pro-

duction plan for motors, with some new lines of information added.

PRODUCT FAMILY: MOTORS

- FAMILY -	JAN	FEB	MAR	APR	MAY	JUN
PRODUCTION PLAN	150	150	150	160	160	160
NET DEMAND	80	120	140	185	200	170
ADJUSTMENTS	0	0	0	0	0	0
ITEM "TRIAL" PRODUCTION PLANS	80	120	140	185	200	170
FAMILY BUILD +/-	70	30	10	-25	-40	-10

Figure 8

The Production Plan and Net Demand values in Figure 8 came from previous figures. A new line, Item Trial Production Plans, is the sum of Net Demand and another new line, Adjustments. Adjustments will be described later in more detail. Since the example assumes a start-up environment, all adjustments are zero, and therefore the Item Trial Production Plans are equal to Net Demand.

Family Build +/- represents the difference between the Production Plan and the Item Trial Production Plans (Production Plan - Item Trial Production Plans). The objective of the master scheduler is to drive the Family Build +/- values to zero. This is achieved by making adjustments to item production plans that cause those plans to balance with the family production plan. For example, the Production Plan in Figure 8 calls for 150 motors to be produced in January. The Item Trial Production Plans (Net Demand + Adjustments) for January shows only 80 units. If the production plan is to be met in January, an additional 70 units must be built, as shown by the Family Build +/- line. The Family Build +/- values serve as both a measurement and a guide.

The adjustments called for by the Family Build +/- line are made at the item level, and can be applied to one or more items in the family. In the example, all adjustments will be made to motor M3. The current status of motor M3 is shown in Figure 9 together with the Family Build +/- guidelines from Figure 8. Figure 9 can be viewed as a type of "load board" for the production family. The objective is to apply the Family Build +/- numbers to one or more items in the family, using adjustments. An adjustment to an item is algebraically added to the Adjustments line and subtracted from the Family Build +/- line for the period in which it is applied. The Item Trial Plan (Net Demand + Adjustments) is then changed by the amount of the adjustment.

ITEM: M3   ITEM PRODUCTION PLAN

On Hand: 50	JAN	FEB	MAR	APR	MAY	JUN
NET DEMAND	0	40	50	70	80	50
ADJUSTMENTS	0	0	0	0	0	0
ITEM TRIAL PLAN	0	40	50	70	80	50
FAMILY BUILD +/-	70	30	10	-25	-40	-10

Figure 9

Figure 10 shows the item trial production plan for motor M3 after adjustments have been applied. The original Family Build +/- values have been added to the Adjustments line, and the Family Build +/- values cleared by this action. At this point, the sum of the item trial plans for all members of the family equal the aggregate production plan.

ITEM: M3   ITEM PRODUCTION PLAN

On Hand: 50	JAN	FEB	MAR	APR	MAY	JUN
NET DEMAND	0	40	50	70	80	50
ADJUSTMENTS	70	30	10	-25	-40	-10
ITEM TRIAL PLAN	70	70	60	45	40	40
FAMILY BUILD +/-	0	0	0	0	0	0

Figure 10

The development of item production plans is basically a process of applying adjustments to different items in the family until the Family Build +/- values are converted to zero. In actual practice, this may not always be possible without resulting in a negative impact on schedules. The important task is to attempt to bring the variance between item production plans and the family production plan to zero, altering as few item plans as possible. The minor differences can be ignored in many cases, or resolved on a cumulative basis.

After all adjustments have been applied, the "trial plans" for each item can be designated as the current Item Production Plans. These are the targets that are used in developing and maintaining the master schedule.

MASTER SCHEDULING USING THE ITEM PRODUCTION PLANS

The Item Production Plans tell the master scheduler exactly what should be produced each period. The master scheduler must now assign specific due dates and quantities to each item, recognizing more specific capacity constraints and other factors such as product changeover efficiencies and time fences. Figure 11 is the master schedule for motor M3, with a comparison to the item production plan.

ITEM: M3   MASTER PRODUCTION SCHEDULE
LEAD TIME: 10   CUM L/T: 52   ON HAND: 50

DATE	MPS ORDER	QTY	PROD'N PLAN	VARIANCE
1/3	M2496	20		
1/10	M2514	25		
1/31	FIRM	25	70	0
2/14	FIRM	40		
2/28	PLANNED	25	70	-5
⋮	⋮	⋮	⋮	⋮
6/13	PLANNED	25		
6/27	PLANNED	25	40	10

Figure 11

Two released manufacturing orders together with a firm planned order make up the schedule for January for motor M3. The three orders' total quantity of 70 is equal to the item production plan. In contrast, the schedule in February of one firm planned order and one planned order is 5 less than the item production plan, and scheduled production in June is 10 units more than required by the plan. The master scheduler can make adjustments with firm planned orders to meet the item production plans, but another consideration must be made.

Even though the item production plans are developed to meet net demand, the timing of the master scheduled orders within a period may result in stockouts. Therefore, in addition to establishing schedules that meet the production plan, the master scheduler must also keep an eye on the projected inventory balance.

ITEM: M3   MASTER PRODUCTION SCHEDULE
LEAD TIME: 10   CUM L/T: 52   ON HAND: 50

DATE	MPS ORDER	QTY	PROD'N PLAN	VAR	DEMAND	PROJECTED INVENTORY
1/3	M2496	20			20	50
1/10	M2514	25			10	65
1/17					10	55
1/31	FIRM	25	70	0		80
2/7					15	65
2/14	FIRM	40			10	95
2/21					15	80
2/28	PLANNED	25	70	-5	10	95
⋮	⋮	⋮	⋮	⋮	⋮	⋮

Figure 12

Figure 12 is similar to Figure 11, with the addition of demand data and the calculation of projected inventory. The data shown in Figure 12 is the basic information needed by the master scheduler. Working with this data, the master scheduler can establish schedules that serve the dual purpose of meeting the production plan and meeting the customer service objectives.

CLOSING THE LOOP

The linkage between the aggregate production plan and master schedule has now been made. If the master schedule is met, the production plan will be achieved. However, nothing happens as planned..... except by accident or coincidence.

In order to react intelligently to changes, the actual performance during a period must be tracked and used as feedback in the next planning cycle. A simple "report card" of January's planned and actual results for motors is shown in Figure 13.

PRODUCT FAMILY: MOTORS   -JANUARY RESULTS-

DEMAND	ACTUAL	PLAN	VARIANCE
M1	24	20	4
M2	98	100	-2
M3	41	40	1
TOTAL	163	160	3
PRODUCTION			
M1	0	0	0
M2	78	80	-2
M3	70	70	0
TOTAL	148	150	-2
INVENTORY	130	135	-5

Figure 13

THE IMPACT OF TIME

As each period passes and actual shipments, receipts, and other transactions are recorded, the planning cycle begins anew. Based on new forecasts and backlog, and the previous period's results, net demand is recalculated for each item. The adjustments that existed for an item have not changed. Therefore, the item "trial" production plans (net demand + adjustments) will now differ from the item production plans and the family production plan developed last period. Top management must now reevaluate the family production plan, ensuring that it still meets the objectives of the company. In most situations the production plan will require only minimal changes. Changes to the plan should be avoided in the early periods.

Figure 14 represents the status of motor M3 at the beginning of February. Although the data for the other motors and the family production plan is not shown, it is assumed that the production planning process has been completed and no change has been made to the family production plan other than the addition of data for July.

ITEM: M3   ITEM PRODUCTION PLAN
On Hand: 77
Held: 70
Avail: 7

	FEB	MAR	APR	MAY	JUN	JUL
DEMAND (New)	50	60	65	80	45	50
NET DEMAND	43	60	65	80	45	50
ITEM ADJUSTMENTS	30	10	-25	-40	-10	0
ITEM TRIAL PLAN	73	70	40	40	35	50

	FEB	MAR	APR	MAY	JUN	JUL
ITEM PROD'N PLAN	70	60	45	40	40	0
VARIANCE	3	10	-5	0	-5	50

	FEB	MAR	APR	MAY	JUN	JUL
FAMILY BUILD +/-	-3	-8	-10	8	5	20

Figure 14

Several new data elements are introduced in Figure 14.
Held inventory is a value that represents Item Adjustments
from periods passed. It is nothing more than an arithmetic
"control number" that keeps track of adjustments through
time.
    Item adjustments are used to bring item production
plans into line with the family production plan. Positive
adjustments represent production that will serve future
demand, while negative adjustments represent demand to be
served from current inventory or earlier production. As
time passes, the adjustments cannot just disappear; they are
accumulated as "held" inventory. Held inventory represents
future demand that must be filled from current inventory.
Thus, the adjustment of 70 in January for motor M3 has been
added to M3's prior held inventory of zero.
    Because held inventory is a form of adjustment, and
adjustments are removed from the net demand calculation,
the held inventory is subtracted from the on-hand inventory
prior to netting.
    The Item Production Plan in Figure 14 is the "current"
plan, developed in the previous planning cycle. The Variance
line is the difference between the new trial plan and the
current item production plan.
    Because of the changes in net demand, M3's trial plan
now varies from its item production plan. If the trial plan
is accepted without changes and designated as the item production plan, the master schedule will have to be changed
to produce an additional 3 units in February, 10 in March,
5 less in April, and so on. The master scheduler wants to
keep the schedule stable within the item's cumulative lead
time; through March in this example. In later periods,
changes can be made with little or no impact on material
plans.
    As a result of the production planning process, a new
Family Build +/- has been calculated (Figure 14). This line
represents the difference between the family production
plan and the total of the new item trial plans. As in the
previous planning cycle, these numbers should be driven to
zero by applying them as adjustments to one or more items
in the family. In Figure 15, adjustments have been applied
to motor M3 to keep the item production plan stable in
February and March, and to satisfy the family production
plan in later periods.

- M3 -

	FEB	MAR	APR	MAY	JUN	JUL
CHANGES TO ADJ'MNTS	-3	-10	-10	8	5	20

	FEB	MAR	APR	MAY	JUN	JUL
NET DEMAND	43	60	65	80	45	50
ITEM ADJUSTMENTS	27	0	-35	-32	-5	20
ITEM TRIAL PLAN	70	60	30	48	40	70

	FEB	MAR	APR	MAY	JUN	JUL
ITEM PROD'N PLAN	70	60	45	40	40	0
VARIANCE	0	0	-15	8	0	70

	FEB	MAR	APR	MAY	JUN	JUL
FAMILY BUILD +/-	0	2	0	0	0	0

Figure 15

    Stabilizing the plan for M3 in March, by reducing the
item adjustment by 10, causes the Family Build +/- value in
March to now call for 2 additional units to be built. These
might possibly be applied to one of the other items in the

family where additional production would not have a negative
impact.
    The item trial plans, once approved, will become the
current item production plans and serve as the input for
revision and extension of the master schedule. In each
planning cycle, the objective is to alter the item production plans by using adjustments until the sum of these item
plans is equivalent to the family production plan.

SUMMARY

    Production planning is an excellent tool for management
to use in accomplishing the company's goals. It provides
measurements of past performance, a picture of present
status, and visibility into the future. The level of detail
and the volume of data can be quickly understood and easily
managed by executives. Translating these high-level, aggregate plans into workable master schedules has always posed
a challenge. The use of item production plans provides the
linkage between aggregate production planning and master
scheduling, resulting in:

° Master schedules aligned to the production plan

° Stabilization of the master schedule

° Commitment to a single goal

° Meaningful performance measurements

° Increased involvement of top management

...... and, finally, improved control of the business.

ACKNOWLEDGEMENT

    The author wishes to extend his appreciation to
Mr. William Robinson of IBM for his invaluable assistance
in providing suggestions and editorial advice during the
preparation of this paper.

About The Author

    Lloyd Andreas is currently an Industry Administrator
with IBM's Industrial Sector Market Development organization in Atlanta, Georgia. He is certified by APICS at the
Fellow level, and has conducted certification workshops in
MRP and Production Activity Control for the Atlanta Chapter.
Lloyd currently serves on the Inventory Management Committee
of the APICS Curricula and Certification Council. He was a
speaker at the annual APICS Conferences in both 1984 and
1985. In addition, Lloyd has been a frequent speaker on the
subject of manufacturing planning and control at local and
national conferences sponsored by IBM.

Blackburn, Joe H., "A Manual System for Master Scheduling Configure-to-Order Products," 27th Annual Conference Proceedings (1984).

This article presents a manual system for master scheduling in an assemble-to-order (ATO) environment. This article provides approaches to the master production schedule (MPS) and a means for understanding ATO problem issues. The firm considering modular bills of material and ATO approaches will find it useful to analyze one of its product lines with the techniques and issues identified in this paper. Thereafter, comparing results with those provided by packages software should be beneficial. Some of the terminology is not the same as that used in popular textbooks and software packages, but differences are minor and easy to understand.

The author relates his experiences in the installation of an MRP II system; master planning was left until last. The manual system described filled the void.

An example planning bill of material is provided where the components are classified as common material, either/or options, true options, variable quantity options, and options to options. (True options are referred to by other terminology in some of the other papers in this monograph. Included are add-on options and attachments.) Quantities for these components are either standard (direct functions of the order quantity), fixed (fixed regardless of the order quantity), or as required (quantity determined from source other than the planning bill).

An order/shipment forecast form is provided that has many of the features of the standard MPS approaches using available-to-promise logic. A difference is incorporation of an offset from forecasted order dates to forecasted shipment dates. Firm shipments (customer due dates) can be compared to both forecasts.

A customer order form illustrates how a specific order is configured. It also provides the basis for detailed shop scheduling and tracking of the order. Specific routings and due dates are determined for each component and the assembly process.

The primary tool used by the master scheduler is a supply/demand status form. This is essentially a normal material requirements planning record to keep track of all customer orders, replenishment of MPS quantities, and projected inventory positions. Supply/demand status forms are kept for each option, and the master scheduler has to keep actual orders synchronized across options. All interlocking dates and quantities have to be monitored continually.

The author believes that the manual system can be used effectively by small firms as well as by larger firms on an interim basis while implementing a computer-based system. He advocates using all of the forms provided, with minimal change, as a way to learn how ATO approaches can best be applied at a particular company.

Reprinted from 1984 APICS Conference Proceedings.

A MANUAL SYSTEM FOR MASTER SCHEDULING CONFIGURE-TO-ORDER PRODUCTS

Joe H. Blackburn, Jr., CPIM
NCR, E & M Clemson

OBJECTIVE

The author was recently involved in the installation of a computerized material management system that involved several modules implemented over a relatively long period of time. Following the usual sequence the bill of material module was installed first, followed by routings, standard cost, inventory control, MRP, and so forth. As in most such projects, the "top end" of the system involving sales forecasting and production planning was left for last. Such an installation sequence is often followed because most companies without good automated systems benefit more quickly in financial and practical terms from having accurate, shared bills of material and inventory records, than from having improved forecasting and master scheduling. And yet the practitioner must manage the sales forecast, order acceptance and master scheduling functions in a manual mode. Perhaps the most difficult environment for managing these functions is when stocking level assemblies are master scheduled based on a sales forecast and then configured from stock to each individual customer order.

As an interim step in the installation of the computerized Materials Management system, the author designed and implemented a manual configure-to-order system. This paper is designed to allow a prospective user to adapt the system to his or her needs in the absence of an existing computer system. The following methods and forms can be used in a manual configure-to-order environment to perform the following functions:

- forecast product families and options
- convert the forecasts into specific master schedules
- configure individual customer orders
- determine cost and availability
- manage and schedule customer orders

PLANNING BILLS OF MATERIAL

One of the first activities in the life cycle of a configure-to-order product is the construction of a planning bill of material that specifically and unambiguously determines the possible configurations of the new product. Several different disciplines must become involved very early in the development of a new, configure-to-order product. Engineering, who must bear the ultimate responsibility for the accuracy and completeness of the planning bill, must determine what configurations of required and optional parts are possible and desirable. Marketing must make sure that the developing configuration of the new product is marketable in terms of price, features, and lead time. Of course the manufacturing group (including materials) must make sure that the product is manufacturable and that an efficient materials plan can be developed.

To illustrate how a planning bill is developed, the product structure illustrated in Figure I will be used.

The possible components that make up radio transmitter AM-1 consist of:

- The basic or common material, that is used on every transmitter Model AM-1 and only on transmitter Model AM-1. One of the most common errors in structuring configure-to-order products is the failure to identify a unique and required item for each product family.

- Two different power supplies, one required for domestic use and another required for use overseas due to power line differences. One or the other of these supplies must be chosen but not both. The situation is like an automobile that requires either a four or a six cylinder engine but obviously not both.

- A display panel that is a true option. The transmitter may be configured either with or without this panel. The quantity of this option is fixed at one; i.e. either zero or one panel must be chosen.

- An input matcher that is used to adapt the transmitter to any of several different input signals. The quantity of this option is variable. The purchaser can choose either zero, one, two, or a maximum of three of these matchers depending on the variety and types of signals to be fed to the transmitter.

- An extender cable that can be used as an option with each input matcher to mount the matcher in a remote location. Zero or one cable may be selected for each input matcher depending on whether the input matcher is remotely located.

Figure II is an example of a planning bill for the AM-1 Model. As previously mentioned, it is originated and maintained by Engineering. The initial bill and subsequent revisions must be approved by Marketing/Sales, Manufacturing, and Materials Management. Note that there is a part number as well as a model number for the AM-1 Model, allowing engineering to change the part number if needed for internal configuration control reasons without forcing Sales and Marketing to change the model number on all the sales literature.

The item number column is a reference that the used-with column on the right refers to. Use of the item number column will be explained below.

Naturally, each part on the bill has a unique part number and description. The parts listed on a planning bill are typically master scheduled items.

The quantity per and quantity type columns are used together to indicate the quantity needed for each customer order configuration. Quantity type is defined as follows:

Standard - the quantity is multiplied by the order quantity.

Fixed - the same, fixed quantity is chosen regardless of the order quantity. An example might be a tube of glue or a packing check list.

As Required - indicates that the quantity information comes from some source other than the planning bill. Examples might be a select-in-test component or a variable quantity option like item number 0005, to be explained later.

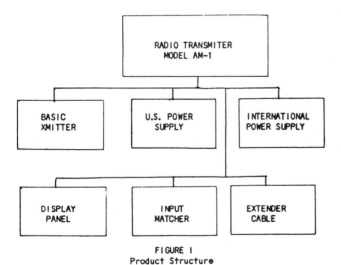

FIGURE I
Product Structure

FIGURE II

PLANNING BILL OF MATERIAL

PART NBR. 6400   DESC. AM TRANSMITTER   PAGE 1 OF 1
MODEL NBR. AM-1
REV. LEV. C   REV. BY SAM ENGINEERING   DATE REV. 03/01/84

ITEM NBR.	PART NUMBER	DESCRIPTION	QTY. PER	QTY. TYPE	COMP TYPE	GROUP	USED WITH
0000	6302	SCHEMATIC	0	AR	REF		
0010	3820	BASIC XMITTER	1	STD	STD		
0020	7135	U.S. POWER SUPPLY	1	STD	RO	A	0010
0030	7136	INT'L POWER SUPPLY	1	STD	RO	A	0010
0040	5640	DISPLAY PANEL	1	STD	FO		0010
0050	2271	INPUT MATCHER	3	AR	VO		0010
0060	2350	EXTENDER CABLE	1	AR	VO		0050

QTY. TYPE	COMPONENT TYPE	
STD-STANDARD	STD-STANDARD REQ'D.	RO-REQ'D. OPTION
FIX-FIXED	NEG-NEGATIVE	FO-FIXED OPTION
AR-AS REQUIRED	REF-REFERENCE	VO-VARIABLE OPTION

The component type column determines how various required and optional parts may be selected in configuring an order. Component type is defined as follows:

    Standard Required – Indicates parts that must be chosen for each order, in a specific quantity.

    Negative – not illustrated on the example but used to indicate that a part is to be removed from another part and returned to stock.

    Reference – Indicates that a part is not physically required to build the product but supplies information that applys to the product.

    Required Options – Indicates that one or more of several parts must be chosen. The two power supplies are a good example.

    Fixed Option – Indicates that if the optional part is chosen, then the quantity shown as the quantity per must be chosen.

    Variable Option – Indicates that if the optional part is chosen, then any quantity up to the quantity per may be chosen.

The group column indicates options that are mutually exclusive, an "either-or" situation.

The used-with column indicates which item number a part is used with. In the example, the power supplies, display panel, and input matcher are used with the basic radio while the extender cable is an option that must be used with an input matcher.

If a product structure or configuration can not be accurately represented by this planning bill structure, then the product is probably not correctly designed for efficient sale, production, and final configuration-to-order.

ORDER/SHIPMENT FORECAST

During the new product development process, a forecast of order bookings and shipments of the new product must be developed by Marketing and a production plan must be developed to support the shipment forecast. The forecast form should be reviewed by top management on a regular (probably monthly) basis and signed off by all concerned: Engineering for new product development commitments, Marketing for a production and inventory plan, and Finance for the financial impact of the overall plan. Typically, only the end product is specifically forecasted; the optional parts are forecasted using option percentages as will be explained later.

Figure III is an example of a sales forecast for the new product. This forecast was prepared at the end of March, right before the first planned shipments began in April. Some of the less obvious entries are explained below.

Production plan peg number–indicates the part number on the planning bill that is required and unique to the model, in this case the basic transmitter. This entry is used to clearly and specifically link material usage (the basic transmitter) to product sales.

Safety stock–determines the minimum projected inventory allowed. This quantity must be determined analytically based on estimates of demand variability and based on management's service level goals.

Leadtime offset–indicates the estimated time from a planned order booking until the shipment of that order.

FIGURE III

ORDER/SHIPMENT FORECAST

MODEL NBR. AM-1   PREP. BY Tom Market   DATE April   PAGE 1 OF 1
PART NBR. 6400   DESC. AM Transmitter   COST $10K   SELL $20K
P. P. PEG NBR. 3820   SAFETY STOCK 2   LT OFFSET 3 mos.   CUM LT 6 mos.

YR TO DATE		J	F	M	A	M	J	J	A	S	O	N	D	PLAN	ACT	J	F	M	A	M	J	J	A	S	O	N	D	12 MO
5	ORDER FCST				1	2	3	3	3	4	4	5	5	40	35	5	5	5	5	5	5	5	5	5	5	5	5	50
0	SHIP FCST						2	1	2	3	3	3	4	25	23	4	5	5	5	5	5	5	5	5	5	5	5	37
	FIRM SHIP				2	2	1																					
	PROD PLAN				10				20								20				20				20			
	PROJ INV				8	6	4	2	20	17	14	11	7			3	18	13	8	3	18	13	8	3	18	13	8	
	AV. TO PROM.				5				20								20				20				20			

ENG. APP _____   FIN. APP _____   GM APP _____

MAT. APP _____   MKT. APP _____

Note that the single order booking forecasted for April is reflected in a shipment in July and so forth.

Cumulative lead time-indicates the total lead time required to order material, manufacture, and ship the product. This lead time indicates how much investment has been committed to the quantities shown in the production plan. The sixty units planned for next year are all outside the six month lead time so no money has been invested in them, and changes in response to forecast variation are easy to make. The 20 units planned for August are five months away so that some purchased material has been ordered, but manufacturing has probably not begun. The initial production quantity of ten shown in April should be essentially complete.

The order forecast line reflects Marketing's best guess as to the quantity and timing of customer order bookings. This line can be used financially along with the ship forecast line to predict the sales backlog.

The shipment forecast line reflects Marketing's best guess as to when the booked orders forecasted above will actually ship. The order and shipment forecast lines only reflect orders that are not yet firm. When an order is formally firmed up and booked, it is deleted from both the order and shipment forecast lines and reflected only in the firm shipment line.

The planned, actual and 12 month columns are used in conjunction with the order and shipment forecast lines. At the beginning of the financial year in January, a plan was developed for 40 orders and 25 shipments of AM-1 for the coming year. Adding together the five orders booked year to date and the 30 orders forecasted to be booked from April through December yields a current actual estimate of 35 orders for the year. Counting both forecasted and firm shipments yields a current actual estimate of 23 shipments for the year, two less than originally planned. The 12 month column simply looks at forecasted and firm orders and shipments over the 12 month period from April to May. All of these columns are useful to management in determining how well the sales plans are being met and whether the forecast is increasing or decreasing over time.

Once the demand pattern has been established, time phased order point techniques are used to develop the production plan and projected inventory lines. Since this is a new product, the inventory prior to the first production lot of ten in April is zero. After the first production lot of ten, a fixed order quantity of 20 has been chosen and scheduled so that the projected inventory line never drops below the safety stock of two units.

The available-to-promise line is used by Sales and Marketing to determine how many units are uncommitted to customers out of each production plan lot. Out of the first lot of ten, there are five firm shipments scheduled before the next order of 20 is available in August. Therefore, there are ten minus five or five units available from that lot.

CUSTOMER ORDERS

Now that we have the framework of a planning bill and a sales forecast, let us review a typical customer order that has been booked. Refering to the sales forecast, the order that we will be looking at is shown in the firm shipment line in July. The customer order form is shown in Figure IV. Note that when the order was entered back on April 15, the scheduled due (shipment) date was June 15. Now at the beginning of April, the order is due to ship on July 12. The reason for the delay will be revealed shortly.

Once the overall system is in place and running smoothly, it can be used as a powerful tool in order promising. Many firms with configure-to-order products are forced to quote a standard order lead time such as "90 days after receipt of order". As will be illustrated later, the proposed system allows a specific delivery

PAGE 1 OF 1
ORDER NBR. 30350
PART NBR. 6400
MODEL NBR. AM-1
REV. LEVEL C

ORIG. DUE DATE 06/15/84 CURR. DUE DATE 07/12/84
CUSTOMER NAME HENERY CUSTOMER
DESC. AM TRANSMITTER
PREPARED BY JIM ORDER ENTRY
DATE PREP. 04/10/84 DATE ENTERED 04/15/84

ROUTING

WORK CENTER	WORK DESCRIPTION	START DATE	LABOR HOURS
ASSEMBLY	CONFIGURE ORDER	06/15/84	32.4
TEST	FINAL TUNE AND TEST	06/20/84	65.7
PACK	TEARDOWN AND PACK	07/10/84	6.0

COMPONENTS

ITEM NBR.	PART NUMBER	DESCRIPTION	QTY. REQ'D.	QTY. ISS	DATE REQ'D.	DELIVER TO
001	3890	BASIC XMITTER	1		6/15	ASSY
002	7135	U.S. POWER SUPPLY	1		6/15	ASSY
003	2271	INPUT MATCHER	2		6/23	TEST
004	2350	EXTENDER CABLE	1		6/15	ASSY

quote based on actual capacity and material availability.

A routing is included to indicate the flow of the order through the manufacturing process. Start dates are specified by Manufacturing for each work center and an estimate is made of the direct labor hours required for each work center since each order can be configured differently and no standard times are available. These labor hour estimates should have been approved by Manufacturing personnel and also should have been used to develop the pricing strategy for the order when it was originally quoted to the customer.

The components listed on the order are determined from the planning bill. In addition to the basic transmitter, this customer has chosen the US power supply, two input matchers and one extender cable. He has not included a display panel. The quantity issued column is used to indicate material issued to the order from stock. The date required and deliver to columns schedule and direct the delivery of component material to the order. The input matcher is not due to be issued until about a week later than the other components, and it is to be delivered to Test rather than Assembly. Either the test foreman doesn't want the matcher until after testing has started on June 20 or the first input matcher production order will not be available until then. If the input matcher is late, that may account for the delay of the order shipment from June 15 to July 12.

SUPPLY/DEMAND STATUS

The heart of this manual scheduling system is the supply/demand status. Really a manual MRP form, the S/D status is maintained by the master scheduler for each part on the planning bill. Each time a change occurs to the demands for a part (either shipment forecast or customer orders) or to the supplies (inventory or production orders), the master scheduler reviews the impact of the changes and, if necessary, reschedules the forecast demand, the customer orders or the master schedule orders.

Figure V is the S/D status for the basic transmitter. Demands are shown for all five firm customer orders, as well as the shipment forecast. The forecast demand line indicates that the basic transmitter is used one per in 100 percent of each order as indicated in the planning bill. The due date for demands is the date that the part is needed on the customer order to begin configuration. For planning purposes, a lead time offset of four weeks has been assumed between the shipment quantities shown on the sales forecast and the due date on this form. This planning offset allows for the final configuration and test lead time.

Each of the five booked orders are listed next as demands. The original and current due date columns in this case signify the date that a basic transmitter is needed on the customer order. These dates should obviously be maintained in concert with the component required dates on the customer orders. The zero in the demand block for customer order 29430 indicates that the basic transmitter has already been issued from supply order 6983 whose quantity has been reduced to nine. The demand quantity for order 29430 has also been set to zero at the top of the form indicating that that demand is satisfied.

Listed below the customer order demands are the master schedule or supply orders. In this case, the original and current due dates signify the date the order is due to be completed and made available for use.

To the right of the form is a graphical display of the supplies and demands for the part. The first 13 columns are weekly buckets, in this case representing the calendar weeks in April (14-17), May (18-21) and June (22-26). The next nine columns represent the months July through March. Each demand and supply quantity is shown in the column representing the respective demand or supply date. At the top of the form is a summary of the supplies and demands. A straight forward MRP projection is then calculated showing the projected available inventory balance. The supplies and demands for this part are in alignment until January, when the projected inventory drops to a negative two. Since the

problem is occurring ten months in the future, the master scheduler can reschedule supply order 3204 into January without causing any problems.

As time passes, the master scheduler updates and reschedules supply and demand orders. As master schedule supply orders are completed and turned into stock, the quantity shown in the right hand grid section is reduced until it reaches zero. In similar fashion, the demands are reduced to zero as parts are issued to the customer orders. Obviously these forms should be done in pencil since changes will occur often. Depending on the activity of the item, the S/D status form is recopied and the calendar grid adjusted every one or two months.

Figure VI is the supply/demand status sheet for the input matcher. A little study will reveal why customer order 30350 is late. The first supply order for the input matcher was entered late on March 15, 1984, probably due to late design completion. It was originally scheduled for completion on May 10, only two months after it was entered. The current realistic due date is June 23 thus explaining why the date required for the input matcher on customer order 30350 is June 23.

The forecast line for the input matcher was calculated based on the following:

- The maximum quantity of three per copied from the planning bill is shown in the Qty/Opt % column.

- Also shown in the Qty/Opt % column is the option percentage for the item. This percentage is negotiated between the master scheduler and marketing forecaster and and is often heavily weighed toward a historical percentage. The correct way to think about this percentage is that ten percent of the AM-1 models sold will have three input matchers.

- Once the quanity/percentage relationship to AM-1 sales is established, the shipment forecast, offset by the planned configuration lead time of four weeks, is multiplied by three and then by 10 percent (or by 0.3). Booked orders including the input matcher must be subtracted,

FIGURE V
SUPPLY/DEMAND STATUS

PART NBR. 3820 DESC. BASIC XMITTER PREP. BY MIKE MATERIAL DATE 1/3/84 PAGE 1 OF 1

COST $7K CUM LT 5 MOS.

SAF STK 2 REJ INV 0

S/D	ORDER NUMBER	PART NUMBER	QTY/ OPT%	L/T OFF	DATE ENT'D	ORIG. DUE	CURR. DUE	14	15	16	17	18	19	20	21	22	23	24	25	26	J	A	S	O	N	D	J	F	M
	DEMAND							0	1			2	1		1						2	3	3	3	4	5	5		
	SUPPLY							9																20					20
	INVEN							9	8	8	8	6	5	5	4	3	3	2	2	2	17	14	11	7	3	-2	13	8
D	FORECAST	6400	1/100	4wk								2			1						2	3	3	3	4	5	5	5	5
D	30350	6400	1		04/15/84	05/10/84	06/15/84										1												
D	30150	6400	1		04/10/84	05/30/84	05/30/84						1																
D	30100	6400	1		04/01/84	05/15/84	05/15/84					1																	
D	29684	6400	1		03/15/84	04/20/94	04/15/84		1																				
D	29430	6400	1		03/05/84	04/07/84	04/07/84	0																					
S	6983		10		11/03/83	03/18/84	04/02/84	9																					
S	4377		20		02/10/84	08/17/84	08/17/84																	20					
S	3204		20			02/11/85	02/11/85																						20

FIGURE VI
SUPPLY/DEMAND STATUS

PART NBR. 2271   DESC. INPUT MATCHER   PREP. BY MIKE MATERIALS DATE 4/3/84 PAGE 1 OF 1

COST $200   CUM LT 4 MOS. | DEMAND | SAF STK 3   REJ INV 0 | SUPPLY | INVEN.

S/D	ORDER NUMBER	PART NUMBER	QTY/OPTS	L/T OFF	DATE ENT'D	ORIG. DUE	CURR. DUE	14	15	16	17	18	19	20	21	22	23	24	25	26	J	A	S	O	N	D	J	F	M
D	FORECAST	6400	3/10	4WK																									
D	30350	6400	2		04/15/84	05/10/84	06/13/84												2										
S	3782		5		03/15/84	05/10/84	06/23/84												5										
S	3103		5		03/15/84	09/12/84	09/12/84													5									
S	3065		5		03/15/84	02/05/85	02/05/85																					5	

and the resultant entered as the forecast demand.

As discussed earlier, accurate S/D status sheets for all of the items on a planning bill allow a master shceduler to accurately predict the availability of material for a proposed customer order. Each part on the proposed order can be checked to determine the date that uncommitted material is available for the order. The master scheduler can then check with production personnel to determine when capacity is available to assemble and test the material.

FUNCTIONAL ORGANIZATION

The manual scheduling system that has been proposed above requires a great deal of close coordination and communication if all the interlocking dates and quantities are to be kept accurate and synchronized. The master scheduler using the S/D status form is the focal point. He or she must meet regularly with Order Entry, Marketing and Engineering as well as Production and Materials. Changes to the planning bill, sales forecast, master schdule or customer order data must be quickly analyzed and solutions to problems negotiated and then reflected on the S/D status sheets.

APPLICATION

A manual production and inventory control system for configure-to-order products has been presented that can be used by companies too small to use a computer system or by larger companies on an interim basis until a computer system becomes available. The system includes planning bill of material, sales forecast, order entry and master schedule functions. Before modifying and adding to the system, potential users should thoroughly understand the basic mechanics of configure-to-order materials management and scheduling. Users should also make rough drafts of the forms illustrated and use the forms as is for a trial period on a representative

product. The forms and system provided contain all of the data and mechanics required. Additional complications should be closely examined to make sure that they represent true requirements as opposed to "not-invented-here" or "we've always done it this way" requirements.

BIOGRAPHICAL SKETCH

Joe H. Blackburn, Jr., is Materials Manager for the Personal Computer Division of NCR Corporation in Clemson, South Carolina. He was previously Director of Materials at the Broadcast Division of Harris Corporation in Quincy, Illinois where he participated in a project to install an MRP system. He has a BS degree in Electrical Engineering from North Carolina State University and has previously worked in quality control and production testing.

ROUGH-CUT CAPACITY PLANNING—
WHAT IT IS AND HOW TO USE IT

Kenneth L. Campbell, CPIM
Digital Equipment Corporation

OBJECTIVE

The purpose of this presentation is to describe what Rough Cut Capacity Planning (RCCP) is, how it fits into a closed loop manufacturing system, what is required to make it work and why one should include it in their operations.

BACKGROUND

For many of us, the phrase "closed loop manufacturing systems" conjures up a vision of a series of geometrical figures and arrows, one of which is labeled "MRP". (See Figure 1)

The increased use of material requirements planning (MRP) has brought such systems to front stage center and they are the focal point of many of the other presentations at this conference.

This diagram (Figure 1) is meant to protray the importance of feedback - of a system that detects "unsafe" conditions and emits warning signals to alert the user. They are considered the early warning systems of the manufacturing world. In this diagram, there are two feedback loops.

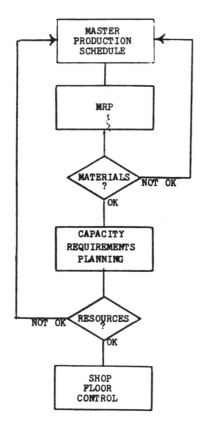

FIGURE 1

The first is from MRP to the Master Schedule. This loop warns of any imbalances of material. The method reporting the imbalance is generally an action report giving move-in, move-out, order and cancel messages.

The second feedback loop is of more interest to us since it concerns capacity. It is the one shown flowing from the block titled Capacity Requirements Planning (CRP) back to the Master Schedule. This loop warns of problems with resources: machines, tools and people.

However, as systems were developed which contained these two loops, it became evident that there must be a better way to test the validity of the Master Schedule relative to the availability of resources.

The problem which surfaced was the long "turn around" time required to validate the availibility of resources. Both MRP and CRP are relatively long runs: both in elapsed time and computer usage. If it was necessary to adjust the Master Schedule, another lengthy loop was required.

Rough Cut Capacity Planning is the technique which has been recognized as an alternative to these lengthy loops. This presentation will explore RCCP in detail.

RCCP AND THE CLOSED LOOP SYSTEM

When RCCP is introduced, the familiar diagram takes on a new appearance. (See Figure 2)

In this diagram, we see a feedback loop between the block titled "RCCP" and the Master Schedule. Since this occurs before MRP, it is obvious that considerable time can be saved in detecting resource problems.

Perhaps we should look first at how Rough Cut Capacity Planning differs from Capacity Requirements Planning.

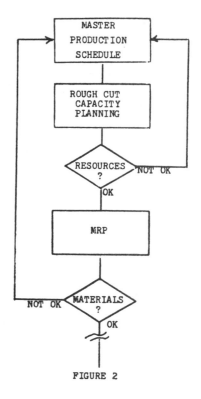

FIGURE 2

Because CRP occurs after the MRP, it (CRP) can be considered a "netted" system that works directly from the Planned Orders, Firm Planned Orders and Scheduled Receipts associated with the MRP programs. These are the result of extensive level-by-level processing.

Rough Cut Capacity Planning is, as the name implies, unnetted. It does not take into consideration any existing inventory. It simply explodes the quantities in the master schedule.

Because it is unnetted, RCCP is not as accurate, and therefore not as reliable, for the short term planning interval. However, in most cases, the Master Schedule extends out well beyond the lead time for most self-manufactured components and products. For this reason, netting has little effect. Consequently, Rough Cut Capacity Planning is considered a medium to long range planning tool.

BASIC DEFINITIONS

Before attempting to further discuss Rough Cut Capacity Planning, a few terms should be defined.

CPIM Master Planning Reprints

Capacity -
The ability to do work. Sometimes stated as the calculated value. In other cases, it is considered the demonstrated output of a work center. It is usually expressed in hours.

Load -
The work to be done and for which capacity is reserved. It is the equivalent of demands or requirements in a material situation. Load is generally expressed in hours.

Bill of Resources -
A list of the resources required to produce a product. It defines the resources required and the quantity (hours) of those resources. It may also contain a "lead time off set" value.

Master Schedule -
A statement of what is to be manufactured. It is expressed in terms of product units and time periods.

FUNDAMENTALS OF RCCP

The concepts of Rough Cut Capacity Planning are straight forward.
1. Determine the Capacity of the Resources (Work Centers) involved.
2. Determine the Load by time period, represented by the products and quantities in the Master Schedule.
3. Compare the Capacity and Load, time period by time period, noting any significant differences.
4. Report the Differences.

The calculation of the capacity of a resource is not difficult.
It is the product of such variables as:
1. Number of units (people, tools, machines) in the work center.
2. The hours per day when the work center functional.
3. The number of working days in the period.
4. Allowances for personal fatigue, machine maintenance, etc.

In the literature, some authors' suggest that the demonstrated capacity averaged over several time periods should be used.
Others suggest using the calculated capacity using the factors shown above. The allowances can be used to adjust for inefficiencies.
In either case, it is the same capacity as you would use for Capacity Requirements Planning.
Determining the load is somewhat more complicated and does require a different data base than is used in CRP.
In general, the data required is contained in a file known as a Bill of Resources. The make-up of this Bill will depend upon what is in the Master Schedule. If you master schedule options, the Bill of Resources would be based on options. If you master schedule major product families, the BOR would be based on these product families.
If the Master Schedule includes an independent demand for service parts and components, the process sheet or master routing data for those items may also be used for RCCP as they are in CRP.
Later in this presentation, we will examine how a BOR for a product family can be developed. However, before we get to that, we will continue the discussion of how the load is generated

THE EXPLOSION PROCESS

From the Master Schedule, we extract a list (ie. Computer File) of identification numbers, dates and quantities. Using the identification number, the appropriate BOR can be located for processing.
Since the BOR identifies each of the resources (work centers) required and the time per piece (or other appropriate unit), one can calculate the total extended time required of the resource. If present, the time required for setup can be added to the extended time.

Also, if present, the lead time set back value can be used to "adjust" the Master Schedule date. Then the extended values and adjusted dates, along with the work center identification, can be outputted to a file (computer record) for later processing.
The process just defined is called "exploding".

THE REPORTING PROCESS

When the entire Master Schedule has been exploded, the resulting records are sorted by work center and date. They can then be summarized by work center and week and the summarized load compared to the planned capacity for the work center.
When a significant difference exists between the summarized load and the work centers planned capacity, the user should review his options.
If the load is somewhat less than capacity, it indicates that the work center is not likely to be fully utilized. Perhaps the capacity of the work center can be adjusted downward by working fewer shifts or re-assigning personnel to other work centers. Another alternative would be to adjust the Master Schedule to provide more of a load to the work center for the week(s) in question.
If the load is significantly greater than the work center's capacity, it indicates that work will not be done on schedule and the user is obligated to take action.
Again, there are two basic options. If practical, the capacity can be increased, perhaps by adding overtime or re-assigning personnel from an underloaded work center. If the overload is indicated to be present for a number of periods, the user may find it necessary to increase capacity by adding machines and/or tools.
When there is no other practical solution to the overload, the user should alter the Master Schedule to eliminate the overload.

TEST THE ADJUSTED MASTER SCHEDULE

When the user has found it necessary to adjust the Master Schedule, a new Rough Cut Capacity Planning run is advisable. This is particularly true if the quantities have been shifted or if any new quantities have been added.
Even if quantities were only reduced, the user may wish to re-run RCCP in order to determine if any work center(s) is significantly underloaded.
It is this re-running that makes Rough Cut Capacity Planning advantageous as compared to Capacity Requirements Planning.
As previously pointed out, to re-run RCCP, it is not necessary to go thru the entire MRP run.
Also, since RCCP employees Bills of Resources (as compared to routing files or process sheets) it is a "single level" explosion process and requires much less time than CRP.

STRUCTURING A BILL OR RESOURCE

As mentioned earlier, the make-up of the Bill of Resources (BOR) will depend upon what is Master Scheduled. If the master scheduling is done by product family, the BOR's should represent the same product families. If the Master Schedule includes options, the RCCP should include BOR's for options.
Of course, the Master Schedule is most frequently stated in specific products. In this case, the BOR will represent the specific product.
Before getting into more specifics about the structure of a BOR, it should be stated again that in all cases, the BOR is a "single level" structure. Even if the unit master scheduled is the upper level of a multilevel Bill of Material, the corresponding BOR will include the resources required for fabrication and assembly of all levels of the BOM.
To illustrate the steps in structuring a BOR, we will borrow an example used by another author in one of the trade journals.[*] In that article, the author selected the (hypothetical) Little Red Wagon Company which could produce nearly 6500 different end products from 32 basic parts and some common hardware.
For example, the company offers a small red wagon with wheels of four(4), five (5), or six (6) inch diameter. It also offers this same wagon with different handles, some of which are painted and others are plated with chrome.

For planning materials, the company developed a Planning Bill of Materials based on the popularity of each of the various options.

In doing this, they might determine that the popularity of wheel size could be charted as shown in Figure 3.

Since all wagons require wheels, it is understandable that the sum of the popularities for wheels (21+56+23) must represent 100% of all wagons assembled.

Likewise, since each wagon requires one handle, the popularity of the painted handles (74%) and the popularity of chrome handle (26%) represents 100% of all the wagons assembled.

They also offer cushions as an "optional extra". Only 8% of the wagons have cushions.

POPULARITY CHART SMALL RED WAGONS	
OPTION	% of SHIPMENTS
4" Wheels	21
5" Wheels	56
6" Wheels	23
TOTAL	100
Painted Handles	74
Chrome Handles	26
TOTAL	100
Cushion	8
No Cushion	92
TOTAL	100
(Note: Partial List)	

FIGURE 3

In a planning BOM, the "per quantities" for the items mentioned would appear as follows:

ITEM	QTY/1 WAGON
4" Wheels	.21
5" Wheels	.56
6" Wheels	.23
Painted Handles	.74
Chrome Handles	.26
Cushions (Purchased)	.08

This same concept can be used to develop a Bill of Resources for the small red wagon.

If we review the "routings" for each of the items previously listed, we might find the following:

WORK CENTER	DESCRIPTION	TIME(hours)
4"WHEELS		
S1	Stamping	.01
W2	Welding	.04
P3	Painting	.05
5"WHEELS		
S1	Stamping	.01
W2	Welding	.05
P3	Painting	.06
6"WHEELS		
S1	Stamping	.01
W2	Welding	.05
P3	Painting	.07

WORK CENTER	DESCRIPTION	TIME(hours)
PAINTED HANDLES		
S1	Stamping	.01
F1	Forming	.02
W2	Welding	.05
P3	Painting	.06
CHROME HANDLES		
S1	Stamping	.01
F1	Forming	.02
W2	Welding	.05
E4	Electroplating	.10

CUSHIONS
Purchased; therefore no routings

Given the popularity of the various options, as used in developing the planning BOM, and remembering that each wagon has four wheels, the Bill of Resources (as related only to the items listed) would be developed as follows:

For the Stamping Work Centers (S1), the required time for one small red wagon would be:

4" Wheels: 4 x .21 x .01 = .0084

5" Wheels: 4 x .56 x .01 = .0224

6" Wheels: 4 x .23 x .01 = .0092

P-Handles: 1 x .74 x .01 = .0074

C-Handles: 2 x .26 x .01 = .0026

TOTAL .0500 hrs/wagon

For the Welding Work Center (W2), the required time would be:

4" Wheels: 4 x .21 x .04 = .0336

5" Wheels: 4 x .56 x .05 = .1120

6" Wheels: 4 x .23 x .05 = .0460

P-Handles: 1 x .74 x .05 = .0370

C-Handles: 1 x .26 x .05 = .0130

TOTAL .2416 hrs/wagon

When the same pattern is used for the other options and work centers, a BOR will result. The completed BOR (relative to the items listed) would appear as shown in Figure 4. It should be noted that the times shown are related to one (1) small red wagon.

BILL OF RESOURCES		
PRODUCT: SMALL RED WAGON		
WORK CTR	OPERATION DESCRIPTION	STANDARD HRS/WAGON
S1	Stamping	0.0500
W2	Welding	0.2416
F1	Forming	0.0200
P3	Painting	0.0444
E4	Electroplating	0.0260
(Partial List)		

FIGURE 4

A similar BOR could be developed for other families: for example, a large red wagon. If we refer to the article mentioned, we would note that not all the wagons offered by the Little Red Wagon Company are red. Some are painted blue, some green and some black. If we make the assumption that the times required for production are independent of color, one BOR for each size (small and large) sould be practical.

If they should require different resources because of color, for example a different paint booth for black paint, it would then be necessary to factor in the popularity of color.

REPORTING FORMATS

There are three basic reporting formats which can be conveniently applied to Rough Cut Capacity Planning.

The first is a tabulated report as shown in Figure 5. This format reports more precisely than the others since it shows the actual numbers derived for each time period.

The second format is a simple graphic display as shown in Figure 6. This format suggests that the load is a "continous" function. However, since it is generally summarized in time periods, a graphic display is not as representative as is the bar graph shown in Figure 7.

In either of these last two forms, the planned capacity of the work center is shown as a dashed horizontal line. When the planned capacity is changing, the dashed line is not as convenient. In this case, and if color is available, it might be useful to represent the planned capacity by a different color. This can be done by shading the background or, in the case of the bar graph, a second bar representing the capacity in the period.

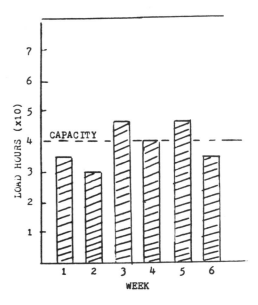

WORK CENTER: P3 PAINTING

FIGURE 7

ROUGH CUT CAPACITY REPORT
WORK CENTER: P3 Painting

	WEEK					
	1	2	3	4	5	6
CAPACITY	40	40	40	40	40	40
LOAD	35	30	45	40	45	35
VARIANCE	-5	-10	+5	0	+5	-5
% (L/C)	88	75	125	100	125	88

FIGURE 5

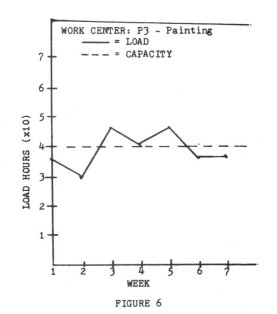

FIGURE 6

SUMMARY

Rough Cut Capacity Planning is rapidly becoming one of the planner's best tools. Since it can be executed prior to the MRP programs, it is less time consuming than Capacity Requirements Planning. For medium to long range planning, RCCP can be as accurate as CRP.

References

1. Richard C. Ling, "MASTER SCHEDULING in a MAKE-TO-ORDER ENVIRONMENT", Inventories & Production (July-August 1981), pg. 17

ABOUT THE AUTHOR

Kenneth L. Campbell has been active in APICS for over fifteen years. He has spoken at several other National Conferences and has contributed articles to the Quarterly. Ken is a Past President of the Worcester County (MA) Chapter. He is employed as a Manufacturing Systems Consultant by Digital Equipment Corporation.

FINAL ASSEMBLY SCHEDULING IN AN OPTION
SENSITIVE PRODUCT ENVIRONMENT
Vinnie Chopra, CFPIM
Resource Management Associates

Reprinted from 1989 APICS Conference Proceedings.

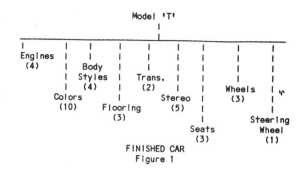

FINISHED CAR
Figure 1

INTRODUCTION

Final Assembly Scheduling represents one of the most important planning and control tools in an assemble-to-order environment, specially one that offers a multitude of options. Yet it happens to be one facet of a closed-loop MRP II system that is neither fully understood nor effectively applied and executed.

In fact, it is ironical that in many companies, while enough attention and importance is given to other schedules, like the master production schedule, material requirements planning and the daily shop schedule; the final assembly schedule-- the one that gets the final product out the back door-- gets a very superficial and informal treatment.

The entire material planning and control cycle will be discussed in this paper beginning with component planning utilizing a two-level master schedule and planning bills. This will be followed with how the sales order entry process is used to create the customer bill of material which becomes the basis for developing the final assembly schedule. This in turn will be used to not only schedule the final product, but also to provide visibility to stock room personnel, in the form of a work center oriented, time-phased pick list; to deliver the right components to the assembly line or area.

Several state-of-the-arts innovative concepts will be discussed with extreme practical value.

THE APPLICATION

Final assembly scheduling takes on a real complex dimension when a product can be configured in a multitude of ways. This typically occurs when various options exist within several families. While some of these options may not be mutually exclusive, the customer for the most part can pick and choose any of these options. The resulting combination of options can result in literally hundreds of thousands of end items.

To further complicate the planning and scheduling problem many times it is virtually impossible to forecast the customer demand for the end item. It is precisely in this environment that many of the concepts discussed in this paper apply offering some break-through solutions.

THE DILEMMA

Imagine an automotive company that offers a variety of options. Figure 1 shows an abbreviated illustration of what these may be. Four different types of engines, ten different colors, four different body styles, three floor options, two transmissions, five different stereo and sound systems, three seat options, three different wheel styles and one type of steering wheel. Assuming all options to be mutually exclusive, that is to say, the customer can pick any one from each of the families, the total number of cars that can be configured is: 4 x 10 x 4 x 3 x 2 x 5 x 3 x 3 x 1 = 43,2001. Of course, as soon as the company offers one more steering wheel option the end item combination increases geometrically to 86,400.

Imagine the dilemma of such a company in planning and scheduling their product when their total production plan calls for only 100 cars per week. Which 100 out of the 86,400 is the question. This, of course, is the classic problem for all products with option sensitive sale assemblies.

This would at first glance appear to be a perfect application for the modular or planning bill of material. However, before jumping the gun, two conditions bear examining. The existence of either condition could still bail us out of this dilemma.

These are: 1. If the delivery lead time based on the market conditions happens to be, say 35 weeks and the cumulative lead time is only 30 weeks; and 2. If somehow we had a crystal ball that could fairly accurately forecast the 100 end item configurations that we expect to sell per week.

Wishful thinking indeed! In all probability the delivery lead time, because of customer and competitive pressure, is apt to be more like 5 weeks. And as for the second condition, it has been appropriately stated that 'there are only two types of forecasts - lucky and lousy'.

So a product structure becomes a perfect candidate for the modular bill of material application if:
1. The delivery lead time is less than the cumulative lead time.
   AND
2. End item forecast is not feasible.

MODULARIZING THE BILL

Companies faced with these conditions in the past would throw up their hands in frustration and conclude that MRP II just was not for them. They claimed that since they could not even begin to come up with a 'build schedule' --- a prerequisite --- they could not drive material or capacity planning. Looked at from that perspective that certainly appeared to be true!

And then came the breakthrough!

It came in the form of what was termed as the modular bill of material approach. The approach literally forced you to lower your planning sites at least a level below the end item. Stated in the MRP jargon, it involves two basic steps:

1. Disentangle the combination of options.
   AND
2. Separate the common from the unique parts. Once modularized, the resulting product structure, at the top level is variously referred to as the planning bill, S bill, Super bill et al. This bill becomes the basis for master scheduling, sales order entry and final assembly scheduling. Again, this approach applies only if you have the problem --- end item forecast is not feasible AND delivery lead time is less than the product end to end lead time.

Utilizing this approach, the automobile's planning bill in its abbreviated form would look like Figure 2.

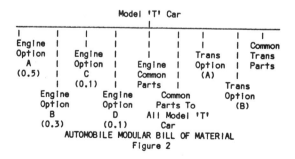

AUTOMOBILE MODULAR BILL OF MATERIAL
Figure 2

Two significant aspects to keep in mind during modularization process are, how far down in the product structure to carry the modularization; and the quantity per relationship.

Referring to Figure 2, the four (4) engine options could have been structured as stand alone buildable assemblies; or as is shown, they may be modularized further by segregating all the parts common to each of the engine options and attaching them to the product structure as a kit of common parts.

The criteria to use in determining the level up to which to modularize, if feasible, involved trade offs. End the process one level below the automobile reduces the final assembly scheduling but increases inventory investment in the event overplanning is done and the customer demand does not materialize. Modularizing deeper in the bill the opposite conditions would prevail.

The quantity per relationship has extreme significance. This represents the quantity that will be utilized for all option planning. The numbers used are often the popularity that option represents of the total product demand. In other words, in our example, engine option A has been determined based on part sales and any future extrinsic information to have a popularity of fifty (50) percent. That is to say, 50 percent of all model T sales are expected to ask for engine option A.

The structuring of a planning bill such as the one described represents an extremely crucial step. This bill quite literally becomes the framework on which the entire planning, scheduling and order entry is going to hang.

THE TRADITIONAL APPROACH TO MASTER SCHEDULING WITH THE MODULAR BILLS.

The planning bill using the modular approach as illustrated in Figure 2, winds up with a series of options and common parts kits, none of these being buildable items. These are referred to as psuedo part numbers. It is at this level, more than likely, that the master production schedule is going to be set. With traditional single level master scheduling, the production plan --- top managements authorization --- will be created at level 0 --- the generic family called Model T. This production plan will be broken down into, what in essence, is the production plan for each of the psuedo options and common parts kits using the popularity percentages. This is the planning visibility that the master scheduler has for creating firm planned lots, according to the production strategy, within the planning time fence.

Utilizing the engine option A, with a popularity percentage of 50, and a production plan of 100 per week for the model T automobile, the planning logic for master scheduling is illustrated in Figure 3.

ENGINE OPTION A --- 50% POPULARITY

Week	1	2	3	4	5	6	7	8
Production Plan	50	50	50	50	50	50	50	50
Customer Demand								
Available To Promise	100		100		100		100	
MPS	100		100		100		100	

MASTER PRODUCTION SCHEDULE REPORT
Figure 3

In our example, the master scheduler has settled on bringing in 100 engines A every other week in order to satisfy the engine A production plan of 50 every week. All such master schedule firm planned lots must first be validated for material and capacity availability (where applicable) by running these quantities through the material and capacity requirements planning modules.

THE PITFALLS OF THE SINGLE LEVEL MPS

Using the traditional single level master scheduling approach, companies become extremely

vulnerable to significant inventory build ups and reduction in customer service levels. Here is the scenario that leads to these conditions:

Let us assume we are operating in a back log mode with an order bank of six (6) weeks. For these first six weeks, the master scheduler has taken the necessary corrective action and adjusted the engine option A master schedule to the actual booked demand. In other words, we are starting with a clean slate, as illustrated in Figure 4.

MPS - ENGINE OPTION A

Week	1	2	3	4	5	6	7	8
Production Plan	50	50	50	50	50	50	50	50
Customer Demand	30	40	20	60	25	75		
Available To Promise	0		0		0			
MPS	70		80		100		100	

THE MPS REPORT SHOWING THE BACKLOG
Figure 4

Let us suppose that two more orders arrive. Customer A wants 100 automobiles model T for delivery in week 7 with only 30 of them requiring engine option A. Customer B also orders 100 model T for delivery in week 8 with a call out for only 10 engine A options. This, of course, is a perfectly real world situation. Inspite of a 50 percent popularity of engine option A, the random nature of customer demand could easily cause such a situation to occur.

And here is where the problems begin! Examine Figure 5. The available-to-promise in week 7 drops from 100 to 60, since 30 engine option A in week 7, and 10 in week 8 have just been sold. The master scheduler, however, lacks total visibility (other than a manual log), that no more 'T' model automobiles can

MPS - ENGINE OPTION A

Week	1	2	3	4	5	6	7	8
Production Plan	50	50	50	50	50	50	50	50
Customer Demand	30	40	20	60	25	75	30	10
Available To Promise	0		0		0		60	
MPS	70		80		100		100	

THE A-T-P IN A SINGLE LEVEL MPS
Figure 5

be sold since the total production plan authorized (100 each of the two weeks) has been completely sold out.

Lacking this vital information there is a strong probability that 60 engine option A that are not required (since no more T model autos can be sold in those two weeks) will stay in the plan driving up the inventory levels and utilizing critical manufacturing capacity (if engines are in fact manufactured by the company).

Therein lies the crux of the problem!

The traditional single level master scheduling approach completely fails to keep the schedule of options in synch with the saleable end item --- the automobile --- as sales materialize.

MULTI LEVEL MASTER PRODUCTION SCHEDULING

The multi level master scheduling approach allows the master schedule to be set simultaneously at two or more successive levels. While technically feasible to select several levels, the most common approach used involves two levels --- the generic model (model T in our example) level and the next level below (the common and unique parts psuedos).

In essence, the multi level MPS ties the various options to the end item generic parent and as customer orders materialize, the MPS lots, originally set at the option level, are modified, if necessary.

Utilizing the previous example, we wind up with two distinct sets of master schedules --- one for the generic automobile model T and the other for each of the unique and common parts pseudo numbers.

Referring to Figure 6, the production plan for model T is 100 per week. The master scheduler sets up firm planned orders for these same quantities which represents the master schedule for the automobiles. Starting with no orders in the order bank, the A-T-P for model T is as shown.

MODEL T   (1st Level)

Week	1	2	3	4	5	6	7	8
Production Plan	100	100	100	100	100	100	100	100
Customer Demand								
A-T-P	100	100	100	100	100	100	100	100
MPS	100	100	100	100	100	100	100	100

ENGINE OPTION A - 50%   (2nd Level)

Week	1	2	3	4	5	6	7	8
Production Forecast	50	50	50	50	50	50	50	50
Customer Demand								
A-T-P	100		100		100		100	
MPS	100		100		100		100	

THE TWO LEVEL MASTER SCHEDULE
Figure 6

The critical aspect of multilevel master scheduling involves understanding that the A-T-P at the model T level represents future or anticipated orders. Consequently this represents the only quantities of automobiles that are subject to a forecast for the option demand. Hence the A-T-P at level 1 becomes the basis for the production forecast at level 2. The production forecast at level 2 is therefore calculated by exploding the A-T-P from level 1 and multiplying it with the popularity percentage for each of the level 2 MPS items.

It is precisely this link that allows multi level master scheduling to be such a powerful tool for planning and scheduling by keeping option planning in synch with the production plan of the family as orders materialize.

To illustrate this point refer to Figure 7.

MODEL T   (1st Level)

Week	1	2	3	4	5	6	7	8
Production Plan	100	100	100	100	100	100	100	100
Customer Demand	100	100	100	100	100	100	100	100
A-T-P	0	0	0	0	0	0	0	0
MPS	100	100	100	100	100	100	100	100

ENGINE OPTION A - 50%   (2nd Level)

Week	1	2	3	4	5	6	7	8
Production Forecast	0	0	0	0	0	0	0	0
Customer Demand	30	40	20	60	25	75	30	10
A-T-P	0		0		0		60	
MPS	70		80		100		100	

KEEPING THE OPTIONS IN SYNCH WITH THE MODEL
Figure 7

Let us pick up on the single level MPS example from Figure 4. Recall that we had a back log of six (6) weeks, meaning that all one hundred (100) of the production plans in each of the first six weeks has been fully sold, with engine option A demand as shown.

As indicated before, the MPS lots have already been adjusted in the past, to be compatible with the actual demand for this particular option.

Again using the previous scenario, two customer orders arrive. Customer order A for 100 model T in week 7 called for 30 engine option A; and customer order B for 100 model T in week 8 called for only 10 engine option A.

As orders for the model T are entered in week 7 and week 8; the customer demand line at level 1 goes to 100 in each of the two weeks and at level 2 goes to 30 in week 7 and 10 in week 8. Since the A-T-P line at level 1 has dropped to zero (0) --- no more autos being available for future sales --- The production forecast at level 2 also goes to zero (0).

Again referring to Figure 7, the master scheduler now has clear visibility that he has 60 engine option A too many in the plan. He may now review the alternatives and most likely will reduce his MPS lot in week 7 from 100 down to 40, thus preventing useless and costly inventory build up for the wrong options.

This process thus becomes the means with which to keep the option planning in synch with the model sales affording an opportunity to significantly reduce inventory investment and at the same time improve customer service levels.

SALES ORDER ENTRY

As customer orders arrive and are checked against the available-to-promise for each of the options requested to insure availability; they are entered into the system. This triggers three major occurrences. They are:

1. A customer bill is structured which represents the unique configuration of the end item sold. This in turn becomes the basis for the pick list for the parts to be delivered to the assembly line.
2. The configured end items with scheduled start and finish dates becomes the basis for final assembly scheduling for building each unique model T car, and
3. The quantity of each option and common parts kit that is entered against the customer order, consumes from the master schedule firm planned lots, recalculating and revising the available-to-promise quantities for each master scheduled level item. The revised A-T-P, of course, becomes the basis for delivery promise for the next customer inquiry.

A feature that can be built into the planning bills that can greatly facilitate the order entry process is a series of prompts. These prompts which have to be built into the product structure with special codes have no planning function but can really make the order entry process relatively simple. An example of this is shown in Figure 8.

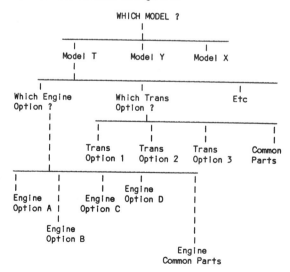

OPTION ORDER ENTRY BILL
Figure 8

These prompts can further be coded such that if a required option, such as engines is involved, the order entry person is forced to specify one of the options.

Options such as air conditioning may of course, be by-passed. Common parts associated with required options can be automatically attached to the customer bill.

An example of the resulting configured automobile is shown in Figure 9.

Model T
C - 1001

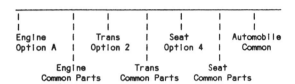

UNIQUE CUSTOMER BILL
Figure 9

FINAL ASSEMBLY SCHEDULING

As stated before, the customized and configured customer bill now becomes the basis for final assembly scheduling. The final assembly schedule, a level above the MPS, is driven off of the customer orders that have been booked. Based on the assembly lead time and the due dates for deliveries, the final assembly schedule can now be set in the form of firm orders. As these firm orders are released, pick lists, referencing the customer bills of material, will be generated allowing the stock room to deliver the required unique and common parts to the line. By specifying the individual work centers on the bills, stock room personnel can get visibility on the pick lists as to where, physically, the parts should be delivered on the assembly line. Additionally, lead time offsets may also be specified on the bills of material allowing the parts planning and delivery to the line to be in synch with the true need dates.

BIOGRAPHY

Vinnie Chopra is a Principal of Resource Management Associates, an International consulting firm that he founded. The company, with clients in the U.S., Europe, Canada and Mexico, specializes in assisting clients in implementing manufacturing, and distribution planning and control systems. Among the services provided are business counseling, in-house education, and project management assistance.

Mr. Chopra, who holds a BSME and an MSIE from the University of Houston, has over eighteen (18) years of experience, both in line management, in the areas of manufacturing, materials, and engineering, as well as in consulting. He is a sought after speaker by various national and international societies, having spoken at APICS International for the last seven years. He led a highly successful delegation of American businessmen to Japan in 1983 at the invitation of a consortium of Japanese companies. He is certified as a CFPIM by the American Production and Inventory Control Society and teaches their AMES education classes.

CAPACITY MANAGEMENT
PART TWO

AN EXPANSION OF 'CAPACITY MANAGEMENT'
FROM THE 1979 APICS
ANNUAL CONFERENCE PROCEEDINGS

James T. Clark
IBM Corporation
Manufacturing Industry Education
Poughkeepsie, N.Y.

This paper is an expansion of the paper "Capacity Management" included in the APICS 22nd Annual Conference Proceedings (Page 191). If this paper is not available to the reader, one will be mailed by the author on request.

The initial paper addressed three capacity management topics: The financial payoff, a closed loop capacity management system and its relationship to priority management, and an outline of various capacity management techniques.

The major principle that was developed was that manufacturing companies are driven by a series of schedules ranging from the long range formal business plan to the detailed short range operation sequence or dispatch list. A derivation of this principle suggests there must be a series of priority systems and a series of capacity systems associated with each of the many scheduling systems.

This is recapped in figure 10 of the 1979 proceedings.

(Please note that the schedules listed and the corresponding diagram of a closed loop system in the 1979 Capacity Management paper imply that the final assembly schedule and master production schedule are synonymous. This is often the case in manufacturing build to order as well as make to stock products.

It is necessary however, in some manufacturing environments to separate the final assembly schedule from the master production schedule. The obvious example of this is assembled to order products that depend on a customer order dictating a mix of options for specific end-product configurations.

The scheduling system matrix would then include the final assembly schedule between the production plan and the master schedule. In the closed loop flow: customer order servicing would be input to the final assembly schedule, forcasting would be input to the master production schedule for option forecasts and there would be two way communication between the final assembly schedule and the master production schedule. The master production schedule would continue to feed MRP.)

The objective of this paper is to expand on the details of the series of capacity management systems.

The following topics will be addressed:

A. Resource Requirements Planning and Rough Cut Capacity Planning

B. Input/Output Monitoring and Control

C. Manufacturing Activity Planning

. Capacity Requirements Planning
. Completion Time Estimating
. Operation Sequencing

In the heirarchy of capacity management systems that support the heirarchy of scheduling systems a number of techniques and approaches have been employed.

It is impossible to identify a single specific technique with a specific level of schedule or level of planning and control for all manufacturers. One manufacturer for example, might use a detailed operations schedule and weekly bucket loading system for capacity management as it relates to the production plan. Another manufacturer might find this impractical because of the data and data processing volumes, and utilize resource load profile simulations. A consumer packaged goods manufacturer might use linear programming to optimize production schedules while this technique would be totally impractical in a job shop.

The definition of short, medium and long range vary by manufacturer and even by product as does the definition of the level of detail relative to the elements of time, product, capacity, etc.

In addition, the proliferation of terminology is overwhelming. Consider: Resource planning, load profile simulations, bills of resources, bills of labor, infinite loading, rough cut capacity planning, job shop simulations, etc.

To minimize this confusion, Figure 1 introduces the terminology of this paper as well as a relative placement of the capacity systems on the axes of planning horizon length and level of detail.

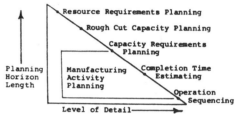

figure 1.

A. Resource Requirements Planning and Rough Cut Capacity Planning

Resource requirements planning, or simply resource planning, has been defined as the process of determining long range resource or capacity needs. The resource planning horizon is at least as long as the lead time to acquire the resource. The horizon should also include sufficient additional time to determine if the need will exist for a long enough period to justify capital commitments.

Rough cut capacity planning has been defined as an analysis of the master schedule to assist in evaluating capacity requirements for critical manufacturing facilities. It falls between resource requirements planning and detailed operational level capacity requirements planning (CRP). Rough cut capacity planning is by definition less detailed than capacity requirements planning and is generally done less frequently.

The major distinction between resource requirements planning and rough cut capacity planning is that the former is associated with the business plan and production plan while the latter is associated with the master production schedule. This implies differences in horizons, level of detail, frequency of evaluation, etc.

Capacity management approaches can vary from econometric models to load profile simulations to long range runs of CRP. The exact same technique might be used for both resource requirements planning and rough cut capacity planning, or the same technique but at different levels of detail, or entirely different techniques.

The technique of product load profile simulations is presented here. It presumes that the operational level CRP system involves too much detailed data, too detailed a forecast and too much data processing to be practical for long-range planning.

The steps involved in resource requirements planning include:
a. Defining a typical product structure.
b. Defining the resources that must be considered
c. Determining the "product load profile" for each typical product, that is, how much load is imposed on the resources by a single unit of an end product.

d. Extending these product load profiles by the
    quantity called for in the production plan or
    master schedule, and thus determining the total
    load or "resource requirement", on each of the
    production facilities and other resources.
e. Simulating the effect of different production
    plans or master schedules in order to make the
    best possible use of resources.

Figure 2. Depicts a typical product structure.

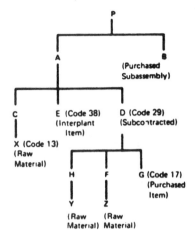

figure 2.

Product P is generally a product group to take
advantage of the improved accuracy of aggregate forecasting. Product groups also decrease the amount of
data to be considered and processed. The product
group must be developed not only to allow aggregate
forecasting but must group products that utilize similar resources.

Product P could be a group of machines including
a statistical mix of options, it could be a single
unique product or it could be an 'average' product
that is never really built.

The next step is to identify critical resources
consumed in the manufacture of P. Figure 2 specifies
certain critical materials which are offset over lead
time in Figure 3.

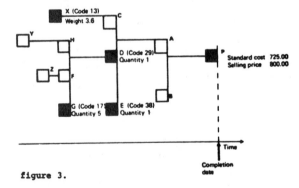

figure 3.

Critical labor is identified and offset over the
lead time of product P in figure 4. This is often
referred to as a bill of labor.

Other critical resources could include design
engineering time, long lead time components, warehouse cubeage, cash, quality assurance, very expensive components, final assembly and test cells, etc.
The objective is to include the truly critical
resources but to keep the list to a manageable number.

Multiple individual resource profiles make up the
product resource profile of Product P. This is depicted in Figure 5.

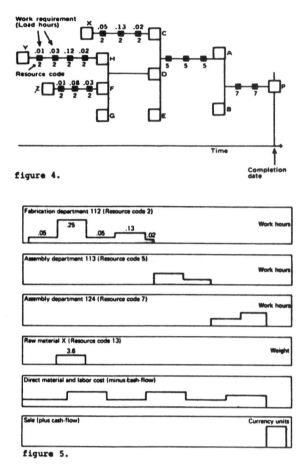

figure 4.

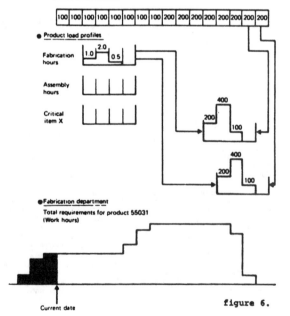

figure 5.

Figure 6. Demonstrates how the profiles are
extended by the quantity in the production plan or
the master schedule. The calculated total requirements profile could now be modified by other factors
such as learning curves or be used to derive the profiles of related resources.

figure 6.

The advantages of the product load profile approach are:

a. It overcomes the data and data processing impracticalities often associated with using the CRP System for long range planning.
b. Its simplicity and speed of processing allows extensive simulation. The result is the ability to develop the probable results of many different possible courses of action. A simulation might indicate for example, that a product group forecast could vary by up to 15% before a major capital formation commitment was shifted into a different fiscal reporting period.
c. A completely computerized bill of material, MRP, routing and scheduling system is not necessary (although the availability of any of this data would obviously be helpful).
d. It allows for the identification of the specific "typical" finished product that created load problems (this may not be practical within the detailed CRP operational system).

The disadvantages include:

a. It is primarily a planning system and does not accomodate measurement and control.
b. The profiles are developed for the manufacture of one unit of the typical product so lot sizing assumptions must be made. A one for one lot sizing approach would usually produce a smoother load than the eventual load produced by the operational level MRP and CRP systems. This is not a serious deficiency for long range planning but could create some problems if the technique were employed in the nearer term. Capacity requirements for set-up would also have to be estimated. Another approach involves using current data from the operational level lot sizes and loads.
c. Available inventories and committed capacities are not considered. This problem is similar to the lot sizing problem and is of minimum consequence for long range planning. Utilizing the approach in the short range, again demands caution.
d. It is not exact. This is more a statement of fact than a disadvantage. The technique is not intended to be exact. If the user realizes this, then there should not be a problem.

B. Input/Output Monitoring and Control

Input/output monitoring and control can be utilized to support various levels of management in manufacturing. Input/output monitoring and control is as useful in production planning and master production scheduling as it is in supporting the management of individual work centers. The examples used here are oriented to a work center since this is the simplest form of input/output monitoring and control. As simple as it is, though, its use is ignored in far too many factories.

A sample input/output report is illustrated in Figure 7.

INPUT/OUTPUT

	PERIOD	1	2	3	4	5	6
INPUT	PLAN	500	500	500	550	550	550
	ACTUAL	450	520	580	540		
	DEVIATION	-50	+20	+80	-10		
	CUM. DEVIATION	-50	-30	+50	+40		

	PERIOD	1	2	3	4	5	6
OUTPUT	PLAN	500	500	500	550	550	550
	ACTUAL	470	480	530	550		
	DEVIATION	-30	-20	+30	-		
	CUM. DEVIATION	-30	-50	-20	-20		

figure 7.

It is important to understand the data elements in input/output monitoring and control.

a. Planned input is the most critical element and the most challenging to manage. Input must be managed. It is not simply taken blindly from a CRP computer report.
b. Actual input as well as actual output are measured values. Accurate and timely shop reporting is essential. Actual output establishes the true available capacity of a work center.

c. The planned output is an estimate into the near future from the work center foreman. It is based on his knowledge of machine and worker capability and availability, job characteristics and mix, and anticipated input.

Actual input and output will have some variability so the cumulative deviation is monitored as well as period deviations. This provides the first indication of whether a work center has an input or an output problem. Cumulative deviation is monitored relative to a specified band or tolerance. Action should be taken when the tolerance is exceeded.

Problems in input force the examination of upstream work centers or in the case of gateway or primary work centers the examination of the order release system and MRP system. The gateway work centers are easier to control in terms of input, particularly if a machine load report and MRP system are available. Order release dates must be managed to insure a steady and realistic flow into the gateway work centers. The order release system is extremely important because it provides a unique opportunity to manage gateway work center input. In fact, it also represents the last opportunity.

The input to secondary or intermediate work centers and to final assembly are more difficult to control because input load is coming from multiple sources. The availability of machine load reports and planned orders from MRP will also support this effort.

Some operation scheduling systems, utilizing combinations of forward and backward scheduling, have been used to accomodate bottleneck work centers, but the discussion of this is beyond the scope of this paper.

In some manufacturing environments the uncoupling of the final assembly schedule from the master schedule is a method of managing input to final assembly. Inventories of assemblies just below the final assembly are justified to maintain controlled input to a high volume final assembly line.

Problems in output are problems with capacity (unless of course they are the direct result of input problems) and the solution of the output problem is an effective capacity planning system. A realistic production plan and master schedule, should be developed with support from resource requirements planning and rough cut capacity planning. The master schedule is input to the MRP and CRP systems and the managed output of CRP develops capacity requirements. Capacity requirements essentially define output requirements. This obviously doesn't eliminate all output problems but hopefully it will minimize them. The short and intermediate range solutions to output problems such as alternate work centers, overtime, subcontract, buy vs. make, etc. will continue to support output management.

The monitoring portion of input/output monitoring and control is relatively simple to implement. It remains for management to provide the dimension of control. Input/output monitoring and control can be completely manual because computerized MRP and CRP is not a prerequisite. Readily available data from any current MRP and CRP systems, would of course, be helpful.

There is no legitimate reason why input/output monitoring and control is not a part of every factory's operation.

C. Manufacturing Activity Planning

Manufacturing Activity Planning, as depicted in the closed loop manufacturing system in the 1979 paper, is down stream from MRP and is the operational level or detail level capacity management system. This system is extremely critical to many interrupted flow manufacturers (job shop or discrete manufacturing) but of minimum importance in continuous flow manufacturing.

Manufacturing Activity Planning is subdivided into capacity requirements planning, completion time estimating and operation sequencing. Figure 8 below, as well as Figure 10 in the 1979 paper, put these systems in perspective.

MANUFACTURING ACTIVITY PLANNING			
	Level of Detail	Planning Horizon	Objective
Capacity Requirements Planning	Week	Months	Develop feasible capacity and material plans
Completion Time Estimating	Day	Weeks	Measure performance against due dates
Operation Sequencing	Hour	Days	Develop detail shop operating plan

figure 8.

It is essential to understand and accept the following premises before pursuing the details of these capacity management systems.

  a. Interrupted flow manufacturing is characterized by the presence of work in process inventory, or queues.
  b. The fundamental challenges of this type of manufacturing involve deciding on what in the queue to work on next and determining if capacity is available to work on it. (priority and capacity management).
  c. Capacity requirements planning and other shorter term detailed capacity management systems essentially involve scheduling by operation and loading by work center.
  d. The capacity requirements planning system can only be as good as the scheduling system.
  e. Scheduling orders and operations demands an understanding of manufacturing lead time.
  f. Manufacturing lead time in job shop or discrete manufacturing (interrupted flow) is made up of set-up and run and interoperation time.
  g. Interoperation time consists of queue for work, queue for move (wait time) and move time. In interrupted flow manufacturing this typically represents 80%-90% of manufacturing lead time.
  h. Queue time is the major ingredient in interoperation time and can easily represent 95% of interoperation time (or 75%-85% of manufacturing lead time).

Assuming that these premises are acceptable then a fundamental conclusion emerges that strongly suggests that capacity requirements planning demands the understanding of, the monitoring of, and the management of work in process inventories and queues.

The following details on capacity requirements planning, completion time estimating and operation sequencing develop progressively increasing refinements in the understanding of and the management of queues.

Capacity Requirements Planning

Capacity requirements planning consists of order scheduling and work center loading. This is often referred to as infinite loading since capacity is not considered in the scheduling or the loading.

Figure 9 is a simple example of scheduling an order by individual operations. The top portion of Figure 9 is input from MRP and includes the part number, quantity, due date and average lead time. The operation schedules are derived by backward scheduling from the due date using a simple scheduling algorithm.

1200 5's due in week 11 (shop calendar day 450)
Lead time = 25 days
order release = day 425

ROUTING OPERATION	WORK CENTER	STANDARD HOURS	START DATE	DUE DATE
			ORDER RELEASE	425
10	A	3.4	428	429
20	B	9.6	432	434
30	C	2.7	437	438
40	D	5.8	441	442
50	E	6.5	445	446
60	F	7.6	449	450

For scheduling:

Assume 3 day queue and move between operations and round standard hours up to the nearest 8 hour day.

figure 9.

A feasible schedule must be developed before the loading step can proceed. Figures 10 illustrate various scheduling situations.

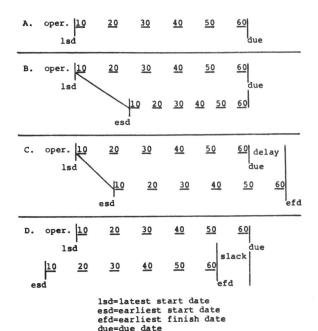

lsd=latest start date
esd=earliest start date
efd=earliest finish date
due=due date

figure 10.

Figure 10A is another way to view Figure 9 and it assumes the order can and will be started on the latest start date.

Figure 10B illustrates a situation where the earliest the order can be started is later than the latest start date. This could be caused by material availability for example. Since the available time is less than the lead time, the interoperation times have been compressed to meet the due date.

Figure 10C is a similar situation showing the delay that would result if interoperation times were not compressed. This decision may have been made in the initial schedule with the intent of compressing interoperation time after order release (expediting) or to simply be late on the order.

Figure 10D illustrates an early start date that is earlier in time than the latest start date and therefore slack is developed. This situation provides an option of starting on the earliest or latest start dates.

These many scheduling possibilities would obviously result in different work center loadings from a timing standpoint. Another key point is that a work center cannot be loaded in the past, so feasible start dates must be developed through logical scheduling.

Capacity requirements of all operations are accumulated for each work center in a given time period based on the results of order scheduling. Figure 11 displays the loads in weekly time buckets for work center C.

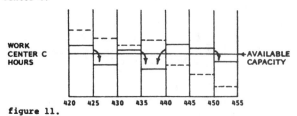

figure 11.

Load profiles can be developed for both early start dates and late start dates. In addition cumulative load should be presented and related to cumulative capacity over some specified horizon.

The load is compared to available capacity to pinpoint potential underload and overload problems. Another important consideration is the cumulative load to capacity measurement and the distribution of that load. If cumulative load is equal to or less than cumulative capacity, an evenly distributed load can probably be leveled. (Solid load lines and arrows in Figure 11). If there are extensive periods of overload or a "moving wave" of current period overloads (dashed load lines in Figure 11) then the ability to level is minimized or eliminated all together.

Capacity requirements planning has a quantity accuracy as good as the standards and a timing accuracy as good as the schedule. Industrial engineering techniques and data collection have long been utilized to define and adjust standards. Unfortunately not enough attention has been given to scheduling, and in particular queue times which is the largest time element in scheduling.

Figures 9 and 10A illustrates a schedule that assumes the same average interoperation time (primarily queue) for all operations and all work centers. This simplifying assumption can probably be tolerated in the longer range, but it can have serious consequences in the timing of load in the near term.

Another important point is that average lead time based on average queue time assumptions tend to be self fulfilling prophecies. (Assuming queues and lead time are not totally out of control). If MRP uses an average planning lead time then it will schedule order due dates and release dates with this average time. Since the planned lead time assumes queues and allows for them, execution to the planned schedule will develop the same queues. This is supported by one of the laws of queue, or backlog, which states that once a queue has been built it will tend to remain at a fixed level unless there are significant changes in personnel, equipment or the health of the business.

Breaking into this loop by reducing queues and lead times is a major challenge, and it also represents a very significant potential for overall improvement in a manufacturing business. The result can be a better competitive position via shorter lead times, less WIP inventory investment, more effective capacity utilizations, less scrap, fewer E.C. problems, etc.

A first step then toward improved capacity management is to evaluate queues by individual work center. This will support more accurate scheduling as well as pinpointing those work centers that have too little or too much queue.

The data gathered in input/output monitoring and control (Figure 7) can be utilized along with the value of the starting queue (prior to period 1) to develop a period by period measurement of queue. If the starting queue were 300 standard hours the queues for periods 1 through 4 would be as illustrated in Figure 12.

	QUEUE			
Period	1	2	3	4
Planned Q	300	300	300	300
Actual Q	280	320	370	360
Deviation	-20	+20	+70	+60

figure 12.

Figure 13 is a plot of the distribution of queue values in four different work centers.

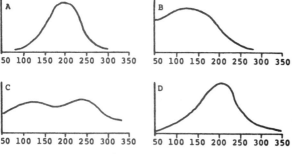

figure 13.   Queues in standard hours

Work center A has an average queue of about 200 hours and over the period of our data has never had a queue less than 80 hours. Clearly we could reduce the queue by almost 80 hours and still in all probability never run out of work in that work center.

Work center B however has a high incidence of idle time because of a frequent occurance of zero queue. Work center C shows a wide range of data and an indication that queues may be out of control

Work center D appears to represent the best situation, but even this distribution could be improved upon. Figure 14, progressing from a to b to c shows this improvement.

figure 14.   50 100 150 200 250 300 350

Queues can be viewed in a statistical sense like safety stock in finished goods inventory. The variability of input and output is similiar to the variability of demand (vs. forecast). The ability to manage and decrease this variability through input/output monitoring and control can result in more stable queues and decreased queues with all the associated benefits.

The evaluation of queues by work center will give the ability to introduce more accurate average queue times per work center in the scheduling algorithm. It will also draw managements' attention to work centers with queues that are too large or too small and to work centers with too great a variability in input and/or output.

Completion Time Estimating

Completion time estimating is the scheduling and loading system in the medium range. The previous level, capacity requirements planning, highlights potential capacity problems, while completion time estimating shows which individual orders are affected. This is the first system to consider finite capacity availability.

Each order is loaded considering latest start dates in priority sequence to the finite capacities of each time period for each work center. The order is loaded beginning with the first operation. If capacity is available, the operation is loaded. If capacity is not available, the operation is delayed until capacity is found. If an order is available, it can be pulled early to take advantage of any available capacity. In the event of delays interoperation time can be reduced.

The sequence of scheduling and loading of orders is dictated by order priorities initially determined in capacity requirements planning. These priorities can then be modified by other factors such as delay, slack, the amount of interoperation compression and external priorities.

Completion time estimating must also consider the results of operation sequencing which is the short range scheduling system

Completion time estimating develops an estimate of order completion time for orders based on the priority of the order and availability of capacity. Additionally, an individual order's contribution to any bottleneck conditions will be detailed.

Operation Sequencing

Operation sequencing is the short range scheduling and loading system and like completion time estimating, considers finite capacity availability. Completion time estimating and capacity requirements planning took into account only the total capacity within a time period without considering the sequence of operations. In contrast, operation sequencing considers the capacity and operation sequence each shift and computes a queue of operations for each machine.

Essentially, operation sequencing is a job shop simulation. It calculates a workable sequence of operations for each single machine considering the existing situation. This involves considering the capacity and the existing load of each individual machine, as well as operation due dates.

More advanced considerations could include alternate routings and operations, alternate work centers, operation splitting, overlapping, time critical operations and grouping related operations.

The objective of operation sequencing is to sequence the operations in a queue, therefore an operation priority must be established to determine the ranking of the operations. Some elements considered include operation in process, successive operations on the same order in the same work center, splits for this operation in process, operation belongs to high priority order and user specified priorities.

The scheduling techniques of developing a prioritized queue of operations for each machine significantly increases the probability of meeting schedules and maximizing capacity utilization.

The operation sequencing system should help manage release of orders into the shop and provide a priority controlled leveling of loads and a realistic dispatch list.

Supporting these three subsystems of Manufacturing Activity Planning is three levels of increasing refinement of queue management. This increased ability to manage queues was defined earlier as a critical prerequisite to better capacity management. This is detailed in Figure 15.

The capacity requirements planning system utilizes average queue time in its scheduling. This should be an average queue time by specific work center.

Standards, of course, are used for set-up and run times for all levels of manufacturing activity planning. An average move time is depicted for capacity requirements planning but the move time matrix shown for completion time estimating and operation sequencing could easily be used.

Completion time estimating introduces a logical refinement of queue times. It recognizes that some orders have longer than average queue times while others have shorter than average queue times in a given work center. The degree of "longer" and "shorter" is arbitrary and in our example there is four levels of detail. This approach demands rigorous record keeping and data collection because it is based on the measurement of actual queue time experienced by all orders and the relationship of the queue time to order priority. Completion time estimating is dependant on order priorities so the presence of priorities is assumed. The priority groups could be determined by simply stratifying the range of priorities.

The table indicates that orders in priority group 4 in work center B had an average queue time of 38 hours This data from past intermediate range history will be used as projections for queue times for scheduling in the future intermediate range of completion time estimating. The single average queue time for this work center in capacity requirements planning could have been 22 hours.

This approach is identical for queue for move (wait) and the move time matrix is used for transit time.

The final refinement is the actual calculation of expected queue time in the operation sequencing function. Since a queue prioritized by operation exists for a work center, it is a simple matter to calculate specific operation and order queue times in a work center. The expected queue time for any operation is simply the total of the standard set-up and run times for all preceeding operations in the queue. The fourth operation in queue in the operation sequencing example will wait 15 hours, which is the sum of the standard set-up and run time of the preceding three operations. The estimate of queue for move is still a refined average because we assume no standards exist for transit time.

Summary

The capacity management systems defined here represent a wide range of systems to support a range of schedules from the formal business plan down to the dispatch list. These systems represent a natural sequence starting with gross and rough cut planning over long horizons and evolving down to very detailed job shop simulations over very short horizons. An essential element of this is the increasing levels of refinement in the understanding of and the management of work-in process inventories and queue times.

Clearly these approaches do not apply to all manufacturers. The systems described here, for example, would be more appropriate for interrupted flow manufacturing. Even within interrupted flow manufacturing, the classical build to order job shop might utilize some refined techniques that are beyond the needs of a build to forecast manufacturer. There is even a greater contrast in capacity management approaches when interrupted flow manufacturing is compared with process or continuous flow manufacturing.

Regardless of the industry, better capacity management should be a high priority for all manufacturers. The rewards are immense. Better capacity management will result in higher productivity, lower costs and shorter lead times, all of which are essential in an increasingly competitive world marketplace and in a U. S. economy that is plagued with productivity problems. Indeed, better capacity management may be the key to survival for many manufacturing enterprises.

			OPERATION LEAD TIME																	
	HORIZON	QUEUE (WORK)					SET-UP	RUN	QUEUE (MOVE)						MOVE					
CAPACITY REQUIREMENTS PLANNING	'LONG' RANGE (MONTHS)	AVERAGE					STANDARDS		AVERAGE						AVERAGE					
COMPLETION TIME ESTIMATING	INTERMEDIATE RANGE (WEEKS)	REFINED AVERAGE					STANDARDS		REFINED AVERAGE						REFINED AVERAGE					
			WORK CENTER							WORK CENTER				FROM		TO			
		PRIORITY	A	B	C	D			PRIORITY	A	B	C	D			A	B	C	D
		1	12	16	14	10			1	1	5	3	2	A	-	2	1	4
		2	17	19	19	13			2	3	8	6	3	B	2	-	1	6
		3	21	26	22	17			3	4	10	8	6	C	1	3	-	2
		4	29	38	34	20			4	7	12	11	8	D	4	5	1	-
OPERATION SEQUENCING	SHORT RANGE (HOURS)	CALCULATED					STANDARDS		REFINED AVERAGE						REFINED AVERAGE					
		OPERATION SEQUENCE	STANDARDS	QUEUE						WORK CENTER				FROM		TO			
									PRIORITY	A	B	C	D			A	B	C	D
		1	6	0					1	1	5	3	2	A	-	2	1	4
		2	4	6					2	3	8	6	3	B	2	-	1	6
		3	5	10					3	4	10	8	6	C	1	3	-	2
		4	3	15					4	7	12	11	8	D	4	5	1	-

figure 15.

REFERENCES

'Master Production Schedule Planning Guide', IBM Publication GE20-0518

'Capacity Planning and Operation Sequencing System-Extended', IBM Publication GH12-5119

'Hot List', R. D. Garwood, Inc., January/February 1978, March-June 1978:
    'The making and Remaking of a Master Schedule'

'Hot List', R. D. Garwood, Inc., September-December 1978:
    'Capacity Planning'

'Communications Oriented Production Information and Control System-Master Production Schedule Planning', IBM Publication G320-1976.

'Communications Oriented Production Information and Control System-Manufacturing Activity Planning & Order Release', IBM Publication G320-1978

'Asset Management and Long Term Capacity Aquisition Planning', Frank O. Sunderland, 1979 APICS Annual Conference Proceedings.

'Manufacturing Scheduling', R. L. Lankford, A Paper presented at the University of Wisconsin, 1973.

'Short Term Planning of Manufacturing Capacity', R. L. Lankford, 1978 APICS Annual Conference Proceedings

'Master Production Scheduling-Principles and Practices', William L. Berry, Thomas E. Vollmann and D. Clay Whybark, APICS, 1979

Biography

Mr. Clark is a Senior Instructor in IBM's Manufacturing Industry Education Center in Poughkeepsie, New York. He has eight years of marketing experience and eleven years of manufacturing education experience in IBM.

Mr. Clark teaches manufacturing courses and consults with IBM customer executives throughout the United States. He has taught in Europe, Japan and Canada. He is the co-author and co-producer of IBM's Material Requirements Planning (MRP) Video Course which is currently in use worldwide.

He has been presenting to APICS Chapters across the United States for the last seven years. He was a topic coordinator and speaker in the 1977 and 1979 APICS Annual Conference and a speaker in the NCPDM National Conference in 1976 and 1980.

Reprinted from 1990 APICS Conference Proceedings.

Advanced Available-to-Promise Concepts/Techniques

Peter Clay, CFPIM

INTRODUCTION

Available-to-Promise (ATP) applications originated as means of controlling the allocation of finished goods inventory and improving the quality of delivery promises to customers. It has since developed into a major operational tool which supports the management of customer demands, safety stocks, product lead-times and the definition of promise dates for even unique build-to-customer-order product configurations.

Properly designed, ATP is demonstrable evidence of the tremendous synergic opportunities available within integrated manufacturing planning and control systems. Unfortunately, though easily understood by most users and characterized by relative technical simplicity, many companies defer the development and/or implementation of ATP. In practice, ATP so clearly and visibly links the definition of external commitments to the supporting manufacturing plan that it serves to positively promote the implementation of the more rigorous and technically demanding applications.

The techniques and variations described below illustrate important ATP concepts. All have been programmed and successfully implemented at a Michigan manufacturer. This manufacturer is a MAPICS user and operates three highly interdependent plants with substantial variety within both process and product. Some of the alternatives presented may be of little value to your organization for this reason. Be aware that differences between planning systems will probably require that you modify most of the techniques described if you wish to incorporate them into your own systems.

For purposes of this discussion, the Master Production Schedule is an independently defined series of requirement quantities and dates for items which are controlled as MPS items. The material planning system is driven by this schedule to produce MPS items in MPS quantities on MPS dates using an MPS order planning technique which does not recognize inventory, allocations or non-MPS requirements. The MPS schedule is consumed by replenishment orders which are opened. Manually entered changes to the MPS are the exclusive means of altering the replenishment plan for MPS items.

ATP FUNDAMENTALS

The major functional characteristic which differentiates ATP application complexity is that of multi-level availability support. Single-level ATP logic defines the availability of an item based exclusively upon its existing material plan. Multi-level ATP supplements an item's existing material plan with selective elements of component availability. In this manner, it enhances item availability and draws significant product planning activity directly into the customer service function.

For purposes of simplicity we will initiate our detailed exploration of ATP issues using a single Master Scheduled end-item. This is a single-level ATP problem which involves a fixed production plan. Once we have established basic ATP principles we will proceed to develop and examine some of the more complex issues involved in multi-level ATP.

Single-Level ATP of an MPS Item

Figure 1 illustrates a typical ATP position. 45 units of a Master Scheduled assembly are physically on-hand. 30 of these have been promised to customers prior to the MPS replenishment of 100 units which is scheduled for day 12. This leaves only 15 uncommitted units which can be promised for shipment prior to day 12. During the interval between the Current date and day 12 only 15 units are available to promise.

In the interval between day 12 and day 22 (when an additional production lot of 100 units is planned), 60 units have been promised to customers. Of the 100 units to be received on day 12, then, only 40 have not been promised and remain available to promise. These 40 units and the 15 units which remain available from the current on-hand balance provide a total of 55 units available to promise on day 12. 15 units can be promised prior to day 12. 55 units can be promised as of day 12. 130 units are available to promise on day 22. This pattern continues out through the schedule horizon illustrated.

WORK DAY	MASTER PRODUCTION SCHEDULE QTY	BOOKED CUSTOMER BACKLOG	CUMULATIVE AVAILABLE TO PROMISE
CURRENT	45 ON-HAND	30	15
12	100	60	55
22	100	25	130
28	200	30	300
35	250	35	515
42	240	40	715
50	120	10	825

Figure 1: ATP FOR A MASTER SCHEDULED END-ITEM

ATP Intervals

Note that for purposes of calculating and expressing available to promise values, the only dates of interest are the current date and dates for which replenishments are scheduled. The reason, of course, is that these are the only dates on which a change in the available to promise can occur. In Figure 1, the ATP value is 15 on each and every date from the current date until day 12. The ATP is 55 on day 20 just as it was on day 12. The intervals established between dates of planned product replenishments are known as ATP intervals. For purposes of efficiency and clarity we maintain and display most ATP information on the basis of ATP intervals.

Interactive ATP displays

There is no 'right way' to present an interactive ATP display for inquiry or commitment but Figure 2 illustrates a display which is certainly acceptable. The heading area provides descriptive, pricing, planning and inventory information about the item. The body of the screen presents information about each ATP interval and supports the addition or maintenance of product commitments.

On screen illustrated in Figure 2, quantities entered under NEW COMMITS will be added to the COMMITTED column and the AVAIL/PROMISE column re-calculated based on the newest commitment position. A Refresh option is provided to restore the item to its commitment position prior to any changes having been entered. Commitments can be backed out by entering a negative value in the NEW COMMITS column. Command key access to commitment detail and safety stock information are also supported.

```
          AVAILABLE TO PROMISE COMMITMENT SCREEN        5/01/90

   Item: 1002-A    Desc: CLUTCH              List:  175.00
   Inv:      45    U/M: EA    W/H: C         Plnr:  121
   Alloc:     0                              Eng:    42

   NEW COMMITS    DATE INTERVAL    AVAIL/PROMISE    COMMITTED
   _____        CURRENT             15             30
   _____        5/17/90             55             60
   _____        5/24/90            130             25
   _____        6/04/90            300             30
   _____        6/13/90            515             35
   _____        6/22/90            715             40
   _____        7/23/90            825             10

   CMD1-EXIT CMD2-DETAIL CMD3-SAFTY CMD19-REFRESH CMD24-EOJ
```

Figure 2: A TYPICAL INTERACTIVE ATP SCREEN

Forward and Backward Logic

A significant variation to the example in Figure 1
arises when product commitments made for later ATP
intervals draw upon replenishment quantities produced in
earlier ATP intervals. Such a situation is illustrated
in Figure 3. The only change to commitments and
replenishment quantities here is that an additional 100
units have been committed in the third ATP interval.
This has, of course, decreased the available to promise
within the third interval by 100 units but notice that
it has also reduced ATP within the second interval from
55 to 30 units.

The reason that interval two available has been
affected is that the 125 units now committed in interval
three exceed the replenishment quantity at the beginning
of interval three. The shortfall must come from
material which remains available from preceding
intervals. In this case the latest preceding interval
with availability is interval two.

Mechanically, to proper calculate ATP balances, the
application must first sequentially process each ATP
interval from the current date to the end of the
planning horizon. Then it must determine if any
interval requires use of replenishments which precede
the interval. In other words, it must first make a
forward pass using one logic, then a second, backward
pass using another logic. The backward logic examines
the ATP in any interval and if it is less than the ATP
in the preceding interval, it reduces the preceding
interval ATP to the lower value.

WORK DAY	MASTER PRODUCTION SCHEDULE QTY	BOOKED CUSTOMER ORDER QTY	CUMULATIVE AVAILABLE TO PROMISE
CURRENT	45 (ON-HAND)	30	15
12	100	60	30
22	100	125	30
28	200	30	200
35	250	35	415
42	240	40	615
50	120	10	725

Figure 3: ATP ILLUSTRATING BACKWARD LOGIC REQUIREMENT

Pegged Commitments and Demand Management

An orderly visual presentation of ATP values is a
tremendous tool but when an item's available to promise
is insufficient to satisfy all demand, simply knowing
availability is not enough. The successful supplier
must be capable of evaluating competing demands and if
necessary, restructuring existing commitments to satisfy
the most critical demands.

Major customers who are JIT, production-line driven
or sole-sourced must be protected in conditions of
limited product supply. This may not mean that any
customer goes without. It is the supplier's
responsibility to manage the competing demands to assure
an uninterrupted supply of product to all customers.
Many demands are computer generated orders driven by
order-point inventory systems. Even orders defined by
time-phased material planning systems are somewhat
arbitrary; sized to meet a container, handling or
shipping multiple or perhaps even a negotiated minimum
order size. Pegging capability within the ATP
application can maximize customer satisfaction under
such circumstances by quickly focusing upon which
demands are at risk and which are the most likely
candidates for review or re-schedule.

Figure 4 illustrates information typical of a
pegged ATP inquiry. In this case, one which details the
existing ATP commitments of Figure 3. If an OEM
requests an additional 40 units to ship on work day 18,
it is clear from Figure 3 that this is a problem. These
units are not available in that quantity until work day
28. The pegged inquiry, however, suggests a number of
alternatives which may prove effective solutions:

If the commitment to OEM #4 for 45 units were deferred
just one day (from day 27 to 28), these 45 units would
then draw from the day 28 ATP interval, freeing up the
needed units in the day 12 ATP interval.

Since OEM #1/PLANT-A has a shipment for 30 units
scheduled for work day 24 and the next shipment is not
until day 37, it's possible they would accept shipment
of 20 units on day 24 and an additional 10 units on
day 28. This too, provides the desired ATP increase
within the day 12 ATP interval.

Distributor #12 has a shipment of 40 units scheduled
for day 12. Perhaps they would have no difficulty
with a lesser shipment at that time and another
shipment on day 28.

There are other possibilities as well. Whichever
alternative is pursued, the process is one of prudently
managing the competing demands for product in a manner
entirely consistent with our existing replenishment
plan.

WORK DAY PROMISED	WORK DAY REQUESTED	QTY PROMISED	CUSTOMER
5	5	20	OEM #1/PLANT-A
7	7	10	DISTRIBUTOR #49
12	12	17	OEM #1/PLANT-B
12	10	40	DISTRIBUTOR #12
20	20	3	DISTRIBUTOR #30
24	24	50	OEM #2
24	24	30	OEM #1/PLANT-A
27	27	45	OEM #4
31	31	30	OEM #8
37	37	35	OEM #1/PLANT-A
44	44	40	DISTRIBUTOR #16

Figure 4: ILLUSTRATION OF PEGGED DEMANDS

Negative Cumulative ATP

Circumstances sometimes cause the cumulative ATP
value to become negative. This occurs when customer
service overcommits product to customers but it can also
arise from inventory adjustments, quality rejections,
shrink, unanticipated product consumption or a failure
to produce product to plan. Such a position is
illustrated in Figure 5.

WORK DAY	MASTER PRODUCTION SCHEDULE QTY	BOOKED CUSTOMER ORDER QTY	CUMULATIVE AVAILABLE TO PROMISE
CURRENT	45 (ON-HAND)	30	-15
12	50	80	-15
22	100	25	100
28	200	30	270
35	250	35	485
42	240	40	685
50	120	10	795

Figure 5: ILLUSTRATION OF NEGATIVE ATP BALANCES

Negative ATP positions are extremely serious occurrences for they reflect situations were the PLAN is TO FAIL. That is, if the existing replenishment plan is successfully executed, some commitments will not be satisfied. The importance of reconciling negative ATP positions promptly cannot be overemphasized.

The customer service group may be unable to increase the supply of product but they most definitely control the distribution of product quantities which are available. Prompt action and good judgement will often provide satisfactory coverage to all customers. It is not acceptable that critical product ship in arbitrary quantities to secondary customers at the risk to major customers. Another consideration is that if replenishment schedules must be changed, costs associated with these changes will be lessened the earlier these changes can be determined. By the same token, early determination of these changes enhances the ability of purchasing or production to successfully effect the changes.

Safety Stock Logic

Safety stocks help assure an adequate supply of product to meet customer demands and insulate manufacturing and purchasing from the disruptive effects of customer demand in excess of forecast.

An appropriate handling of safety stock should assure that a flag is raised when the safety stock level is reached so that a prompt and informed evaluation of the item's position can be made. In addition, care should be taken to assure that safety stock inventory is not promised to the first customer who would draw upon it. An OEM production schedule may very well be jeopardized by sending critical product into the aftermarket product channel.

A very effective method of handling safety stock within the ATP application is illustrated in Figure 6. The safety stock inventory objective (which is a value which must have been defined and reside in the database) is deducted from the calculated cumulative ATP position. Negative ATP positions caused by this deduction are covered by applying whatever available ATP safety stock is required to restore a cumulative ATP of zero.

In the Figure 6 example, it was necessary to apply 25 units of safety stock in the current interval and 5 units in the second ATP Interval to maintain the minimum ATP of zero. Note that the available safety stock balance is always replenished (mathematically, since there is no physical differentiation of the inventory) before displaying a positive ATP quantity.

The 'AVAILABLE SAFETY STOCK' column is displayed only in response to a command key request by the user. This additional keying step helps assure that the user does not unintentionally commit safety stock and reduces the use of safety stock as a first alternative in solving demand problems. If a specific customer situation warrants consideration of safety stock consumption, the user has immediate access to the available safety stock position and a display which reflects it's impact upon the cumulative ATP. It is wise to clearly define your policy with respect to the use of safety stock to support of customer demands.

BEGINNING ON-HAND: 45 UNITS
SAFETY STOCK OBJECTIVE: 40 UNITS

WORK DAY	MASTER PRODUCTION SCHEDULE	BOOKED CUSTOMER ORDER QTY	CUM AVAIL TO PROMISE	AVAIL SAFETY STOCK
CURRENT	45(ON-HAND)	30	0	15
12	100	80	0	35
22	100	25	70	40
28	200	30	240	40
35	250	35	455	40

Figure 6: ATP FOR A MASTER SCHEDULED END-ITEM WITH A SAFETY STOCK OBJECTIVE DEFINED

ATP For Non-End Items and Non-MPS Items

ATP calculations for non-end items require that manufacturing allocations be subtracted from the on-hand balance in the CURRENT interval. In addition, material requirements which have been generated in MRP by parent items must be added to the component item's customer commitments and included in the commitment totals for each ATP interval. To properly support the demand management function, commitment pegging should include standard MRP requirements pegging in addition to the customer commitment pegging described above. ATP positions for non-end items tend to be more dynamic than those of end-items because changes in the plan for any parent can affect component ATP.

ATP intervals for non-MPS items are established by the CURRENT DATE, all ORDER DUE DATES within the CMLT, and the CMLT itself. Order due dates include those for open, firm planned and planned orders. The CMLT (Cumulative Material Lead Time) is the length of time it takes to replenish a product assuming that no material is available. Figure 7 illustrates this definition of ATP intervals through time.

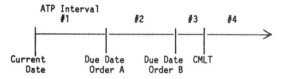

Figure 7: ATP INTERVAL DEFINITION FOR A NON-MPS ITEM

The CURRENT interval ATP position for non-MPS items is calculated as on-hand inventory less manufacturing allocations less CURRENT interval commitments (customer orders and all generated material requirements from parents which occur in the interval). For calculating subsequent interval ATP positions, order quantities increase the ATP position while generated requirements and customer orders within the interval reduce the ATP position (all treated as commitments).

At CMLT, full planning lead-time is provided for the product replenishment cycle in support of any additional product commitment. For purchased items the CMLT is identical to the normal planning lead time. In theory, it is at this point that replenishment order quantities can be revised or launched in support of additional customer commitments without planner review. Although such logic makes serious and potentially inappropriate assumptions about the ability and/or willingness of the company to allocate substantial resources without planning management review, I have used CMLT as a time-fence for open ATP exposure in support of purchased items without major difficulty. Use of the CMLT in this manner for manufactured product without the means to test capacity constraints is not recommended. Capacity tests are available with multi-level ATP logic. The convention used to express an ATP without limit at the CMLT is arbitrary. I have always used all nines for the ATP value when no ATP constraints exist. Figure 8 illustrates the ATP calculation for a non-MPS component.

BEGINNING ON-HAND: 45 UNITS
MFG ALLOCATIONS: 8 UNITS

DAY	ORDER SCHEDULE	INTERVAL GEN REQMTS	INTERVAL CUSTOMER ORDERS	CUMULATIVE AVAILABLE TO PROMISE
CURRENT	37*	5	20	12
6	100 (Open)	15	45	52
15	120 (Firm)	12	60	100
28	110 (Plan)	16	25	169
40	100 (Plan)	6	25	238
50	CMLT	148	80	999999

* On-hand less allocations

Figure 8: ATP FOR A NON-MPS COMPONENT

The Source of Availability

Only projected item balances in excess of ATP requirements provide ATP availability. Further, it is differences in requirements handling between MRP and ATP that provide these excesses. Some requirements are used as 'consuming' (use up projected available inventory) requirements in MRP but ignored by ATP. Others are treated just the opposite or treated as consuming requirements in both applications. For example, MPS requirements are treated by MRP as consuming requirements and they drive the production of product. ATP, on the other hand, treats only generated requirements and customer orders as consuming requirements. The difference between the replenishment plan (driven by the MPS) and the commitments (customer orders and generated requirements) provides an ATP balance.

Some companies use sales forecast requirements to drive production of product and disregard them within ATP. Customer orders are used by some to drive production of non-MPS items and also as consuming requirements within ATP. In most systems, generated requirements are ignored by MPS items within MRP yet are treated as consuming requirements by ATP. Note that ATP balances are randomly created by order lot-sizing techniques which plan replenishments in excess of known requirements.

MULTI-LEVEL ATP LOGIC

The Need for a Multi-Level Solution

Since ATP is a tool which supports the orderly commitment of excess (uncommitted) product, then an ATP position exists only to the extent that the plan is to produce in excess of commitments. The clear shortcoming, of course, is that few companies enjoy the luxury of producing all products simply in anticipation of future customer commitments. Most have many products which they produce discretely to customer order from 'common' components. The latter supporting a variety of end-items and product variations.

Multi-level ATP recognizes that additional availability for an item may reside at component levels. Indeed, that for some products all pre-commitment availability resides at component levels. Within a multi-level ATP application, an assembly can be promised to a customer if all components evaluated are available and sufficient lead-time is provided in which to produce the parent from components. Constraints dictated by process or critical resources can be supported by including processes or resources in the component definition.

Master Scheduling discrete end-items is becoming less common as manufacturers strive to replace finished goods inventory with manufacturing flexibility and bills of material are further flattened as part of expanding JIT programs. In addition, Master Scheduling suffers

from being resource intensive and inherently resistive to change. The more parts that are planned in this manner, the less successful the planning function becomes. There are other issues as well. Most detailed product schedules reflect arbitrary quantity and date decisions. Master Scheduling intervention required to manipulate these schedules in response to demands tends to be unproductive and creates undesirable delay within the customer service function. Even worse, customers sometimes unnecessarily accept commitments short of their requests.

These issues have increased efforts to shift Master Scheduling from specific end-items to more generic product levels. Common alternatives include Master Scheduling major sub-assemblies (which comprise basic building blocks of many end-items), Master Scheduling raw materials and Master Scheduling process or line rates for end-item families. In some cases, the material issue is left entirely to such tools as planning bills.

When an end-item (or any parent) is not Master Scheduled, its availability is limited to its existing replenishment plan unless supplemented by additional availability translated from component levels. Multi-level ATP performs this translation of component availabilities into additional availability at the parent level. This involves two major ATP issues beyond those discussed thus far. First, how to translate inter-level availability and second, how deep into the component structure to go in reviewing component availability.

The Component ATP implosion

Translating component availability to availability at the parent level (any number of levels up the product structure) involves a technique reciprocal to the standard MRP explosion, called an ATP implosion. In this process the inter-level quantity relationships in the product structure and the single-level lead-time are used to 'implode' availability back to the parent level.

Consider the product structure illustrated in Figure 9. 'A' is an end-item with three components, 'B', 'C' and 'D'. 'B' is an MPS sub-assembly which is MPS controlled because it is very costly, has a substantial CMLT and draws upon significant manufacturing resources. Two (2) 'B's are required to produce one (1) 'A'. The single level lead-time for 'A' is two (2) days. For the moment we will ignore the availability issues of both 'C' and 'D'.

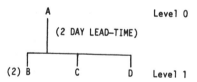

Figure 9: END ITEM 'A' WITH AN MPS COMPONENT 'B' (2 REQ)

An MPS for 'B' is shown is Figure 10. Translating the availability of 'B' into an ATP contribution position at parent 'A' requires that we offset 'B's ATP interval dates by the single-level lead-time and factor the ATP quantities by the product structure quantity relationship. 'B's contribution to 'A's availability is provided in column 1, Figure 11.

WORK DAY	MASTER PRODUCTION SCHEDULE QTY	COMMITMENTS (CUST ORDS+ PARENT REQ)	CUMULATIVE AVAILABLE TO PROMISE
CURRENT	45 ON-HAND	30	15
12	100	60	55
22	100	25	130
28	200	30	300
35	250	35	515

Figure 10: ATP FOR MASTER SCHEDULED SUB-ASSEMBLY 'B'

Column 2 in Figure 11 presents a hypothetical ATP for 'A' based only upon its own replenishment plan. Column 3 illustrates the impact of including 'B's contribution to 'A's ATP.

WORK DAY	column 1 ADDITIONAL CUMULATIVE ATP FOR 'A' FROM 'B'	column 2 'A' ONLY CUMULATIVE AVAILABLE TO PROMISE	column 3 COMPOSITE CUMULATIVE AVAILABLE TO PROMISE
CURRENT	0	5	5
2	7	0	12
14	27	0	32
24	65	0	70
26	–	10	80
30	150	0	160
37	257	0	267

Figure 11: ATP FOR END-ITEM 'A' AS IMPLODED FROM 'B'

'This Level' Available Values

The ATP values in column 2 are 'This Level' values, independent of contributions from component levels (other than those implicit in the replenishment plan at this level). In fact, the values in column 1 which stem from item 'B' are really This Level values from 'B' which have been translated into their parent level equivalency. The composite ATP, shown in column 3 of Figure 11 is the sum of 'A's This Level ATP values and the component This Level ATP values converted to 'A's equivalency.

If additional orders are opened or planned for 'A', the single-level ATP for 'A' will be increased by the order quantity. Simultaneously, the contribution from component 'B' would decrease by an equivalent value due to either a lower on-hand balance (if already issued to the parent order for 'A') or increased allocations (if not yet issued to an open order for 'A') or a generated requirements (if a planned order for 'A'). Both of the latter would be commitments in calculating 'B's ATP values.

Netting This Level ATP

We can explore another important Multi-level ATP issue if we define 'D' as another MPS component of 'A' item with an MPS and ATP as illustrated in Figure 12.

WORK DAY	MASTER PRODUCTION SCHEDULE QTY	COMMITMENTS (CUST ORDS+ PARENT REQ)	CUMULATIVE AVAILABLE TO PROMISE
CURRENT	0 ON-HAND	0	0
8	20	0	20
28	30	25	25
38	30	0	55

Figure 12: ATP FOR MASTER SCHEDULED SUB-ASSEMBLY 'D'

Translating 'D's This Level ATP into it's contribution to 'A's ATP requires only the two day offset for lead-time since the product structure is one (1) per. The result of this translation is illustrated in Figure 13. Also shown is the ATP contribution data previously calculated for component 'B'.

WORK DAY	AVAILABLE TO PROMISE FOR 'A' FROM 'D'	WORK DAY	AVAILABLE TO PROMISE FOR 'A' FROM 'B'
CURRENT	0	CURRENT	0
10	20	2	7
30	25	14	27
40	55	24	65
		30	150
		37	257

Figure 13: ATP FOR 'A' IMPLODED FROM 'D' AND 'B'

It is clear in Figure 13 that the required components are not contributing an equal availability to 'A'. In fact, the additional 7 units of 'A' available from 'B' on day 2 are of no value until day 10 because we need both 'B's and 'D's to produce 'A's and day 10 is the earliest that 'D' can support additional availability of 'A's. In addition, on day 10 we can't take full advantage of the additional 20 units of 'A' which are supported by 'D's because we are constrained by limited 'B's. This example serves to illustrate that it is necessary, before attempting to pass availability from one level of the product structure to another, to reduce or net availability at the lower level to it's lowest common denominator. The result of this netting for Level 1 components in our example is illustrated in Figure 14.

WORK DAY	AVAILABLE TO PROMISE FOR 'A' FROM LEVEL 1	CONSTRAINING COMPONENT THIS DATE
CURRENT	0	BOTH 'B' and 'D'
10	7	'B'
14	20	'D'
30	25	'D'
40	55	'D'

Figure 14: NETTED LEVEL 1 ATP CONTRIBUTION TO 'A'

The Multi-Level process for determining availability of a parent is to calculate the ATP contribution available from each single-level component and net these availabilities among those single-level components included in the analysis. The netted composite ATP can then added to the This Level ATP of the parent.

If we chose to make a commitment at the parent level in a pure net change MRP environment, the additional generated demands placed upon component availabilities will immediately be evident. In a regenerative environment it is necessary to maintain a record of the availability which has been committed since the last planning run. These commitments are retained in an ATP file which is organized by the part number from which the availability has been obtained.

In our example we have dealt with only a single product structure level. In fact, the process of gleaning availability from components is reiterative and can be applied, bottom-up, to every leg of every level of the product structure. The process of chasing the product structure chain downward ceases only when we reach a purchased part or an MPS item. Purchased parts have no components which can lend additional availability. Master Scheduled items have been Master Scheduled to dictate the quantity to be produced and changes to that schedule require planning management review.

Multi-Level ATP Depth/Breadth

The price for full Multi-Level ATP support includes computer resources and slower user response time. Depending upon the nature of your products, the depth and breadth of your product structures and how you use Master Scheduling, it may be appropriate to consider means of limiting the extent of Multi-Level ATP activity. In some cases, non-MPS items are of limited financial significance (i.e., adapters, fasteners, labeling) or their lead-times are short (relative to the customer order lead-time) or their predictability is very high. Under such circumstances, consider simply excluding these components from the ATP issue as we have done with 'C' in our example above.

Another solution is to limit the number of component levels within the product structure to be considered in the Multi-Level ATP process. If Master Scheduling no more than 2 levels deep, consider using Multi-Level ATP only to a low-level code of 2 to assure that any MPS availabilities are included in the parent ATP being constructed. Another alternative is to flag items (ATP significant components) which are to be included in Multi-Level ATP analysis. Piggy-back upon regularly scheduled implosions (such as cost roll-ups) to carry a flag from these components up to their parents. With this technique, when an ATP inquiry is made one need only search component chains for which the parent has been flagged as a parent of items to be included in the ATP analysis.

The ATP File

The Multi-Level ATP process of 'rolling up' component ATP contributions to parent levels is a reiterative activity which involves the chase of product structure chains, calculating This Level ATP information about each part included in the process and manipulating (imploding, netting and summing) this data. By far the most time-consuming element of this process is calculating the This Level ATP information.

Significant benefits can be obtained by calculating This Level ATP values in batch as part of the MRP run and storing these values in the ATP file for later use by interactive users. The response time for interactive ATP inquiry is far faster, the computer resources used are off-shift batch, and the processing task itself is reduced because calculations are performed only once for each part, each MRP run.

ADDITIONAL ATP ISSUES

Production Constraints within Multi-Level ATP

Thus far we have discussed the use of component availability by Multi-Level ATP from the perspective of providing additional parent ATP. As significant is the ability of this same logic to constrain parent ATP in a desired pattern.

Most production planning issues involve assuring the adequacy of material and the uniformity of requirements for non-material resources. The MPS mechanism in a Multi-Level ATP environment can be used to assure that customer commitments are made in a manner fully consistent with defined production, line or process rates. It is only necessary that a component be defined which is common to all parents that draw upon the critical resource. Multiple resource issues require that multiple 'resource' components be included in the product structure, one for each resource. These components are then Master Scheduled to reflect the line, rate or process limit. The component item may an intermediate item within product structures (in which case it also serves as a material driver) or it may be a phantom with no components (in which case it can serve to control the commitment of a significant resource).

I am involved with a plant that produces injection-molded nylon fans. We are staffed on two shifts to produce 1200 fans per day off two molding presses. Fans are produced strictly to customer demand. Fans require molding followed by a secondary finishing operation with capacity matched to the rate of 1200 units per day. The fans are made from a single nylon raw material and one of any number of metal discs. Die change issues have prompted us to define each week's die changeover schedule at the beginning of the week. We sell nearly 120 standard fan configurations which are molded in any of 15 dies. These fans differ in both blade count and diameter.

As long as Production has 6000 fans scheduled to produce at the beginning of each week, they aren't concerned about which 6000 fans they are. The die changes are scheduled based upon the specific fan mix required that week. The nylon is purchased with a simple reorder point while the fan discs are planned and purchased to planning bills. The physical components for fans are often available in quantities capable of supporting greater than 6000 fans in any given week due to demand mix planning of discs and reorder point buying of the nylon.

Our solution was to add a phantom component (which we Master Schedule) to the fan bills. The MPS for this non-existent component is 6000 every 5 working days. Multi-Level ATP constrains customer commitments for fans to 6000 per week via the single-level available netting process which occurs at the fan component level. Customer service commits up to but no more than 6000 fans each week. When 6000 have been committed from a given week's production, there is no more availability from than week.

Lead-time Management

Lead-times to customers are not only a significant element of customer service but they reflect the equilibrium which exists between the replenishment plan and consuming demands. ATP lead-times are potentially leading indicators to planning management that imbalances have developed. Movements to either side of target lead-time ranges in the ATP application provide opportunities to address such imbalances before they are allowed to create a crisis.

Interactive vs. Batch ATP

There are important opportunities to remove planning and customer service entirely from order commitment activities. One major example: customer demands from an EDI application. The potential benefits from EDI are seriously undermined by all requirements for manual intervention. The ATP application can be called by applications such as EDI and availability tested as part of the automated loading of demands into the order system. Limited rules for dealing with insufficient availability must be defined but large elements of the standard order promising activity can be absorbed by the system.

End-of-Product-Life ATP

When a product's life is nearing or has reached its end, define it as a Master Scheduled item and provide an MPS that reflects its final replenishment schedule. It then becomes an ATP constraint beyond that schedule.

Customer Access to the ATP function

Customers can be provided access to ATP functions only if limitations are defined for these users. Specifically, safety stock support must not be available and commitment detail should not be displayed.

SUMMARY

You can walk into my office this afternoon and successfully support inquiries from our largest OEM customer concerning availability of any of the 2,500 end-items we manufacture or purchase. Many of these products have very long lead-times and others draw upon critical and limited resources. Some are highly complex, incorporating hundreds of components. In addition, many of these products are not sitting on the shelf waiting for the customer's order. Effective ATP support has evolved the order promising function from one requiring extensive product and process knowledge into a routine clerical function and availability inquiries are answered much more promptly and accurately.

Whether you are a discrete lot, repetitive or process manufacturer, a well designed ATP function can provide these capabilities to your order promising and production planning groups.

ABOUT THE AUTHOR

Peter Clay is Materials/MIS Manager for Kysor Industrial Corporation's Cadillac Division. He was previously with the Emerson Electric Company. He has managed the development of several innovative manufacturing management systems applications.

Mr. Clay is Certified at the Fellow Level and has previously made presentations to APICS chapters and the International Conference.

Reprinted from 1979 APICS Conference Proceedings.

LIVING WITH POOR CAPACITY PLANNING FORECASTS

Robert F. Conti

FOLLETT CORPORATION

Aggregate capacity planning and control are essential elements of a manufacturing system that answer two key questions:

PLANNING - "How much capacity do we need?"

CONTROL - "Is our capacity still adequate?"

In most companies, capacity planning starts with product line or product group forecasts. The role of these forecasts is described by Plossl and Wight (1) as follows:

"Product group forecasts are used to make capacity plans... They are used to determine the manpower and machine capacity requirements for each major product facility. The importance of product group forecasts is to establish production levels. This application makes use of the principle that group forecasts are more accurate than item forecasts."

Product group forecasts are especially important if demand is seasonal since large inventory commitments are often made to stabilize production. The need for accuracy in these forecasts is a major factor in choosing an appropriate method. We must, however, also consider the cost of this accuracy. In most cases, accuracy is increased by the use of more sophisticated methods. This affects two major costs. The costs caused by forecast inaccuracies go down while the costs of using the techniques go up. This is shown in FIGURE 1, adapted from the Harvard Business Review (2).

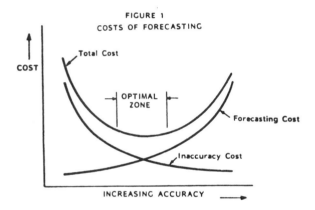

FIGURE 1
COSTS OF FORECASTING

The curve of Forecast Cost vs. Accuracy is affected by diminishing returns and the Total Cost curve shows an optimal zone beyond which improved accuracy is not justified. Once this zone is reached, emphasis should shift from obtaining more accurate forecasts to living with the forecasts that are made. This is a shift from planning to the control phase.

The control objective is to determine the need for forecast revisions and changes in capacity. The requirements to exercise this control are similar to those of a feedback control system:

(1) Definition of desired results

(2) Measurement and feedback of actual results

(3) Detection of errors by comparing actual and desired results

(4) Corrective action if errors are significant.

These can be met by tracking the product group forecasts. Desired results are the forecasted sales, and actual results are the actual sales. Since these inputs are readily available, the key system element is the error detector that signals the need for action. Plossl (3), suggests a tracking system using a graph of cumulative demand versus forecasted demand with control limits as the error detectors. The limits are set at plus or minus a fixed % of the forecast. Since 1964, a version of this approach using statistically determined limits has been used by the Follett Corporation.

Follett manufactures commercial ice making equipment. Sales demand is highly seasonal, and products are stocked for immediate shipment. The forecast tracking system evolved in the early 1960's from efforts to reduce the risk of heavy pre-season inventories. It is based on the premise that the underlying pattern of past demand can be used to forecast future demand and the variability about the pattern can be used to set control limits to detect significant errors.

DESCRIPTION OF METHOD

STEP 1 - Define Past Demand Pattern

For each product line, the cumulative monthly demand is determined for each of the past six years. The data is expressed in % of total yearly sales. Our fiscal year begins in September and TABLE 1 shows the demand data for a simplified example.

TABLE 1
YEARLY DEMAND PATTERN PRODUCT LINE "A" FISCAL YEAR 1972

MONTH	DEMAND/UNITS	CUMULATIVE DEMAND	CUM. % OF TOTAL DEMAND
Sept	80	80	8.0%
Oct	50	130	13.0
Nov	50	180	18.0
Dec	40	220	22.0
.	.	.	.
Aug	90	1000	100.0
	1000 Total		

STEP 2 - Determine Average and Standard Deviation of Pattern

The average cumulative % is computed for each month using the past six year's history. The standard deviation is then estimated using the formula:

$$s = \sqrt{\frac{\sum (x-\bar{x})^2}{N-1}} \qquad \text{where } N = 6$$

TABLE 2 illustrates the historical pattern and statistical results for the first four months of the year for product line "A". The average % values will be used to determine the cumulative monthly forecasts and the standard deviation estimates will be used to determine the control limits. A similar method described by Enrick (4) uses the demand pattern range for determining limits.

TABLE 2
CUMULATIVE % OF TOTAL DEMAND
PRODUCT LINE "A" FISCAL YEARS 1972-77

MONTH	'72	'73	'74	'75	'76	'77	AVG CUM %	STD DEV
Sept	8.0	7.0	5.0	8.0	6.0	7.0	6.8	1.2
Oct	13.0	15.0	9.0	12.0	14.0	12.0	12.5	2.1
Nov	18.0	22.0	17.0	18.0	17.0	19.0	18.5	1.9
Dec	22.0	26.0	23.0	25.0	21.0	25.0	23.7	2.0
.								
Etc.								

STEP 3 - Determine Control Limits

Monthly control limits are set at some multiple of the standard deviation above and below the average %. Therefore the Upper Control Limit will equal $\bar{x} + ks$ and the Lower Control Limit will be $\bar{x} - ks$. Ideally the limits should be set to maintain an in-control condition in the face of random fluctuations but respond quickly to significant deviations. Unfortunately these are conflicting objectives and selecting the value of k involves the typical control system trade off between stability and response. A low k favors response. It will tend to give some false indications that action is required but will seldom miss quickly signalling a true need. On the other hand, a high k favors stability. It will seldom trigger false signals but will react more slowly to significant deviations.

The choice of the value for k is a function of the environment. A company that can tolerate a few false alarms but incurs high costs when a significant change is missed, should use tight limits with a low k. If, however, reactions to false signals are much more costly then a slow response to a need for action, a high k and wider limits should be used. FIGURE 2 gives some of the relevant cost factors and their influence on the selection of k.

FIGURE 2

COST FACTORS INFLUENCING CHOICE OF K FOR CONTROL LIMITS

COMPANY COST CHARACTERISTICS	USE TIGHT LIMITS LOW k (1.5 - 2.0)	USE WIDE LIMITS HIGH k (3.0 - 3.5)
Cost to change production level	Low Cost	High Cost
Cost to carry inventory	High Cost	Low Cost
Cost of Stock Outs	High Cost	Low Cost

The Follett Corporation incurs reasonably low costs in changing production levels, and has high inventory carrying and stock out costs. Therefore we use relatively tight control limits with k = 2.0.

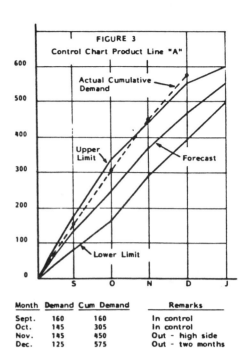

FIGURE 3
Control Chart Product Line "A"

Month	Demand	Cum Demand	Remarks
Sept.	160	160	In control
Oct.	145	305	In control
Nov.	145	450	Out - high side
Dec.	125	575	Out - two months

STEP 4 - Set Monthly Avg. Demand/Control Limits

A sales forecast for the coming year is made for each product line. A variety of methods are available and widely discussed in the literature (2,5,6). Once the forecast is made, it is translated into monthly demand and control limit amounts using the selected value of k and the statistical results of TABLE 2. For purposes of illustration, assume that the forecast for product line "A" for fiscal year 1979 is 2000 units, and k = 2.0. TABLE 3 shows the total forecast translated into monthly values

TABLE 3

PRODUCT LINE "A"
1979 FORECAST AND CONTROL LIMITS BASED ON

Forecast of 2000 units and k = 2.0

MONTH	AVG CUM %	% UCL	% LCL	CUM UNITS	CUM UNITS UCL	CUM UNITS LCL	UNITS MONTHLY
Sept	6.8	9.2	4.4	135	185	90	135
Oct	12.5	16.7	8.3	250	335	165	115
Nov	18.5	22.3	14.7	370	445	295	120
Dec	23.7	27.7	19.7	475	555	395	105

Notes: UCL % = AVG CUM % + 2.0 S
CUM UNITS = AVG CUM % x 2000

The various product line forecasts are used to determine capacity needs and formulate aggregate production plans for the coming year.

STEP 5 - Track Actual Demand with Control Charts

A control chart is drawn for each product line, using the data in TABLE 3. The control chart for product line "A" is shown in FIGURE 3 with only the first few months for clarity. Cumulative demand is plotted monthly on each chart. For our example, the first four month's demand is plotted and summarized below the chart. The demand of 450 units at the end of November is out of control - just above the upper limit of 445. An out of control condition can be caused by random fluctuations. To reduce the probability of this being the cause, it is best to wait for two consecutive months to be out of control before reacting. This is the case after December, with demand of 575 exceeding the upper limit of 555.

At this point there is a high probability that an assignable cause is at work either some factor, such as a competitor's strike, that is distorting this year's pattern or simply an error in the forecast. We must first try to determine whether something is distorting the pattern. Sales and marketing inputs are particularly important. If such a factor can be identified, the magnitude of its effect must be estimated and the system over-ridden to generate a new forecast and production plan. If nothing appears to be influencing the pattern, we can conclude that the forecast is probably wrong and should be changed. Assume that this is the case in our example. The data of TABLE 3 provides a basis for re-forecasting. The demand of 575 units at the end of December is, on the average, 23.7% of the annual total. Therefore, the expected total is 575/.237 = 2425 units. This new forecast will be exploded into monthly amounts and a new control chart drawn.

Waiting for demand to be out of control for two consecutive months can be a problem when the first signal occurs so far into the year that a deadline for taking action is reached. To avoid basing a decision on only one point, it would be helpful to know what can be expected to happen next month. This need at Follett led to a revision of the basic method, combining a forecast for the coming month with the actual cumulative demand.

In the revised method, at the end of each month two points are plotted

1. The actual cumulative demand to date
2. The actual cumulative demand to date, plus an exponentially smoothed forecast of demand for the next month. This is a forecast of next month's cumulative demand.

FIGURE 4 shows the control chart, using the revised method. Actual demand only through November is used, with the December point based on forecasted demand. TABLE 4 shows the development of the December forecast using seasonally adjusted exponential smoothing with trend. Referring to FIGURE 4, at the end of November we see the same out of control condition indicated previously in FIGURE 3, but in addition, we show a forecasted out of control point of 577 units for December. The revised method, therefore, saves one month in response time at the expense of some added risk in reacting to a forecasted point. The result is a broader choice of response and stability trade offs. These range from taking action when only one forecasted point is beyond limits to reacting only after two actual points and one forecasted point are out of control.

CONCLUSIONS

The basic forecast tracking method has been very effective in controlling capacity at Follett for the past fifteen years. The exponential smoothing modification is in its second year of use and initial indications are that the improved system response justifies the extra effort.

We feel the approach has several advantages:

1. It is a graphical technique easily understood by those who use it.
2. It works "by-exception". Management can focus only on those product lines that are out of control.
3. It is easily implemented and maintained, at low cost.

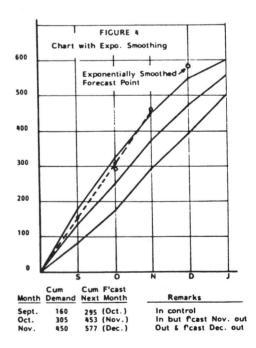

FIGURE 4
Chart with Expo. Smoothing

Month	Cum Demand	Cum F'cast Next Month	Remarks
Sept.	160	295 (Oct.)	In control
Oct.	305	453 (Nov.)	In but f'cast Nov. out
Nov.	450	577 (Dec.)	Out & f'cast Dec. out

TABLE 4

EXPONENTIALLY SMOOTHED FORECAST PRODUCT LINE "A" FISCAL YEAR 1979

Month	Index	Actual Demand	Adj. Demand	AVERAGE DEMAND	Apparent Trend	Avg. Trend	EXPECTED AVG. DEMAND	NEXT MONTH FORECAST
				190		+2.0	198	162
Sept	.82	160	195	191	+ 1	+1.8	198	135
Oct	.68	145	213	196	+ 5	+2.4	206	148
Nov	.72	145	201	197	+ 1	+2.1	205	127
Dec	.62							

1. Index = Avg Mo % / 8.3   for Nov. % = Cum. Nov. % – Cum. Oct. % = 18.5 – 16.5 = 6.0% and Index = 6.0/8.3 = .72

2. Adjusted Demand = Actual Demand / Index   for November = 145 / .72 = 201

3. Average Demand = a (Adj Demand) + (1-a) (Previous Month Avg. Demand)   with a = .2

    for November = .2 (201) + .8 (196) = 197

4. Apparent Trend = Avg. Demand – Previous Month Avg. Demand   for November = 197 – 196 = +1

5. Average Trend =   a (Apparent Trend) + (1-a) (Previous Month Avg. Trend)   with a = .2

    for November = .2 (+1) + .8 (+2.4) = +2.1

6. Expected Average Demand = Avg. Demand + (1-a)/a (Avg. Trend)   with a = .2

    for November = 197 + (.8/.2) (+2.1) = 197 + 8 = 205

7. Next Month Forecast = Expected Avg. Demand x Next Month Index

    at end of November, the December forecast = 205 x .62 = 127

As with any techinque, the tracking system has limitations. The major ones are:

1. It requires a reasonably stable demand pattern. Therefore it works best for products in the mature stage of the life cycle, that also have a seasonal pattern caused by fundamental buying habits. The differences in monthly demand are caused by a combination of a seasonal effect, a trend effect, and the effect of differing numbers of days in the months. Of these three, the days effect is constant except for leap years, a seasonal effect due to basic habits tends to be reasonably stable, and the trend effect is most susceptible to basic change. In a mature seasonal product the seasonal effect is usually dominant, tending to result in a stable pattern. While the technique can be extended to non-seasonal products, its effectiveness depends on whether the trend creates a reasonably stable effect on the monthly pattern. This condition is met, of course, by products having no significant trend.

2. Sufficient historical demand data is required for the specific product groups used to determine the required capacity. In the absence of such data the Plossl method (3) is an alternative.

Our conclusion is that the tracking technique can be an effective aid in making capacity decisions. It would have appealed to Sherlock Holmes who said, "One forms provisional theories and waits for time and fuller knowledge to explode them."

REFERENCES

1. G.W. Plossl and O.W. Wight, Production and Inventory Control, Prentice-Hall, Inc., 1967, pg. 35.

2. J.C. Chambers, S.K. Mullick and D.D. Smith, "How to Choose the Right Forecasting Technique", Harvard Business Review, July-August 1971, pg. 47.

3. G.W. Plossl, "Getting the Most From Forecasts", Production and Inventory Management, 1st Qtr. 1973, pg. 14.

4. N.L. Enrich, "Gearing Production to Seasonal Inventory Needs", APICS Quarterly Bulletin, April 1965, pg. 29.

5. Wheelright and Makridakis, Forecasting Methods for Management, Second Edition, Wiley Interscience, 1973.

6. Gross and Peterson, Business Forecasting, Houghton Mifflin & Co., 1967.

Reprinted from 1974 APICS Conference Proceedings.

CLASS SEASONALITY - A NEW APPROACH

By Glenn Dalhart
Ernst & Ernst

INTRODUCTION

The purpose of this paper is to introduce the concept of class seasonal parameter estimation. The introduction will be made through a discussion of classical seasonal estimation techniques and the investigation of an illustrative example. The practical aspects of implementing class seasonality will also be outlined.

The use of statistical forecasting techniques has expanded dramatically in the recent past. With this expansion, investigation and evaluation of various forecasting techniques has become an important part of the development of production and inventory control systems. Seasonality, defined as variations in the level of activity within a calendar year, is an essential sub-element of the forecasting problem. Seasonal considerations are far reaching in the production and inventory control environment. Some of the important uses of seasonality include:

1.) Improving forecast accuracy.
2.) Measurement of forecast errors.
3.) Computation of economical order quantities, reorder quantities and safety stock.

These potential uses of seasonality in the decision process signifies the importance of seasonal parameter estimation.

CLASSICAL APPROACH

Traditionally, seasonality is analyzed for each item for which forecasts must be produced. This analysis typically utilizes the theory of time series decomposition which serves to break time series data into components of trend, seasonality and randomness or noise. The ratio to moving average technique, which is widely used, effectively isolates the trend component of a time series. After all trend has been removed from a time series, only the components of seasonality and noise remain. This remainder is generally utilized as the basis for the final estimation of seasonal parameters (commonly termed indices or co-efficients) for each item.

The primary weakness of this approach to seasonality is that the seasonal component is never isolated from the noise component. To the degree that noise or randomness is present in the behavior of the item, a distortion in the seasonal parameters will result. This distortion can become significant when this technique is utilized to forecast individual products or stockkeeping units where unpredictable behavior is common.

CLASS SEASONALITY

Class seasonality can be described as the grouping of items and use of the average seasonal behavior of the group for estimation of seasonal parameters for all items in the group. The benefit of utilizing this approach is the elimination of the noise component distortion in the seasonal parameters. Elimination of the noise component is a natural by-product of the averaging process which is fundamental to class seasonality.

The mechanics of applying class seasonality begins with the definition of a seasonal group. All items within the group are then analyzed as in the classical approach. Once the trend has been removed using an appropriate technique, the seasonal parameters for each item are estimated for each reporting period in the calendar year. These parameters are then averaged for the group resulting in the estimated class seasonal parameters. These class parameters are subsequently used for all items belonging to the group.

ILLUSTRATIVE EXAMPLE

The benefits and appropriateness of class seasonality can be effectively demonstrated through the use of an example. The data used in the following example was generated using simulation techniques. The example is structured to highlight the concept of the removal of noise distortions from seasonal parameters. For this purpose, all items in this hypothetical example are assumed to have no trend and to have a consistent underlying seasonal behavior. This behavior is described in Figure 1 by the assumed seasonal coefficients (percent per period) for twelve monthly reporting periods.

Figure 1. Assumed Seasonal Behavior

Reporting Period	Seasonal Coefficient
1	0.054
2	0.063
3	0.083
4	0.104
5	0.113
6	0.125
7	0.113
8	0.104
9	0.083
10	0.063
11	0.054
12	0.041
	1.000

DATA GENERATION

The example data was generated for 100 items (or products), each item having 24 periods of demand data. The annual demand rate was assumed to be 12,000 units per year and distributed as shown in Figure 1. In addition to these assumptions, a random component of noise was introduced to the demand data through the use of a random number generator which provided normal random deviates. These deviates were applied to each of the 100 items in conjunction with an assumed level or amplitude of noise. For purposes of this illustration, the noise amplitude was increased progressively from a minimal level for the first item to a relatively high level for the 100th item. Examples of the demand data that was generated for several items is shown in Figure 2.

Figure 2. Example of Data Generated.

Reporting Period	First Year of Demand Data			
	Item #1	Item #25	Item #75	Item #100
1	525	693	597	655
2	962	573	1,173	215
3	1,069	636	751	1,714
4	1,505	787	28	0
5	1,560	1,477	1,081	1,875

Figure 2. Example of Data Generated - Continued

| | First Year of Demand Data | | | |
Reporting Period	Item #1	Item #25	Item #75	Item #100
6	1,675	2,109	1,793	1,589
7	1,554	1,596	695	458
8	1,759	1,129	1,065	1,285
9	1,307	826	997	1,404
10	520	877	690	515
11	649	589	587	627
12	419	341	412	419
	13,504	11,633	9,869	10,756

RESULTS OF SIMULATION

A set of seasonal coefficients can be computed for each of the 100 items treated in this simulation. In the simplified case of only one year of demand data (12 reporting periods) the coefficients are computed simply by dividing the demand in each reporting period by the total for the year. This computation for Item #1 as shown above would be as follows:

$$\text{Reporting Period #1 Coefficient} = 525 \div 13,504 = 0.039$$

This procedure (as compared with ratio to moving average) is greatly simplified by the assumptions of one year of data and the lack of trend. Because of these simplifying assumptions, the preceeding computations are equivalent to the standard techniques for estimating seasonality distributions. Figure 3 shows the results of estimating the seasonal distribution for each item shown in Figure 2.

Figure 3. Computed Seasonal Coefficients

Reporting Period	Assumed Distribution	Computed Coefficients			
		Item #1	Item #25	Item #75	Item #100
1	0.054	0.039	0.060	0.060	0.061
2	0.063	0.071	0.049	0.119	0.020
3	0.083	0.079	0.055	0.076	0.159
4	0.104	0.111	0.068	0.003	0.000
5	0.113	0.115	0.127	0.110	0.174
6	0.125	0.124	0.181	0.182	0.148
7	0.113	0.115	0.137	0.070	0.043
8	0.104	0.131	0.097	0.108	0.119
9	0.083	0.097	0.071	0.101	0.131
10	0.063	0.039	0.075	0.070	0.048
11	0.054	0.048	0.051	0.059	0.058
12	0.041	0.031	0.029	0.042	0.039
	1.000	1.000	1.000	1.000	1.000

It is interesting to compare the computed seasonal coefficients to the assumed seasonal distribution from which the demand data was generated. The distortion caused by the addition of noise to the demand data is evident in the variation in the seasonal distributions of the individual items as compared with the assumed seasonal distribution. The amount of distortion increases for items whose assumed noise amplitude was relatively large (higher numbered items). In line with the classical approach to seasonality, the computed seasonal coefficients for each item would be used as the assumed seasonality for each item. The class seasonal approach would require the combination (or averaging) of the computed individual item distributions. When this is done for the example data under discussion, the class seasonal distribution shown in Figure 4 results.

Figure 4. Computed Class Seasonality

Reporting Period	Computed Class Distribution	Assumed Distribution
1	0.052	0.054
2	0.065	0.063
3	0.081	0.083
4	0.103	0.104
5	0.113	0.113
6	0.127	0.125
7	0.112	0.113
8	0.103	0.104
9	0.087	0.083
10	0.063	0.063
11	0.056	0.054
12	0.038	0.041
	1.000	1.000

The results in Figure 4 show the effectiveness of the class seasonal procedure in accomplishing the objectives of noise removal and identification of true seasonal behavior. These objectives are strongly emphasized in this example because of the size of the class and the assumption of identical seasonal behavior for each item in the class.

ANALYSIS OF RESULTS

This paper has been primarily directed toward the development and explanation of the class seasonality concept. It is important to quantify the potential benefits of class seasonality. A simple extension of our illustrative example will serve to demonstrate these benefits.

Each of the 100 items in the example had twenty four periods (or two years) of data generated. Only the first of the two years was used to compute each item's seasonal distribution and to compute the class seasonal coefficients. The second year of data was reserved as an independent set of data which could be used for an unbiased comparative analysis.

The use of seasonality in forecasting is one area where improved estimates of seasonal distributions can provide significant benefits. These benefits are realized in the form of lower forecast errors. The comparative analysis of class seasonality versus the classical approach can be summarized as the statement of a forecasting problem:

    Given the following facts:

    · 100 items with 12 reporting periods of history for each item.

    · Approximately 12,000 units will be demanded for each item in the coming year.

    Problem:

    · Provide forecasts of demand by reporting period for the coming year.

The question posed by the following analysis is which technique, the classical approach or class seasonality, is more effective (least forecast error) in solving this problem. A sample of the analysis calculations is shown in Figure 5 for Item #1.

Figure 5.   Calculations for Comparative Analysis

(1) Year 2 Demand Data	(2) Classical Forecast	(3) Classical Absolute Error	(4) Class Seasonal Forecast	(5) Class Seasonal Absolute Error
595	436	159	581	14
839	793	46	726	113
863	882	19	905	42
825	1,240	415	1,151	326
1,284	1,285	1	1,262	22
1,439	1,385	54	1,419	20
1,714	1,285	429	1,251	463
1,134	1,463	329	1,151	17
718	1,084	366	972	254
688	436	252	704	16
693	536	157	625	68
379	346	33	424	45
11,171	11,171	2,260	11,171	1,400

(2)   Computed using seasonal coefficients shown in Figure 3 times 11,171.
(3)   Absolute value of $[(1)-(2)]$.
(4)   Computed using class distribution shown in Figure 4 times 11,171.
(5)   Absolute value of $[(1)-(4)]$.

The above analysis was performed for all 100 items in the example and the results are summarized in Figure 6.

Figure 6.   Summary of Comparative Analysis.

(1) Average Demand Data	(2) Average Classical Absolute Error	(3) Average Class Seasonal Absolute Error	(4) Percent Improvement
651	291	167	42.6
781	288	199	30.9
1,005	402	276	31.3
1,277	444	330	25.7
1,319	510	362	29.0
1,535	530	388	26.8
1,427	589	405	31.2
1,210	449	288	35.9
998	368	271	26.4
784	327	215	34.3
606	269	191	29.0
504	180	143	20.6
12,097	4,647	3,235	

(4) $[(2)-(3)]$ / (2)

The benefits of class seasonality are clearly demonstrated by the results of
the comparative analysis.   The significance of the benefits associated with the
use of class seasonality warrant the serious consideration of use of this concept.

IMPLEMENTATION

The practical matter of implementing class seasonality requires the establishment of classes or groups of items.   This is undoubtedly the most difficult

task associated with the class seasonal approach. In practice, the most sensible method to use for the grouping task is to identify items with natural seasonal tendencies or causes. Oftentimes product coding or some type of classification system will be invaluable in this effort. Once general seasonal classes have been established, mathematical techniques can be useful in the further refinement of the seasonal classes. These techniques include goodness of fit tests and identification modes (or peaks) in the seasonal patterns of individual items.

OTHER CONSIDERATIONS

The use of class seasonality provides additional benefits which are not apparent in the illustrative example discussed above. Data requirements of the classical seasonality approach limit its effectiveness in several ways. Effective application of the classical approach assumes the availability of <u>at least</u> two years of data for each item. This is a serious limitation in many situations and especially when a system is first being implemented and historical data has not been collected in the past. New items are particularly troublesome since reliable seasonal estimates will not be available for at least two years after introduction. Class seasonality reduces the historical data requirements because the technique can be used effectively with one year of data. New items are also readily handled if they can be associated with a previously established seasonal class. Under these conditions, the new item can be assigned a seasonal distribution immediately upon introduction.

CONCLUSION

The use of class seasonality for the estimation of seasonal parameters has been shown to be more effective than classical techniques. This effectiveness results in significant benefits through reduction of forecast errors. Class seasonality can also be useful in reducing data limitations inherent in the classical approach to seasonality. For these reasons, implementation of this technique should be seriously considered whenever seasonality of products is a significant problem.

BIOGRAPHICAL SUMMARY

Glenn Dalhart is a Senior on the Management Consulting Staff of Ernst & Ernst, Chicago, Illinois. He has been primarily concerned with the design and implementation of forecasting systems for production and inventory control. Mr. Dalhart is a graduate of Purdue University with a degree in Engineering and a Masters Degree in Engineering Sciences.

Reprinted from 1989 APICS Conference Proceedings.

BOTTOM-UP ACCOUNTABILITY FORECASTING
Paul N. Funk, CPIM
Alan G. Dunn, Inc.

Put yourself in the shoes of the Regional Sales Manager. He is responsible for the execution of the Company's marketing and sales plans, and to do this he must motivate and supervise his Territorial Sales Reps to achieve their assigned portion of the numbers (popularly referred to as a SALES QUOTA). He also owes an obligation to the Corporate Office: he must keep track of the "big picture" of product mix, and give people at the plant feedback on sales trends of the various product lines so they will have a "head start" in responding to what the customers actually are demanding.

Up to now, this has been a terribly difficult job in most companies. What's worse, the MIS systems in most companies simply were never geared toward the capture and analysis of meaningfully-sorted Sales History and Forecast information. As a result, too many field sales management systems have ended up on manual systems, or on non-integrated Personal Computers. As we all know by now, this situation causes dissension among players in all departments. As Lord Bacon said, "Knowledge is Power." The Sales Manager then said, "...and if I have the knowledge, and you want it, then I have power over you!" Thereafter, many arguments developed over whose numbers were the most correct.

Well, it's time we changed all that. This article describes some simple concepts for integrating the Forecasting/Sales Planning function with the Business Planning function of Top Management, and with the Master Scheduling function at the Corporate Office. Along the way, the author will describe some techniques for measuring sales rep performance, and for giving meaningful feedback on product line performance.

Begin at the Bottom

Let's begin at the lowest level in the process, and go from the BOTTOM UP. The lowest level of control in the Sales function is the Territory Sales Rep. However, in order to properly measure the Territory Sales Rep on his organization skills and sales skills, many companies are going to a level one lower than the Territory Sales Rep: to that of the CUSTOMERS that actually make up his territory. Many salespeople and Sales Managers complain about this level of detail. In fact, in some businesses, it is impractical to forecast at the customer level. But experience has proven that, even if formal forecasts are not prepared, the Regional (or Area) Sales Manager is aware of the potential sales of each and every Sales Rep under his supervision. The usual method of communication of these opportunities is the Call Report. What I propose, and what many companies have adopted

years ago, is a more formal method of communicating customer demands, either real or potential, all the way up the chain to the Corporate Office, so that proper forecasts can be constructed and adjusted to reflect the "real world" in the field. Companies who have adopted this approach, after an initial period of working out the bugs, have always achieved a greater degree of visibility of the marketplace's reactions to Marketing and Sales Plans, and of the capabilities for execution on the part of their sales staffs. There is also a major benefit in improved communications (much more timely, and much more accurate) to those responsible for production planning and inventory control. By concentrating on the balance between supply and demand, buffered properly by judicious placement of inventory, companies implementing this philosophy of doing business have been able to score dramatic gains in customer service levels while achieving corresponding cuts in "just-in-case" inventory requirements.

Let's examine the sales organization of our model company, Fastcool Fan Company:

Figure 1.

The author has intentionally used a very simple organization structure to easily show how the concepts that follow work. These methods have also been installed in multi-division companies, and in companies with many product lines. The key requirement in these more complicated organizations was to reduce paperwork to a minimum. Therefore, the companies went to lap-top computer systems, with built-in modems, pre-programmed with the database and spreadsheet templates of their choice. Once the system had been debugged, the laptops became so popular with the Sales Reps, that they would now be very reluctant to part with their laptops! The use of the laptops was then expanded to include on-line inventory checking, review of the Master Schedule, pricing and discount determination, and actual entry of some Sales Orders from the field. Companies with fewer customers, fewer product lines, fewer end items, etc. may choose to implement this system manually.

Now let's look at the makeup of the company's product lines:

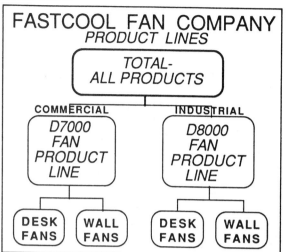

Figure 2.

Are you starting to get the picture? The Corporate Office and manufacturing plant develops Strategic Business Plans and Sales & Operations Plans on a Product Line basis, not on a total revenue basis. Therefore it is critical to involve the Sales Reps in the timely and accurate collection of "intelligence data" on a Product Line basis.

Each Territory Sales Rep is responsible for all customers with facilities in his geographic area. Some customers may have facilities in many different territories; it is up to the Company how commissions and sales credit are handled. But for this example, let's assume that if the sale comes from a Rep's territory, and he had a hand in the sale, he gets the credit. He is than also responsible for forecasting the sale of end items to all known customers in his Territory!

While this may appear to be a radical notion to some of you, consider the way Sales Managers manage their people now: they have the Sales Reps report all potential business on a "call report," then they check with them frequently to see if they accomplished what they said they were going to do.

Now, lest you think that I am about to bury the poor Sales Rep in paperwork, I offer the following tried-and-true solution. The idea is to give the Sales Rep the tools he needs to develop a proper forecast, quickly, and with minimum paperwork. The Corporate Office has collected lots of sales history. The Sales Manager is aware of certain extrinsic conditions that may cause seasonality of the product or some event-based predictable demand pattern. Many larger customers, particularly large aerospace firms and larger municipal/State/federal government agencies, have annual bid cycles which occur at the same time every year. We also have actual booked sales orders information available. The trick is to put all of this information in a database of some kind (preferably in your main

business system computer), for later extraction of relevant data. The data are run against one or more forecast models. Then we prepare a suggested forecast report which is either printed and mailed, or electronically downloaded to each Sales Rep via electronic mail. This happens on a specified date each and every month. The Sales Rep has three to five days to revise this forecast. He will put in all of the knowledge he has at his command to make this forecast as realistic as possible. When he is done, the Rep forwards the forecast directly to the Corporate Office. There Corporate MIS compiles all of the individual Sales Rep forecasts.

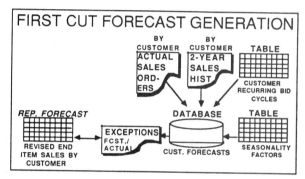

Figure 3.

Aggregating customer forecast data

The next step is to aggregate data from all 80 Sales Reps on a total of thousands of customer sites, into some meaningful information for the Regional Sales Manager. Corporate MIS produces a report showing Territory-By-Territory forecasts as produced by each Sales Rep, in units and dollars. The Regional Sales Manager gets a timely report either sent to him by overnight mail, or electronically downloaded to his office personal computer. Included in this package is a small group of charts which reflect forecast-to-plan numbers for each Sales Rep and for the total Region, and the projections displayed from the Top Producer to the Lowest Producer, and the forecast-to-actual confidence percentage for the last six months of data for each Sales Rep. In addition, Corporate MIS calculates forecasted sales by customer for each Territory, charts them in descending order, and has them available on-line for any Region Manager or for the National Sales Manager or Vice-President Sales & Marketing to review whenever required.

End Item (SKU) vs. Option Forecasting

This method is equally well suited to either environment, although of course forecasting major options on capital equipment systems and machines is far more complex than one SKU of a known configuration. In the option-based company, demand data are captured by a questionnaire completed by the Sales Rep during the quotation/sales cycle. This approach causes the Sales Rep to get closer to the actual needs and expectations of the Customer, sooner in the sales cycle. By capturing demand for popular long-lead-

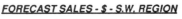

FORECAST - $ - BY PRODUCT LINE
S.W. REGION - NOVEMBER 19__

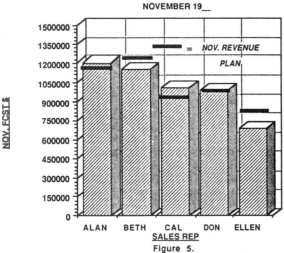

Figure 4.

FORECAST SALES - $ - S.W. REGION
NOVEMBER 19__

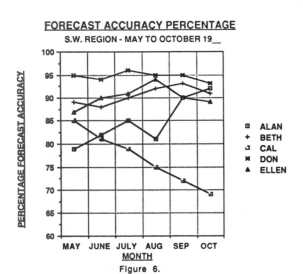

Figure 5.

Similarly, the Regional Manager has access to charts which show Sales Rep forecast accuracy and a list of the top customers in each Territory:

FORECAST ACCURACY PERCENTAGE
S.W. REGION - MAY TO OCTOBER 19__

Figure 6.

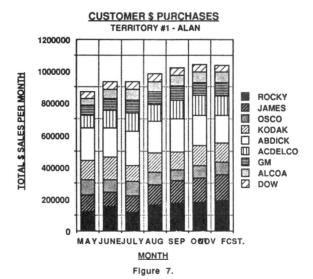

CUSTOMER $ PURCHASES
TERRITORY #1 - ALAN

Figure 7.

time or difficult-to-build options ahead of time, and through the use of effective Master Scheduling, leadtimes can be dramatically shortened for the customer, thus generating confidence and further orders.

Aggregating to the Corporate Level

The information captured in our database is then aggregated and summarized for all Sales Regions, all Sales Reps, and all Customers (real or potential). The information is then available in Units and Dollars by SKU, Option·Part Number (if required), Territory, Region, and Product Line. The last category is then judiciously analyzed by the system. The UNITS of demand for each SKU/Option is compared to the TOTAL UNITS forecast for each Product Line, by month. What results is a new, powerful concept in Master Scheduling: the Time-Phased Planning Bill.

Time-Phased Planning Bills

The problem with stationary planning bills, used often by companies to plan for options, accessories, and SKU product mix, is that they are only a SNAPSHOT of the mix of products or options at any one point in time. Too often they are prepared ONCE, then never updated! No one pays attention to product life cycles, or dramatic rises or dropoffs of demand. This causes companies to waste resources building the wrong things, and to needlessly build inventory in unneeded products and options. The need exists for a more dynamic tool to project demand better during the Master Scheduling process. Enter the Time-Phased Planning Bill (I am indebted to Joseph N. Fields, Vice-President Operations, System Industries, Milpitas, CA, for this concept). With the accurate and timely forecast input from the field presented to your system regularly, you can have the system calculate monthly planning bill percentages for each SKU/Option Part Number. Then, when you explode the Master Schedule for this month, you will get the current product mix. And when you explode it for next month, and the months after, you will get exactly the product mix that Marketing and Sales projects will be sold in those upcoming months.

An Improved Master Scheduling Process

Once we have dynamically-updated (but only once a month is recommended, unless your product's demand is a real runaway) Time-Phased Planning Bills, we can plug these into the Master Schedule for future periods (out beyond where there are firm Sales Orders). The objective then is to run the Master Schedule and MRP in simulation mode, to see what shortages will be caused by these changes in product mix, and also to run a Rough-Cut Capacity Planning analysis to see how these changes might impact resource capacity, tooling, and other constraints. Once the Master Scheduler has reviewed the changes, dealt with the exceptions, and formulated a strategy, the proposed Master Schedule is <u>dollarized</u>, and passed to Finance for review. Finance will check out the aggregate total revenue as described in the Master Schedule, and compare it to the Corporate Revenue Forecast in the Business Plan. If any shortfalls are noted, Finance notifies Marketing immediately, and the problem is resolved in a Forecast Review Meeting (see below for how this meeting is conducted). Once a consensus agreement is reached on the right amount to forecast for each Product Line, adjustments are made to the Master Schedule by adjusting the Time-Phased Planning Bill percentages for a targeted period. The Master Schedule is then approved and executed by the rest of the company.

The following illustration shows the flow of information and decision points in this process:

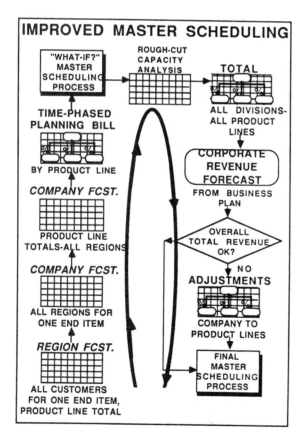

Figure 8.

The Chief Corporate Forecaster's Job

In most companies, the Master Scheduler is just too busy to analyze product mix in as much detail as this process. Most of his/her time is spend in the Order Promising activity. Companies with enough sales volume (or enough grief) have opted to establish a position of Chief Corporate Forecaster. This person may report to Marketing, Operations, or the President. It is his/her responsibility to design the systems to collect the data, operate these systems on a timely basis, and work hand-in-glove with the Master Scheduler to prepare more timely and accurate demand forecasts. One of the major responsibilities of the Chief Corporate Forecaster is the conduct of the Monthly Forecast Review Meeting, which is held just ahead of the Monthly Sales and Operations Plan Meeting.

Monthly Forecast Review Meeting

This meeting is conducted by the Chief Corporate Forecaster. Present are the senior managers of Marketing, Sales, Finance, Manufacturing/Operations, Materials, Engineering, and the Master Scheduler. The Master Scheduler reviews the demand data Product Line by Product Line, showing trends graphically. Changes in SKU or Option product mix within Product Lines are pointed out. Strategies to accomodate these demand changes are developed. Next, a comparison of all of the company's Product Lines to the total demand is made. Each Product Line's contribution to sales and profits is assessed. Upcoming product introductions which may have a major effect on product demand are discussed, along with any production, inventory or quality problems which may be temporary constraints to satisfying demand for any SKU, Option, or End Item. The last agenda item is the dollarizing of the Master Schedule (with the agreed-to changes) for the next 90 days. The monthly shipment projection is compared to the Business Plan Revenue Projection and is adjusted as necessary through negotiation between Marketing/Sales, Finance and Operations. All the facts are there to make good informed decisions which may make the difference between being profitable or not. If capacity is an issue, a Rough-Cut Capacity analysis can be run right there in the meeting and reviewed by all players. If critical raw material/purchased part shortages are the issue, a net-change MRP can be exploded within a couple of hours, and the players can return to the meeting to review the facts. This meeting is the key to effective performance against the Master Schedule.

Accountability for Inventory

If Marketing/Sales gets the forecast data from the Sales Staff in time, and if the Chief Forecaster prepares and analyzes the data on time, and if the Monthly Forecast Meeting is held on time, and if Operations/Materials/Manufacturing properly executes the Master Schedule which results, then the <u>Marketing Department is responsible for inventory levels of finished goods</u>. Putting the responsibility for inventory levels in Marketing's budget increases the emphasis and priority of the Senior Marketing Manager to demand timely and accurate forecast data from Territory Sales Reps.

<u>Using Forecast Data for Managing Sales Reps</u>

It is extremely important for the company's Senior Management Team to communicate the right priorities to field sales people in a timely manner. To do this, I suggest the use of several levels of Time-Phased Planning Bills to convert the overall company-wide forecast to Region sales targets (quotas) and individual Territory sales quotas. Most MRP II software which supports planning bills allows "nested" planning bills, which allow the elegantly simple explosion logic of MRP to rapidly calculate lower-level requirements. Once an agreed-upon Master Schedule is developed, explode the requirements down through Time-Phased Planning Bills by month, and produce simple reports for the Regional Sales Manager (preferably in graphic form). These reports may be printed or downloaded to the Regional Sales Office computer.

FEEDBACK is the Breakfast of Champions. It is especially important to the success of the Bottom-Up Accountability process that Sales Managers and Territory Sales Reps get accurate and timely feedback on Actual Sales compared to Forecasted Sales. Sales Managers must then help their people achieve more accurate numbers.

<u>Conclusion</u>

The process of Bottom-Up Accountability Forecasting is practiced by many high-volume manufacturing and distribution companies today. It offers a much quicker way to arrive at the relevant facts to make good decisions. By applying the concept of Time-Phased Planning Bills and a Monthly Forecast Review Meeting, these companies have yielded much better long-range plans than previously. This has given them yet another competitive advantage in the war for the GRAND PRIZE: Market Share.

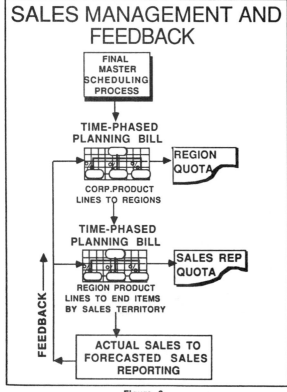

Figure 9.

<u>BIOGRAPHY</u>

PAUL N. FUNK is a Senior Manufacturing Consultant with Alan G. Dunn, Inc. He has more than 10 years of industry experience in positions from Manager,Inventory Planning & Control to Plant Manager. He has over 10 years of consulting experience and has been instrumental in the turn-arounds of many companies, large and small. He is Certified C.P.I.M. by APICS, and is the co-author of the Performance Management chapter of the "APICS Production and Inventory Control Handbook" (2nd Edition)." Mr. Funk presents seminars and workshops on Manufacturing Excellence worldwide.

Reprinted from 1990 APICS Conference Proceedings.

The Master Scheduler's Job Revisited

Paul N. Funk, CPIM

In my previous paper in 1987, "The Master Scheduler's Job: How To Operate While Between a Rock and a Hard Place," (see 1987 International Conference Proceedings) we explored the Master Scheduler's main responsibilities and how he/she could work his/her way out of some very difficult situations that seem to arise very often in a dynamic manufacturing environment. This paper will further explore how the job of the Master Scheduler has changed with the advent of Just-In-Time master scheduling techniques, changes in customer expectations, the huge increase in competitive pressures, and the pressure to reduce inventories and leadtimes. It will also point out what I perceive as some problems that still exist today in the master scheduling process.

The old job

The key characteristic of the job of the Master Production Scheduler, as we discussed before, was CONFLICT. The Master Scheduler was required to be manufacturing-oriented, customer-oriented, engineering-oriented, finance-oriented, and be able to juggle the priorities as they occurred. On top of this he (or SHE--implied) was required to plan the TIMING of events which, when taken together, would achieve everyone's goals. No wonder we said that the Master Scheduler was between a rock and a hard place!

Let's recall some of the personal characteristics of a successful Master Scheduler. He (or SHE--implied) is a thoughtful, analytic, confident individual with a great deal of product knowledge, customer knowledge, and general business sense. He is also capable of presenting himself well, preparing data quickly and verifying its accuracy, and making "ad hoc" presentations to management on short notice. This person has the ability to "sell" ideas and to negotiate compromises based on knowledge of a broad range of alternatives not known to others. He is, by and large, a proponent of formal systems and would rather plan than expedite; however, when certain situations evolve (downhill), he is not above "making deals" to get the product out the door.

Changes in the work environment

Since that paper in 1987, the pace has definitely quickened! The competition from other American producers and from foreign producers has, in many industries, increased tenfold. This usually means that, quality and cost being equal, he that delivers in the shortest lead time wins the business. This has put tremendous pressure on the Master Scheduler to turn around unusual customer requests in the shortest possible time. The luxury of several days time to analyze all the alternatives is no longer available.

Another area of tightening pressure is the new product development cycle. Master Schedulers are increasingly being called upon to contribute their expertise to the reduction of lead time required to bring new products to market. It is another "rock and hard place" situation to try to accommodate trial production runs on production equipment while still trying to achieve a monthly production/revenue target. The Master Scheduler is charged with a massive coordination effort of providing

- manpower

- materials

- manufacturing capability

- money (cash flow) and

- management of all the logistical activities

In direct conflict with the need to get the product to market is the need to continue producing enough of the current best-selling products to meet the goals of customer service. Since the popularity of your products is always a fickle thing with customers, this is a process of never-ending change. The major task of the Master Scheduler is to minimize the impact of these changes.

Changes in customer expectations

Because of the great proliferation in competition, and the transition from a captive U.S. market to a global market, many companies have had to change their approaches in dealing with customers. It's by and large a buyer's market. The customers are in a position to demand more and more concessions on price, delivery, special packaging, etc. Supplier companies who won't go along with these requests usually find themselves having to participate in a round of competitive bidding, where they were "locked in" as a sole source before; or they may lose in the next round of bidding if they were the majority supplier. Think about it! What would you do if you suddenly lost the business of your largest customer?

The winners in this area have enlisted the aid of their customers in helping to develop long-range plans for the benefit of both buyer and supplier. Often this has involved direct contact and the development of camaraderie between your Master Scheduler and the CUSTOMER'S Master Scheduler. Thus we see the Master Scheduler becoming a member of the SALES team for the first time in some companies.

Changes in scheduling technology

Recall from the 1987 paper the steps in formal master scheduling in an MRP II system:

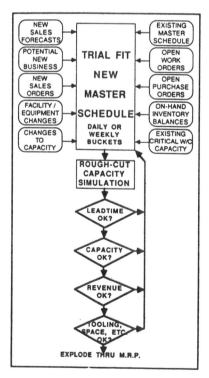

Figure 1

While most of the above steps are still valid and practiced today, there have been several new wrinkles added, with the advent of Just-In-Time production systems. First, contrary to the belief of many, the emphasis is on PLANNING in a J-I-T production system, not EXECUTION via Kanban cards! How do you suppose they know how many cards to put out on the floor, and where? What do they do with short runs? How do they handle unique customer requirements? Well, the good news is, the Master Scheduler's job doesn't go away when you implement J-I-T. In fact, the job becomes infinitely more important. Second, with Total Quality Control and J-I-T generating constant improvements, we can now "tighten up" the scheduling buckets from months to weeks to days to ONE HOUR! The objective is HIGH PRECISION PLANNING with NO CONTINGENCIES! That calls for some new techniques for planning, execution and feedback that our MRP II systems didn't provide. Figure 2 illustrates this:

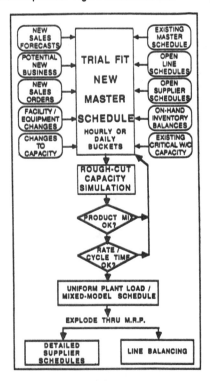

Figure 2

The emphasis in precision Just-In-Time scheduling is not on the contingencies (safety stock, inventory shortages, missing tooling, missing documentation, etc.), since these are already handled by others as a part of accepting responsibility for "delighting the internal customer" in Total Quality Control. The emphasis may now be switched to what counts: improving THROUGHPUT! The best measure of throughput is Sales Dollars (shipped) Per Employee. Do you know your company's throughput yardstick? Why not find out?

Scheduling without work orders is a difficult transition for some Master Schedulers. But once you learn the basics of line scheduling to a RATE and MIX target, the rest is easy. The key to this is the concept of Uniform Plant Loading. This can best be expressed as "make something of everything, every day." The idea is to set up a production schedule of many repeating CYCLES of the most popular products. The proportions are first determined by sales forecasts, then distilled down to weekly, daily and hourly rates. Once the required cycle time for each product has been determined, many companies often set up a schedule for 40 minutes for each hour for these most popular products, and use the technique of Mixed-Model

Scheduling to create repeating cycles, like this:

- Product 'A': 10
- Product 'B': 20
- Product 'C': 5
- Product 'D': 15

- Product 'A': 10
- Product 'B': 20
- Product 'C': 5
- Product 'D': 15

The trick to making this work is total employee involvement of all departments. First, sales and marketing must agree to "time fence" guidelines for 95% of all customer orders. Constant disruption of schedules for emergency customer requirements will defeat the purpose. Engineering changes must not be implemented at random. They must be grouped and incorporated at the appropriate time (the best time is during changeovers from one product to another). Once the Final Assembly Schedule is arrived at, and agreed to by all, the objective is to achieve *linearity* to that schedule: this means the *closest possible adherence* to the Final Assembly Schedule. All of the supporting activity centers who provide material to the final assembly area must be in tune to the Final Assembly Schedule. Thus the *synchronization* of all schedules in the plant is the vehicle that brings precision to the overall process, and allows us to reduce inventory and increase throughput. Once people know they can count on a regular pattern occurring every day, the need for contingencies soon disappears. This is what we mean by schedule linearity.

Why schedule only 40 minutes of each hour this way? To allow for the processing of very small quantities for unique customer requirements. The other 20 minutes is used for this purpose. Through a concerted effort by your management and your supervision and workers, customer leadtimes can often be reduced from weeks to days or even hours!

The process of Rough-Cut Capacity Planning becomes much more meaningful when schedules are linear, because you are including a whole production line or a cellular group of machines in your calculations, not just a few "bottleneck" work centers spread throughout the factory. Visibility is provided, in a very simple form, for current work-in-process and the load against each production line, cell, or individual machine. By treating the entire factory as a cell, loads can easily be "trial fitted" into any available time slot and tested to see if the customer's needs can be accommodated within the constraints of your plant.

Note in Figure 2 how M.R.P. is still used to calculate requirements, but mostly for purchased parts and for manufactured parts which are only occasionally used. The process of *synchronization*, involving all departments who feed the final assembly area, will eventually replace the M.R.P. II Dispatch List and other priority control tools. The feeding activity centers rely on the *linearity* of the Final Assembly Schedule. They then set up their activities to produce each hour the exact number of components needed for the final assembly area. The existence of a firm, cyclical Uniform Plant Load only increases the effectiveness of M.R.P. In short, M.R.P. is used by better than 90% of J-I-T factories to generate medium-range to long-range requirements to communicate to suppliers, and to plan for plant expansion.

The new job

Master Schedulers, this is a direct challenge! You MUST start educating yourself about J-I-T scheduling techniques. Doing things the same way you are doing them now, while it appears to be effective, will achieve the same results you are achieving now, in the future. Meanwhile, there are at least 5 to 50 competitors out there who are looking to beat your company out of its market share. How will they do that? By implementing J-I-T Continuous Improvement production. Heaven help you if you are the LAST in your industry to adopt these important manufacturing philosophies! You may not last that long.

A word about software packages for J-I-T scheduling. They are still not up to the capabilities needed for mix analyses, production rate breakdowns, rough-cut capacity planning, cycle time analysis, profitability/contribution analysis, etc. You Master Schedulers had better learn to use simple microcomputer-based spreadsheet programs for analysis. If you're not using these tools now, you are really behind the power curve. Your competitors are! And they will use the facts and plans gained by this analysis to "eat your lunch!" Also remember: people hate to look at a large spreadsheet full of numbers. Put these numbers into GRAPHS! You will be far more effective at communicating your point with pictures than with columns of numbers.

The biggest change in the Master Scheduler's job is that he(or SHE-implied) is now a more important focal point than ever before for decision-making. When you remove most of the contingencies from the production process (safety lead times, safety stock, move time allowances, queue time allowances, overtime, etc.), your scheduling must become more exact and be followed with precision. Also, the Master Scheduler is increasingly aware of the necessity for IMMEDIATE turnaround of information about alternatives. No longer is he the recipient of Sales Orders put into a shovel and thrown over the wall. He is now a working partner of Sales. Many firms have portable computers in the hands of salespeople, which they now use to dial up the factory and talk to the Master Scheduler ON-LINE! Think about that. What if you were to receive an on-line inquiry from a sales rep. How would you answer it in your current system? The Master Scheduler of today is an innovator. He has designed many "quick response" tools which he can use to get information to the field *in a hurry* to take advantage of a rapidly closing window of sales opportunity with a customer. Quick responses mean quick sales! If the Master Scheduler can provide accurate, quick turn-around of commitments to customers which can be met 99% of the time or better, he is usually worth much more than before, when the organization wasn't synchronized and achieving 75% on-time deliveries was a chore.

The Master Scheduler is increasingly seen as NOT the Materials Manager's "troop," but a working member of the staff of the Senior Management Team. There is a greater tendency to elevate him organizationally to report to a Vice-President or directly to the President. He becomes increasingly more involved in long-range planning and simulation of alternatives. He is also concerned with Performance Measurement of the entire enterprise. Master Schedulers frequently come under attack from one or more departments who perceive their needs not being met. It is up to the Master Scheduler to provide the proof that the system is working better than it did before, and defuse these arguments before they get a chance to fester and grow out of proportion to reality.

Why has the Master Scheduler's job achieved prominence? Because many bright people have taken to the position and creatively enhanced it so that their companies are dramatically more responsive to customers, to setbacks and disasters, to changes, and to market conditions. The Master Scheduler of today uses a combination of

- integrated computer systems
- microcomputer analysis tools and graphics
- MBWA (Management By Walking Around)
- superior communications skills including writing and speaking
- the judicious use of meetings and one-on-one discussions for gathering internal and external intelligence
- negotiation techniques to protect schedule integrity
- and dedication to the principle of continuous improvement

to advance his company to the position of market leader. The combination of a properly motivated, trained and dedicated Master Scheduler, working with an organization committed to linearity of schedules and constant improvement, will eventually destroy their competition.

Where will it lead? The future Master Scheduler

The Commitment to Excellence being made by companies as a competitive strategy for the 1990's will lead to a tragedy of sorts--those companies NOT making the commitment or relying on "the way we've always done it" will begin to decline, and by the end of the decade, over HALF of them will either be bankrupt or acquired by another company. You may think that this "doom and gloom" prediction means there will be less Master Scheduler jobs available. On the contrary! The surviving companies will be forced to introduce new products constantly, at an ever more accelerated pace. Their existing inefficient factories will have to be either "modernized" or closed and replaced with another factory elsewhere in the country.

Master Schedulers have an integral role to play in either of these scenarios. If an old, inefficient factory is to be "modernized," what better place to start than on Master Schedules? The Master Scheduler must introduce new techniques such as Uniform Plant Loading and Mixed-Model Scheduling. He must educate everyone on the benefits of "broadcasting" repetitive-cycle Final Assembly Schedules to internal feeding activity centers and to suppliers. He must become the *de facto* Project Manager to implement these techniques in his plant. Finally, he must pay particular attention to Performance Measurement, insuring that he reports the truth about accomplishments. If the performance is slipping back to previous levels, he must "blow the whistle" and cause the company's management to get involved to go after the next level of excellence.

If the Master Scheduler is involved in a "start-up" operation, he has the perfect opportunity to set the stage for Uniform Plant Loading, Mixed Model Scheduling, Linearity of schedules, flow of Final Assembly Schedule priority information to feeding activity centers and suppliers, and proper Performance Measurement. What he must do is to thoroughly plan all of the tools he will need to perform the three jobs of Customer Service, Change Control and Capacity Management. The emphasis must be on tools which can be used for QUICK response. Then the Master Scheduler must become the "Chief Educator." Starting with the Senior Management team, he must explain to people the value of good schedules which are not changed frequently. Once the benefits of schedule linearity are embraced by Senior Management, they must communicate to all employees that they will not tolerate major schedule disruptions unless it is for a very good reason. Armed with this commitment, the Master Scheduler can be an effective marketing weapon, manufacturing productivity enhancer, protector of the company's assets, and profit enhancer.

We have witnessed a huge explosion in the Body of Knowledge about Master Scheduling. All Master Schedulers should be learners. They need to read constantly. They need to study other disciplines besides Materials Management. It is very important to the negotiating process that the Master Scheduler be able to talk the language of the design engineer, general accountant, cost accountant, manufacturing manager, quality manager, sales / marketing manager, customer service manager, field service manager, manufacturing engineer, materials manager, purchasing manager, President, etc. An excellent vehicle for this is APICS Certification. It should be a prerequisite for all Master Schedulers to be APICS Certified, and to have taken ALL 6 Certification Exams. The upcoming improvements in the APICS Certification program will vastly expand the Body of Knowledge as it relates to the *entire* manufacturing enterprise. Watch for the announcements on this soon. Continuous improvement is the name of the game in Master

Scheduling. Make the commitment to yourself to improve 1% A DAY, EVERY DAY. That will give you about 250% improvement in your skills every year! Every Master Scheduler can do this.

America is going to get involved in a war in the 1990's. But it will NOT be fought with guns. It will be a trade war. Our objective is to **REDUCE OUR BALANCE OF PAYMENTS TO ZERO!**

This means we must build and operate our manufacturing plants at a productivity rate equal to or higher than those in the most productive countries in the world. That's a tall order. But the place to start is in Master Scheduling. The job of the Master Scheduler has never been so important.

BIOGRAPHY

Paul N. Funk, C.P.I.M. is a Senior Consultant with Alan G. Dunn, Inc. of Diamond Bar, CA. He has many years of industry experience in positions from Planner to Plant Manager. He has been a member of the Los Angeles Chapter of APICS since 1977, serving as Vice President of University Programs, Day Seminars, Evening Certification Seminars and as a Director of Education. He has served as an Associate Professor for Materials Management courses for California State University Dominguez Hills, California State University Long Beach, California State University Northridge, and University of California Berkeley. He is the co-author of the Performance Management chapter of the Production and Inventory Control Handbook, 2nd Edition.

Reprinted with permission from <u>Production & Inventory Management Review</u>, Feb. 1982.

Sales Forecasting - Replacing Magic With Logic

by Jack Gips and Bill Sullivan

*T*he forecast will never be *right!* These six words have been bandied about in MRP discussions for years and they have become a great excuse for not addressing a very serious problem. Think about it for a moment . . . With these six words, manufacturing and sales people in many companies have dodged an activity as crucial as assuring inventory accuracy or bill of material accuracy. This attitude, cast in concrete, has caused many companies to make feeble attempts at, or even to ignore, improvement of their sales forecasts.

Yet anyone who has been exposed to MRP logic can tell you that an error in a sales forecast can cause results similar to errors in inventory accuracy -- volatile schedules, excessive inventories and surprise shortages. The inventory error affects the supply side of the MRP equation, while the sales forecast error affects the demand side. Because demand is "uncontrollable," many individuals feel that improvements in forecasting accuracy are impossible.

What makes a forecast error *even worse* than an inventory error is that it occurs predominantly at the highest levels of the product structure in most companies. So this error tends to ricochet through more components causing even greater turbulence in the system.

But before forecasts can be improved, the excuses must be challenged and removed. To continue the analogy between forecasting and inventory accuracy, companies that have accomplished their inventory goal have had to deal with a myriad of excuses for why it could not, or should not, be addressed.

Many excuses relate to the difficulty of achieving inventory goals:
- *"The tolerances are too tight!"*
- *"It's impossible to get high accuracy on hardware and slow-moving items."*
- *"Our volumes are too high."*

Some avoid the problem:
- *"Inventory accuracy has improved. It's up from 55% last year."*
- *"MRP, even with 70% accuracy, will be better than our current system."*

With additional effort and information, better measurement, and more teamwork, the forecasts used in MRP can be made more accurate and can be better managed than they are today in most companies.

Some border on the ridiculous:
- *"Our parts are round and can't be stacked neatly."*
- *"The union won't let us add requirements to the stock handlers' job description that they must be able to count to ten."*

Today, many companies have dealt with these excuses and others, faced up to their inventory accuracy problems, and met their goals. It has been demonstated many times over -- by diverse companies making many diverse products with many diverse processes -- that inventory accuracy can be accomplished. It has been a long and difficult struggle in many cases because there have been some people with attitudes that made them unwilling to address the problems. Instead they have worked unceasingly to find new excuses for not tackling them. But now, in the case of inventory accuracy, it is getting more and more difficult to sell these excuses because there are so many successes being reported. Management people will no longer accept them as quickly as they once did.

Sales forecasting, however, is another area of accuracy where the excuses still run rampant. Today we hear excuses like:
- *"Our customers are too unpredictable."*
- *"Our volume is too low to forecast."*
- *"We can forecast how many end products the customers will buy, but never the options."*

and, of course, the ever popular:
- *"The forecasts will never be right, so why bother . . ."*

It is an area where little effort is being made, and it is an area of even greater potential improvement than inventory accuracy.

Now, we don't intend to claim that most companies can reach the same level of accuracy in their forecasts that they can in inventories. Obviously, there is more uncertainty, more subjectivity. Inventory accuracy is achieved when parts are counted correctly, transactions are processed properly, and physical controls are established. In sales forecasting we are working with an unknown future. Subjective inputs are essential, and control is more difficult (but not impossible) to establish.

We contend, however, that with additional effort, additional information, better measurement, and more teamwork, the forecasts used in MRP can be made more accurate and can be better managed than they are today in most companies.

An improvement in product family forecast accuracy from 70 to 80%, or 85 to 95%, can be translated into significant improvements in the operation of any MRP system. Consequently, there would be more realistic delivery schedules, reduced product costs, and better resource utilization. This may be the single most important effort to make if inventory, bill of material, and open order accuracy are established. A 10% improvement in the forecast is likely to result in greater benefits than a 10% improvement in any of these other categories because of its impact at the highest levels.

So, rather than shy away from this task, we believe that it must be tackled aggressively. Companies must make it part of the MRP implementation process, establish an action plan, and begin the improvement process.

The key to improving sales forecasts is the development of a coordinated company forecasting strategy. This strategy should include:

- *The development of a sales forecasting policy statement, including who in the organization is responsible for managing the forecasting effort.*
- *Selection of the most suitable forecasting techniques for the company's products and markets.*
- *Application of subjective judgements to the results of the mathematical forecasts.*
- *Plans to deal with departures from ordinary business.*
- *Coordinated and informed use of the forecasts once they are developed.*

❝ Unfortunately, much of the literature available today on quantitative forecasting techniques has been written in a way that 'turns off' the average businessman. ❞

The purpose of this strategy is to generate an "official" sales forecast for the company. If this "official" forecast is not formally prepared, then anyone making decisions about ordering materials, expanding capacity, hiring people, or anyone in the process of developing budgets and plans will make his or her own forecasts. These will most often not be coordinated with forecasts made by other people in the organization. This "official" forecast is the only way to provide a consistent basis for all planning activities. Let's look at the elements of the strategy more closely.

Developing A Sales Forecasting Policy

A formal forecast policy statement should clearly specify the objective of sales forecasting in the company. There may be several objectives which could cause several different types of sales forecasts to be defined. Defining the purpose of the forecast helps to set the length of the forecast horizon and the units in which it is expressed. A sales forecast for capital investment purposes would normally be long range, two to five years. At the other extreme, sales forecasts for procuring materials and scheduling production might cover only the next three to six months. Some forecasts, such as those used in setting financial plans, must be stated in dollars, while forecasts to support manufacturing plans may be expressed in pieces, pounds, barrels, etc.

The forecast policy should also include a framework for organizing the key people in the company into a formal forecasting team that meets regularly. It should define the roles of each of the members of that team, the frequency of the forecasting activities, and the measurements to determine how well the forecasting process is working. Finally, it should define the plan for interfacing a mathematically derived forecast based on history with external information and subjective judgement to result in the "official" forecast.

Selection Of The Right "Statistical" Forecasting Techniques

There are two basic considerations in determining which forecasting techniques a company should adopt. *The techniques must fit the nature of the company's business.* Unfortunately, much of the literature available today on quantitative forecasting techniques has been written in a way that "turns off" the average businessman. The derivations of the formu-las and the arguments for their use are presented in mathematical terms, or they have been given esoteric names that would discourage many potential sales forecasters. However, when you analyze these techniques, you find that they are simply a projection into the future of past history with varying degrees of capability to handle seasonal or cyclical relationships. Or, they are techniques that relate a company's future business to forecasts for external factors which affect the business. For example, if it can be proved that a company's sales have been directly linked to the trends for the construction of new housing, then a forecast of the company's sales in the future can be made by looking at the expected trends for future new construction and projecting them into the company's business.

The company's management must be able to understand the techniques. It is important to remember that no technique will work if it is so complex that the users cannot understand it. People will not blindly follow numbers generated by a computer. They must be able to understand where the numbers come from to accept their validity.

To increase their confidence, it is a good idea to test these forecasting techniques to see which best fit your business. This can be done by tracking their performance on a sample of the company's products over a period of time. This will result in a realistic level of expectations once the technique is installed. It is important for management to know how accurate they can be statistically, so they can fully understand the need for the addition of subjective inputs.

Application Of Subjective Judgements

Once the quantitative forecast has been developed, it is necessary to apply the judgements of the best informed people in the company to those results. This is a step that many companies have ignored, and is the cause for much of the dissatisfaction that users have with the mathematical techniques. Most

© American Production & Inventory Control Society

companies' forecasting techniques should not be either totally quantitative or totally subjective. They must be a combination of the two.

The real challenge in forecasting is to organize the subjective inputs from sales and marketing, and integrate them into the "official" sales forecast that will be used for planning purposes. This is not a matter of just asking the sales manager what he thinks the forecast should be. It is much more formal and organized than that. In this regard there are several commonly used types of qualitative or subjective forecasting techniques. Many of them are characterized by concepts and terms that might confuse or scare off the potential user. But the basic approach of these techniques makes a lot of sense.

The Delphi method, for example, draws upon the advice of a group of sales and marketing personnel. The traditional approach to sales forecasting is to obtain many opinions through open discussion and attempt to determine a consensus. However, results of panel discussions are sometimes unsatisfactory because group opinion is highly influenced by dominant individuals, or because a majority opinion may be used to create the "bandwagon effect."

The Delphi method attempts to overcome these difficulties by forcing the experts involved to voice their opinions anonymously through an intermediary. The intermediary acts as a control center in analyzing responses to each round of opinion gathering and feeds back the group opinion to the participants in subsequent rounds. Thus, the Delphi technique is a systematic procedure for soliciting and organizing sales forecasts through the use of iterative responses to a series of questionnaires. Typically, convergence on a consensus forecast by this procedure turns out to be a fine estimator of future sales.

Another technique, subjective probabilities, involves making estimates of the probabilities of different levels of sales occurring. For example, the Vice-President of Marketing might be asked to give his estimate of market share for a given product family next year such that the actual value has a 50 percent

chance of being above or below this number. He might then be asked to give an estimate such that the actual has a 99 percent chance of being less than his estimate, then a 99 percent chance of being above it. The resulting ranges can then be used to set boundaries to compare with the mathematical forecast that has been developed earlier.

There are also a number of specialized forecasting techniques that provide procedures for data collection and analysis to predict future technological developments and the impact these will have on the sales of the company. The basic idea behind all of these subjective techniques is to

---

' ...results of panel discussions are sometimes unsatisfactory because group opinion is highly influenced by dominant individuals, or because a majority opinion may be used to create the 'bandwagon effect'. '

---

apply some human judgement to historical fact to arrive at the best of all possible forecasts in an organized, formal manner.

Departure From The Ordinary

No matter which forecasting techniques are implemented, there will always be cases within a given company that those techniques will not fit perfectly. There should be a different strategy established, for example, in the case of a new product where there are no historical data. This technique may rely on the use of sales data for similar products as an analogy, or on market surveys or expert opinion, or some combination of these. If a new market is established, a different approach may be taken. The most important thing is to understand that no single technique will be perfect for forecasting all products in all markets. Establishing a level of expectations within the

company that is too high is one of the common causes of dissatisfaction with the forecasting system.

Coordinated Use Of The Forecast

Once the results of the different techniques are obtained, internal and external factors must be considered one last time in establishing the sales forecast for the immediate future. Through this point, sales forecasting has been a group effort among sales, marketing, engineering, and manufacturing. As subjective influences are allowed to override the mathematical forecast, a single person should be given the responsibility of monitoring and controlling the combination of "scientific" and subjective forecasts. Actual results should be obtained and compared graphically and numerically with forecasted values. This auditing, or tracking, is necessary for assessing the value and quality of the forecasting effort. The forecasting program should be reviewed periodically and those product family forecasts that do not meet the company's forecasting goals should be carefully scrutinized to determine why this is so.

It is necessary to recognize that sales forecasting is partly a science and partly an art that is learned from experience and knowledge of the market and the product. The key to improving forecasts is to recognize first that they can be improved. Second, any fear of the "scientific" part of forecasting must be overcome. Third, develop formal ways to obtain the best subjective information that can be applied to this "scientific" forecast. And finally, organize this entire forecasting effort into a formal program whose result is an "official" forecast that can be accepted and used by the whole organization. Imagine the results you can get by matching these improved forecasts with a strong MRP system! □

About The Authors

Bill Sullivan of the University of Tennessee has outstanding experience in the field of forecasting. He is co-author of the book Fundamentals of Forecasting - a practical guide to the use of forecasting techniques. He is a full-time professor at the University of Tennessee and has consulted with a number of companies on the installation and improvement of their forecasting systems.

Sullivan has also presented seminars on forecasting and production planning to many manufacturing companies.

Jack Gips is President of Jack Gips, Inc., a firm specializing in high quality education and consulting for manufacturing companies. He has instructed MRP workshops for the past four years and consulted with many companies to help them implement successful MRP systems.

Jack served for ten years as a practitioner with the Warner and Swasey Co. holding the positions of Materials Manager and Manufacturing Operations Manager. He is a frequent speaker at APICS meetings and was Chairman of the 1977 International Conference.

Reprinted from 1972 APICS Conference Proceedings.

BASIC FORECASTING

J. Daniel Hess
The Hess and Eisenhardt Company

Introduction

Forecasting is a term that we as businessmen, managers, or educators are familiar with; but, it also brings us to grips with what many feel is an inexact science. The mental image that we usually conjure is that of the "great crystal ball" which somehow clears and allows us to see into the future. Unfortunately, we haven't been able to find the crystal ball, even though nearly all of us have to do some type of forecasting. Harold Koontz and Cyril O'Donnell in their widely used management text book Principles of Management describe the functions of a manager-planning, organizing, staffing, directing, and controlling - stating that these apply to managers at all levels and with any kind of enterprise. Planning is the first function described, and planning involves forecasting in nearly all managerial disciplines. Accountants plan through the budget - which evolves from the sales forecast, sales managers plan through analysis of their product potential, new products and past performance of current products - which is another way of describing a forecast - and the production control manager plans from longer range forecasts, short range actual orders and material explosions or material requirements planning.

What I'm really saying is that forecasting is a tool that all managers should know how to use if they are going to effectively carry out their functional role of a manager.

This is even more important for our profession of Production and Inventory Control, as a knowledge of forecasting is not only a tool but a knowledge requirement. Plossl and Wight in their text Production and Inventory Control state the objectives of production and inventory control very well when they list:
1. Maximize customer service
2. Minimize inventory investment
3. Efficient (low-cost) plant operation

They go on to state that production and inventory control professionals have begun to recognize basic principles and to know the useful techniques and apply them to the basic elements that make up any production control system. These elements are:
1. A forecast
2. A plan for:
   (a) Inventory levels
   (b) Production rates (capacity)
3. Control - through feedback and corrective action of:
   (a) Production rates
   (b) Input - scheduling and loading
   (c) Output - dispatching and follow-up

Production control deals with the future, and we look at the future through either the forecast or a prediction.

Technically, a forecast is really a projection of past demands into the future, while a prediction is considered to be management's anticipation of changes and of new factors (markets, products, production capacity) affecting the forecasted demand.

We are going to discuss basically the art of forecasting as it now exists. We will do this by first stating some general principles of forecasting and then indicating through examples the types of forecasting techniques best suited for various lengths of future time periods.

Some Basic Principles of Forecasting

Most statistic books say that forecasting is a projection and analysis of
past demand patterns. The demand patterns most often discussed and mod-
eled are:
1. Average level of demand
2. Trend
3. Periodic or seasonal variations
4. Randomness (noise)

When looking at these demand patterns one should also keep in mind these
general characteristics of forecasting:
1. Forecasts are more accurate for larger groups of items.
2. Forecasts are more accurate for shorter periods of time.
3. Every forecast should include an estimate of the error.
4. Test the system and follow-up to compare the actual demand with
   the forecasted demand.

Forecasting Intervals

Forecasting is needed for three main time periods - long range,
intermediate range, and short range.

Long range forecasts deal with a time frame 2 to 5 years in advance. Top
management levels require these forecasts for long range planning of
plant facilities, capital equipment, and market and product planning.
Total sales are normally forecasted.

Intermediate range forecasts deal with a time period of from 1 to 2 years.
They are required for budget preparation, manpower planning, production
leveling and planning, long lead time procurement, establishment of blan-
ket purchase agreements, sales and market analysis, and establishment of
inventory levels. Generally, groups or families of items are forecasted
and preparation of the forecast is either a marketing function, a budgeting function, or that of an economic forecaster.

Short range forecasts generally deal with one to twelve month intervals
and are required for production and inventory scheduling, manpower analysis, cash flow analysis, short term budgeting, and service level determination. Individual items are forecasted and this is the responsibility
of either the production control organization or the sales function if
service level is important.

Techniques

Techniques of forecasting depend first of all on the type demand for the
item. If the item has a demand independent of the usage of other items
such as an end item, the techniques discussed in the latter portion of
this paper should be used. If the usage is dependent on another item,
such as a component part or raw material, a bill of explosion technique
such as Materials Requirements Planning should be used. This basically
takes the demand calculated for the end item and determines the requirements for the components of that end item by breaking down the parts required, comparing these requirements with available quantities and producing the apparent shortages. This is marched out over time periods to
anticipate stockouts and to release orders with adequate lead time and
follow them with up-dated priorities. MRP has received much coverage in
APICS and CAPICS and I'll leave the details for this year's conference
to Ollie Wight.

At this time, we have determined why we need forecasts, what time periods
they cover, who prepares them, and for what reasons. Now how do we forecast?

First, you have to determine the time frame and the type of item - whether dependent or independent. Dependent items are forecasted by exploding their appropriate independent end item. Independent items should first be looked at in terms of time requirements and from that the appropriate technique can be determined. The chart following is a summary of the forecast types and the techniques. Following the chart will be a discussion of the specific techniques recommended.

Type	Long Range	Intermediate Range	Short Range	New Products
Time Frame	2 - 5 years	1 - 2 years	1 - 12 months	Normally 1 mo. to 2 years
What Fore-casted	Total Sales	Groups or families and total sales	Individual Items	Items
By Whom	Top General Management	Marketing or Budgeting Function	Production Control or Marketing	Sales or P&IC
For What Reason	Plant Facilities Capital Equipment Market Planning	Operating Budget Manpower Planning Production Leveling Long Procurement Blanket Purchases Sales Analysis Inventory Levels	Customer Service P&IC Planning Manpower Analysis Cash Flow Short Term Budgets	P&IC Planning Inventory Levels Distribution Applications
Forecasting Technique	Intuitive Economic Regression and Correlation	Economic Regression and Correlation	Average Weighted Average Exponential Smoothing	Intuitive Compare with Like Items Market Survey

General Approaches

A. **The Intuitive Approach** - This is really more of a prediction as we have defined. It is really an intuitive, seat-of-the-pants type guess based on experience, knowledge of the market, and knowledge of general business conditions. It is a valid approach for new products and really should be applied from a common sense standpoint to all forecasts. One should always remember the nature of the person making the forecast - is he an optimist or pessimist? - and keep in mind the fact that people normally over-react to the most current events. If recent sales have been good, the intuitive forecast will probably be influenced by this and in reality will probably be too high.

B. **Economic Analysis** - Economic forecasting in the United States is based upon forecasts of the components of the gross national production and established leading, coincidental, and lagging indicators. Leading indicators tend to lead actual GNP and some correlation has been determined to tie these to changes in GNP. Typical leading indicators are:
   1. Average hours worked
   2. Layoff rate
   3. Durable good orders
   4. Housing starts

5. Common stock prices

Coincidental indicators rise and fall with GNP and verify acutal changes in GNP. These include:
1. Unemployment Rate
2. Industrial Production
3. Personal Income
4. Retail Sales
5. Price Index

Lagging indicators verify an upward or downward trend after it has happened. These include:
1. Unit Labor Cost
2. Manufacturing Inventories
3. Installment Credit
4. Bank Loans Rate
5. Plant and Equipment Expenditures

This area of forecasting requires special expertise in the profession of economics and the elements of gross national product. Along with these indicators, a study of business cycles and GNP cycles can help in predicting general business conditions. These are generally long range forecasting techniques, and have to be studied in the light of the impact of these indicators, components of GNP, and cycles on your company's business and general sales.

C. <u>Statistical Techniques</u> - With statistical techniques we actually forecast from demand history, attempting to find a model of demand patterns that best fits one particular business.

Specific techniques include:

(1) <u>Regression and Correlation Analysis</u>.- Through regression and and correlation analysis, we can predict the value of one or more dependent variables from the value of independent variables and then get a measure of the degree of relationship among the variables under consideration. This is done by inspection or by the least squares method. Dependent and independent data are plotted on a two dimensional (X,Y) basis with X the independent variable.

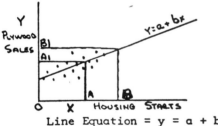

With inspection, a line of best fit is determined through the data. When housing starts were A, plywood sales were A1, if we can forecast housing starts at B, then plywood sales should be B1.

Line Equation = y = a + bx

$$a = \frac{\sum x^2 y - \sum x \sum xy}{n \sum x^2 - (\sum x)^2}$$

$$b = \frac{\sum xy - \sum x \sum y}{n \sum x^2 - (\sum x)^2}$$

The formulae appearing above show the least squares method of calculating the actual equation for the line y = a + bx where y is the dependent value, a is the y intercept and b is the slope. This equation can be calculated through these statistical formulae or now through most computers if historical a and b data can be supplied.

Correlation is expressed as a percent and tells what part of plywood sales (in this example) are correlated or explained by housing starts. For example if the calculation indicates a correlation of .70, it tells us that 70% of plywood sales can be attributed to housing starts, the remaining 30% is due to other causes. Most Computer program libraries include programs to calculate the line of regression and the correlation coefficient if previous independent and dependent demand values can be supplied. This is normally an intermediate to long range forecasting technique.

$$\text{Coefficient of Correlation} = r = \frac{\sum(x-\bar{x})(y-\bar{y})}{\sqrt{\sum(x-\bar{x})^2 \sum(x-\bar{y})^2}}$$

(2) <u>Straight Average</u> - The remaining techniques are used for the short range forecast. This is simply the arithmatic mean and can be used with items that exhibit stable demand. It is probably (unfortunately) still the most widely used forecasting technique. For example:

	Month	Demand	
Recent	1	34	
	2	45	$\frac{234}{6} = 39 = \bar{x}$
	3	40	
	4	30	
	5	40	39 is average forecast
	6	45	for next month
Total Months	6	Total Demand 234	

(3) <u>Weighted Average</u> - This technique allows more weight to be given to certain historical demand data, normally the most recent.

	Month		
Recent	1	34 x .3 = 10.2	
	2	45 x .2 = 9.0	
	3	40 x .2 = 8.0	38.7 is weighted average
	4	30 x .1 = 3.0	forecast for next
	5	40 x .1 = 4.0	month
	6	45 x .1 = 4.5	
	6	234 1.0 38.7	

Try to have summation of weighting factors equal to zero for ease in calculation.

(4) <u>Exponential Smoothing</u> - Mr. Robert G. Brown first developed this technique and achieved a break through from the averaging technique. His basic text is <u>Statistical Forecasting for Inventory Control</u>, and in this work, he developed a technique which is basically a weighting technique but one which weights the forecast error from last month's forecast compared to last month's actual demand. He has developed a smoothing factor which is designated the alpha (α) factor. This alpha factor represents the weight given to the error to adjust the old forecast for next month. The alpha factor can be calculated with a simple approximation formula:

$$\alpha = \frac{2}{n+1} \qquad \text{Where } n = \text{number of time units included in calculation of first forecast}$$

For example: 6 months -

$$\alpha = \frac{2}{6+1} = \frac{2}{7} = .286$$

$$\alpha = \frac{2}{12+1} = \frac{2}{13} = .154 \text{ - 12 month calculation}$$

Most alpha factors fall in the .1 to .3 range.

To calculate the new forecast, using first order exponential smoothing, the old forecast is merely adjusted by adding (or subtracting) the actual forecast error multiplied by the alpha factor. Expressed as a formula,

New forecast = old forecast + α (actual sales - old forecast)

For example if the old forecast was 39 units, the smoothing factor .1 and actual sales last month were 45 units:

New forecast = 39 + .1 (45-39) = 39 + .6 = 39.6

As you can see, this is a lagging forecast if trend exists, but it does not compensate for error as we might be inclined to do as human beings. This is an excellent technique if demand is fairly constant and is not exhibiting excessive trend seasonality, or randomness.

If you feel that trend exists, second order exponential smoothing should be used. In this technique the forecast is calculated through two formulae:

New forecast A = old forecast A + α (Actual Sales - old forecast)

New forecast B = old forecast B + α (New Forecast A - old forecast B)

New forecast B is really new forecast A (the single smoothed forecast) adjusted for trend, where trend is the difference between new forecast A and new forecast B. This is then "smoothed" by applying the alpha factor which allows a portion or percent of trend to be introduced into the forecast. An example of this technique:

Assume New Forecast A = 39.6 from previous example

　　　Old Forecast B = 40 units

　　　　　　α = .1

　　　New Forecast B = Old forecast B + α (New forecast A - Old forecast B)

　　　　　　　　= 40 + .1 (39.6 - 40.0)

　　　　　　　　= 40 - .04 = 39.96 units

Of course you could also adjust for trend by having a very high α factor.

One other technique that is useful if demand changes suddenly is adaptive response exponential forecasting. With this technique, a tracking signal is introduced to detect these sudden changes. This tracking signal recognizes changes and triggers a sub-routine that increases the alpha value to give more weight to recent data. Once the system has stablized, the alpha value is reduced again to help in filtering out random variations in demand. The tracking signal is:

$$\text{Tracking Signal} = \frac{\text{smoothed error}}{\text{smoothed absolute error}}$$

where error is the difference between forecast and actual demand. If the system is in control, this signal will fluctuate around zero. If biased errors occur, the value of the tracking signal will move toward ± 1.0. In order to adopt the response rate of the forecasting system to changes as measured by the tracking signal, the alpha factor is set equal to the tracking signal.

To adjust for seasonality, you need two years of data to really determine a seasonality factor. This factor is then applied to the smoothed forecast to adjust for the cycles of seasonality. Basically we will develop a demand profile:

Month	Recent Year	2 Years Ago	Total	Month Total Average		Seasonality Index
1	20	15	35	$\frac{35}{60}$	=	.583
2	25	20	45	$\frac{45}{60}$	=	.750
3	30	25	55	$\frac{55}{60}$	=	.917
4	35	25	60	$\frac{60}{60}$	=	1.000
5	40	30	70	$\frac{70}{60}$	=	1.167
6	50	40	90	$\frac{90}{60}$	=	1.500
7	50	45	95	$\frac{95}{60}$	=	1.583
8	45	40	95	$\frac{95}{60}$	=	1.583
9	40	30	70	$\frac{70}{60}$	=	1.167
10	30	25	55	$\frac{55}{60}$	=	.917
11	25	20	45	$\frac{45}{60}$	=	.750
12	20	15	35	$\frac{35}{60}$	=	.583
	410 +	310 =	720			

$$\text{Two Year Monthly Average} = \frac{720}{12} = 60.0 \text{ units}$$

Here we see a case of a seasonal trend with sales highest in the middle of the year and low at the end. To calculate the sixth month's forecast you would calculate your single or double exponential smoothed value at the end of the fifth month and then multiply by the sixth month's seasonality index of 1.500.

Randomness in your forecast is handled through the alpha factor first of all as it only weights new values with a small (eg. .1) factor. Another technique is the   demand filter. When the demand is plotted, it may look like this:

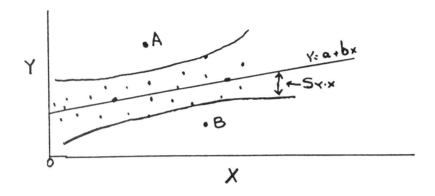

Through statistics, a standard error of the estimate (which is similar to a standard deviation in a normal curve) can be calculated.

$$Sy.x = \sqrt{\frac{(y' - y\ actual)^2}{n}}$$

These are measures of how closely the data falls around the y - a + bx line demand data such as points A and B fall outside this line and are abnormal. They should be reviewed manually before they are included in your forecast history. This demand screening technique is one way of handling the randomness problem.

Summary

Good forecasting, in total, requires the same abilities as other functions of management, namely knowledge of the specific techniques, applied with common sense and the co-operation and participation of all management functions particularly marketing and manufacturing.

Forecasting will always be wrong because it is a science that deals with the future and very few of us have the famous "crystal ball".

Our objectives in preparing forecasts should be to strive continually to make them better as really the whole business system starts with a forecast of some type. How well we forecast has a tremendous impact on our company's profits and ability to compete in today's competitive environment.

SELECTED BIBLIOGRAPHY

1. Robert Goodell Brown, <u>Smoothing Forecasting</u> and Prediction of Discrete
   <u>Time Series</u>, Prentice Hall, Inc., Englewood Cliffs, N.J. - 1963

2. Elwood S. Buffa and William H. Taubert, <u>Production-Inventory Systems:</u>
   <u>Planning and Control</u>, Richard D. Irwin, Inc. - 1972

3. Gene K. Groff and John F. Muth, <u>Operations</u> Management: Analysis <u>for</u>
   <u>Decisions</u>, Richard D. Irwin, Inc. - 1972

4. Harold Koontz and Cyril O'Donnell, <u>Principals of Management</u>,
   McGraw-Hill Book Company - 1964

5. John F. Magee, <u>Production Planning and Inventory Control</u>, McGraw-Hill
   Book Company - 1958

6. C.W. Plossl and O.W. Wight, <u>Production and Inventory Control, Principals</u>
   <u>and Techniques</u>, Prentice Hall, Inc. - 1967

AUTHOR'S BIOGRAPHY

Mr. J. Daniel Hess is a third generation of management in the Hess and
Eisenhardt Company. The company manufactures high quality hearses and
ambulances and custom automobiles including armored passenger vehicles.
Previously he was Manager of Production and Inventory Control at the
Formica Corporation and before that served as a Supply Officer and Unit
Commander with the United States Marine Corps.

Mr. Hess received his MBA from Xavier University and is currently teach-
ing a course there in Production Control in the MBA program. He has
been active in APICS and was General Chairman of the 1970 APICS International Convention in Cincinnati.

Kneppelt, Leland R., "Product Structuring Considerations for Master Production Scheduling," Production and Inventory Management (First Quarter 1984).

Production structuring for the assemble-to-order (ATO) company is a complex problem. This paper provides considerable insights into the issue and the cost/benefits that accompany them. There are also critical differences between bills of materials structured on the basis of how the products are sold and those structured for how products are manufactured.

The author explains the different placement of the master production schedule in the "engineer-to-order (make to order), ATO, and make-to-stock environments. The ATO case is of most interest. The use of catalog numbers to identify customer-selected options leads to a matrix bill of material, from which a super bill can be constructed. The super bill has common parts, either/or options (one must be selected), and attachments (yes or no options).

The concept of a "pseudo" part number is important for the ATO firm. Common parts can be defined as pseudo in that they cannot be built; it is only a bag of parts. Other options may be called pseudos as well. Consider the air conditioner option on a car. It is an option that can be sold with the car. On the other hand, the bag of parts (e.g., dash board accessories) cannot be combined into a stand-alone subassembly.

Another use of pseudo part numbers is to keep track of critical resource constraints associated with some unique customer-specified features. The part number identifies the work center, and customer orders are translated into hours of capacity required. The capacity itself can be analyzed using available-to-promise logic.

The author also explains an interesting issue about the bill of material level at which parts are scheduled. In his bicycle example, if competition forces the firm to ship from stock, all end items must be forecasted and stocked. If a one-week delay is possible, part of the finished items can be assembled from stocks of parts and assemblies. For the lead times given in his example, it would be necessary to stock frames in all sizes and colors. If a two-week delay time is competitive, frames can be painted to order. Also note that an item that is considered as a common part still remains uncommitted to an end item until the final assembly schedule.

Achieving maximum benefits for the ATO firm requires a careful analysis of how the bills of materials are structured. Making this happen depends on a companywide agreement with both the ATO philosophy and the establishment of modular bills and procedures to make it work.

Reprinted with permission from Production & Inventory Management Review, 3rd Qtr. 1984.

PRODUCT STRUCTURING CONSIDERATIONS FOR MASTER PRODUCTION SCHEDULING

Leland R. Kneppelt
Management Science America, Inc.   *Winston-Salem, NC*

INTRODUCTION

The traditional function of a bill of material is the definition of a product from the design point of view only. The format is normally a parts list on the drawing or a formulation in the process industry. The material requirements planning technique altered the function of the bill of material. The bill of material is used under material requirements planning to reflect product content, state of completion, timing, and/or process stage.

Master production scheduling further alters the function of the bill of material. The bill of material must now provide the structure for decision support at the top planning level. It forms the basis for development of forecasts, assembly schedules, and customer order control within the functional area of master scheduling.

The approach to the top level structure should be based on the company philosophy of product offering. A company may offer a product completely engineered to the customer order, a product assembled to the customer order, or a stocked part number for shipment to the customer. Most companies provide a combination of product offerings. The definition of a company policy on product offerings is a key criterion for product structuring to support Master Production Scheduling.

Figure 1 illustrates the major types of product offerings with respect to the level within a product structure at which Master Production Scheduling (MPS) and Material Requirements Planning (MRP) can provide computer systems support. In the engineer-to-order environment, MPS and MRP support is limited to a raw material or purchased part level, since the product structure is developed per the customer order specifications. Advanced material planning through MRP is limited, but as the product structure is developed, MRP can be used to track the critical path toward product shipment.

At the other end of the spectrum in Figure 1, the ship-from-stock environment allows the MPS to be defined in end product part numbers with MRP controlling all raw material, purchased parts, and sub-assembly planning. The third type, assemble-to-order environment, is the most common in companies today. The specific end product configuration is not defined until customer-order specification. The MPS is defined in part

FIGURE 1
Product offering philosophy

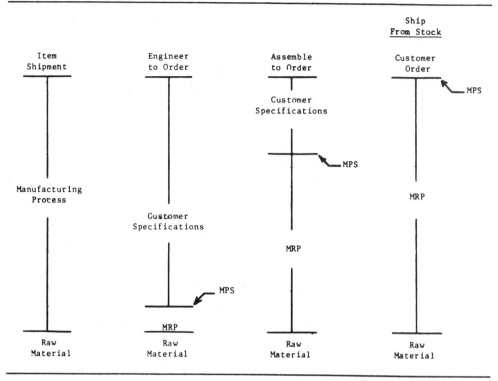

numbers of potential configuration items and MRP controls all raw materials, purchased parts, and sub-assemblies below that level to support master production schedule. The major emphasis of this article is the product structuring considerations for the assemble-to-order environment. However, the concepts and considerations also apply to the other environments.

PRODUCT STRUCTURING GUIDELINES

Many companies in the assemble-to-order environment attempt to plan based upon the assignment of a unique part number for each product configuration. Each unique product part number has a complete product structure. A master schedule is developed for each unique product part number. And, customer order specification is made against that unique product part number, even in cases where the company has adopted a policy to supply a product with options or variations. However, using a unique part number for every possible combination of options and variations makes forecasting, master scheduling, and customer order definition very difficult, if not impossible. Often, a unique part number will be generated for a new customer order when that same combination or configuration has been built one or more times before. This is the result of the traditional function of the bill of material: definition of the product from a design point of view.

The material planning systems (MPS/MRP) use the bill of material for advanced planning. When always building to a unique part number, a forecast is required for each unique product part number. Flexibility of component material assignment to new customer order configurations or new unique part numbers is limited, though they may be similar to those forecasts. The options or variations are buried within the bill of material of a unique part number on the customer order. Thus, when the problem arises that could be covered through a substitution, limited visibility exists except through human inspection on the assembly floor.

As is often the case, marketing will develop a technique to ease the translation of a customer's requirements into the unique part number used by manufacturing. Figure 2 is an excerpt from a typical product catalog. The example illustrates the instructions to develop a catalog number used to order a bicycle. This catalog number then becomes the unique part number for the bicycle which is to be shipped to the customer. The shipping, inventory, planning, and the product structure is based on this unique part number. Whether the product is shipped from stock or the product is assembled and shipped, this unique part number is the basis for inventory, transaction processing, and shipping. The ship-from-stock or assemble-to-customer-order philosophy question is a matter of timing. Manufacturing often does not recognize or know of the technique that marketing used to generate the unique part number and thus, designs and builds to the part number. Marketing may also configure a product based on a sales potential and the result is a product on the shelf. Naturally, forecasting and master scheduling must be based on the unique part numbers at the product level, since this is the entry point for customer demand.

The alternative to a unique part number is to restructure portions of the product structures to aid master schedule planning and ease the customer order configuration task at order entry time. The initial step to restructuring is the recognition that within a family of products, some sub-assemblies and components are always required (common parts). This aids in planning and scheduling since the number of product shipments planned will equate to number of sets of common parts required.

A technique used to assist in defining the extent of common parts within a product family is the definition of a matrix bill of material. The matrix bill of material can be developed using manual tracing, but if the bills of material are computerized, a special computer program can be developed. The resultant matrix bill of material is a table with the unique product part numbers across the top. Sub-assembly, component, and raw material part numbers are listed down the left side of the table. The internal columns of the table illustrate the number of times sub-assembly, component, or raw material part numbers are used in each unique product part number

FIGURE 2
Typical catalog excerpt

Super Silver Bicycle

```
Sizes:     53, 57 and 60 CM
Color:     Silver
Saddle:    Racing or Touring/Men or Women
Wheels:    Clincher or Tubular
Toe Clips and Straps:   Optional

Standard includes Crankset, Pedals, Derailleur, Brakes and
           Handlebar
```

To order, specify catalog number as shown below:

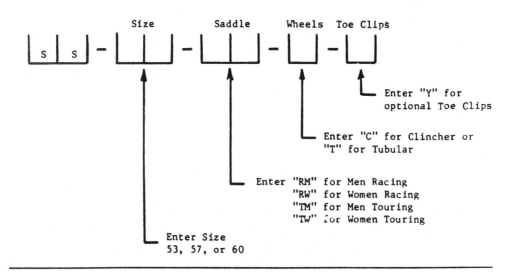

listed across the top of the table. This illustrates part numbers common to products within the family.

Figure 3 is a portion of a matrix bill of material for the bicycle used in Figure 2. As shown, components of the bicycle are listed down the left side and unique part numbers for the bicycle are listed across the top of the table. The table is then completed with an entry for each component used on the bicycle part number at the head of the column.

Analysis of the matrix bill of material for the bicycle yields the concept that many of the kits such as brakes, derailleur, etc. are required and common for every bicycle. Yet, frame size, saddle, etc. are unique to certain

FIGURE 3
Matrix bill of material

Number	Component Description	U/M	Model Number Used on			
			SS-53-RM-C-Y	SS-53-TM-C-Y	SS-53-RM-T	SS-53-TM-T
FR-53-S	Silver Frame (53CM)	EA	1	1	1	1
FR-57-S	Silver Frame (57CM)	EA				
FR-60-S	Silver Frame (60CM)	EA				
SA-T-M	Saddle Touring, Men	EA		1		1
SA-T-W	Saddle Touring, Women	EA				
SA-R-M	Saddle Racing, Men	EA	1		1	
SA-R-W	Saddle Racing, Women	EA				
SE-01	Seat Post (25.8MM)	EA	1	1	1	1
WH-C	Wheel Kit, Clincher	EA	1	1		
WH-T	Wheel Kit, Tubular	EA			1	1
CR-01	Crankset Kit	EA	1	1	1	1
PD-01	Pedals Kit	EA	1	1	1	1
DE-01	Derailleur Kit	EA	1	1	1	1
BK-01	Brakes Kit	EA	1	1	1	1
HD-01	Handlebar Kit	EA	1	1	1	1
TC-01	Toe Clips/ Straps	EA	1	1		

bicycle models. Further analysis illustrates that while the saddle is unique to certain bicycle models, the component, seat post, is always required. A closer look at the wheel kits would also illustrate that the difference between the clincher and tubular is in the rim and tire, but many components such as spokes and hubs are always common. The information on common parts (as illustrated in the matrix bill of material) can form the initial basis for establishing a super bill of material. Figure 4 is a general example of a super bill of material.

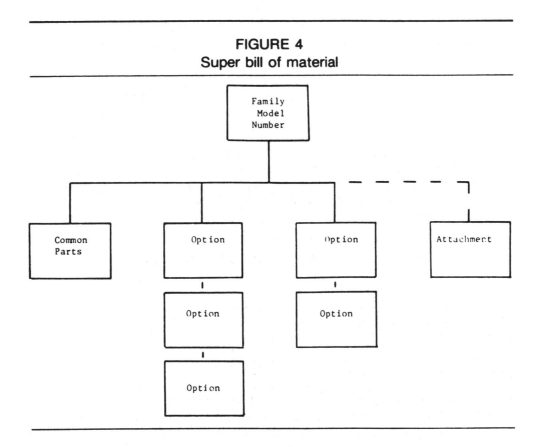

FIGURE 4
Super bill of material

The first step to establishing a super bill of material is to assign a model part number for the product family. This part number is used to identify the family and form the attachment point for the super bill of material structure relationships. It also serves as the entry point for the shipment plan or production plan in terms of the number of units within the family.

A part number to identify all parts common throughout the family is now structured under the model part number. This part number is defined as a "dummy" or "pseudo" part number since it cannot be built. Under this part number is the list of part numbers always used on any model structure for the family. This allows MPS planning to relate to one part number for the parts structured below and plan those parts in matched sets through MRP.

The model part number also has a series of part numbers structured under it which relate to options within the family. As shown in Figure 4, there are a series of option part numbers attached to the model. When shown in a vertical relationship, one option must be selected from the list to build a configuration of the model. These option part numbers may define a stocked part number. They may also be a pseudo part number which defines a part list that when combined with a portion of the common parts provide the unique product. This is where an option differs from a variation, since a series of variations normally contain the same core of parts. The attempt is to reduce variations to a series of option pseudo part numbers which are used to plan only the parts unique to the option.

Another designation on the super bill of material in Figure 4 is the attachment. The attachment merely defines an option which may or may not be selected to define the unique product. The term "attachment" would apply to add-on options, maintenance kits, and service or spare parts. Under the above definitions, the structure of a super bill of material consists of a common parts number, option numbers, and attachment numbers.

Figure 5 is a simple super bill of material definition for the bicycle example. Master schedule planning would be accomplished at the part number level below the model number; common parts, frames, saddles, etc. Structured under the pseudo part number for common parts are all the components and sub-assemblies required to make any model of the bicycle. The options are then structured in vertical relationships to illustrate that a selection of one must be made to complete the bicycle assembly. The toe clip and strap option is linked with a dotted line to signify that it is an attachment. An attachment may or may not be selected for the bicycle assembly. Notice that spokes, hubs and seat post have been structured under common parts rather than under their respective unique options.

When structuring the super bill of material, other considerations include special capacity constraints related to a customer specification, inventory investment requirements, and the competitive lead time situation. Often, a unique product definition will contain a special process which is defined by the customer order. An example may be the printing of the customer information on the product before shipment. The printing may be a capacity constraint which can delay shipment. Under this condition, a pseudo part number may be included in the super bill of material to specify the capacity center required to process the product before shipment. The customer order would then place demand on this capacity center in hours versus the normal quantity demand against the other super bill of material components. This provides visibility of capacity requirements and commitments.

Another example which relates to the bicycle could be that a portion of the bicycle production is sold under a variety of other names. The difference between the standard bicycle and those sold under another name is an additional set of operations to paint stripes and apply a decal. Both the color of stripes and decal are customer specification dependent.

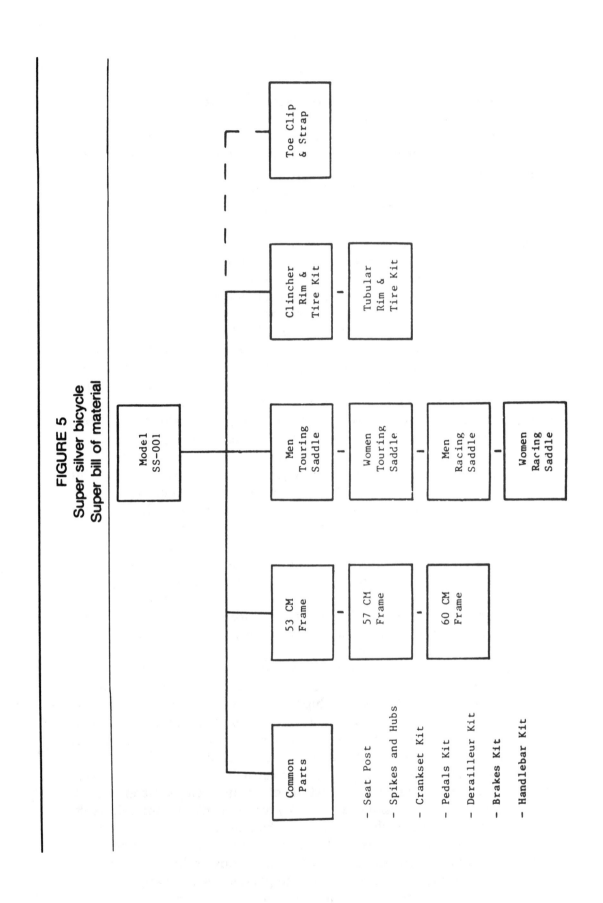

FIGURE 5
Super silver bicycle
Super bill of material

Model SS-001

Common Parts
- Seat Post
- Spikes and Hubs
- Crankset Kit
- Pedals Kit
- Derailleur Kit
- Brakes Kit
- Handlebar Kit

53 CM Frame
57 CM Frame
60 CM Frame

Men Touring Saddle
Women Touring Saddle
Men Racing Saddle
Women Racing Saddle

Clincher Rim & Tire Kit
Tubular Rim & Tire Kit

Toe Clip & Strap

The capacity is limited in the work center where the stripes and decal are added. Therefore, shipments become dependent on the schedule of these additional operations. A pseudo part number option could be added to the bicycle super bill of material which designates this work center and the quantity in hours required for each customer order. As master scheduling and subsequent order promising is accomplished, the master scheduler is able to track next available capacity as well as spot potential shipment problems.

The definition of the super bill of material and subsequent levels should also consider inventory investment. The goal is to develop a unique separation of optional parts from the common parts, and only expend labor to match the parts when actual customer demand dictates. However, if the optional parts are relatively inexpensive, it may be better to invest in extra inventory and always plan for their use rather than making the separation. Competitive lead time is another consideration in the structure analysis. There may not be a choice but to build product on the potential of sales in order to match or beat the competition quoted delivery time. This type of analysis must continue throughout the life cycle for a family of products. A program or procedure can be developed to provide reporting which illustrates the critical path or lead time required to build to the various completion levels of product. An additional important piece of information is the dollar investment in the product at the various completion levels in relation to the lead time to complete and ship. Often, companies will find that the greatest labor investment is made during the last few weeks of product build.

In Figure 6, a portion of the bicycle super bill of material has been turned and drawn to illustrate lead time to shipment. If competition ships from stock, the bicycles may have to be built to forecast and shipped from stock. If a one-week assembly lead time is feasible, the bicycles could be built to the master schedule part level and assembled to a customer order in one week. However, this would require that the frames be built to stock in size and color. If marketing stated they could be competitive with a two-week lead time, this offers additional flexibility. The frames would not have to include color, since in two weeks the frames could be painted and the bicycle assembled. This means the labor value to paint is not added to the frame until customer demand requires it. This is the type of analysis at the super bill of material level which can provide major benefits.

WHY PRODUCT STRUCTURING?

The previous section has briefly defined the super bill of material and some of the considerations for structuring it. The reasons for the structuring effort fall into two major categories: communications and ease of control over the master schedule. One of the critical items of information required for master scheduling is a forecast at the top level. Under the environment

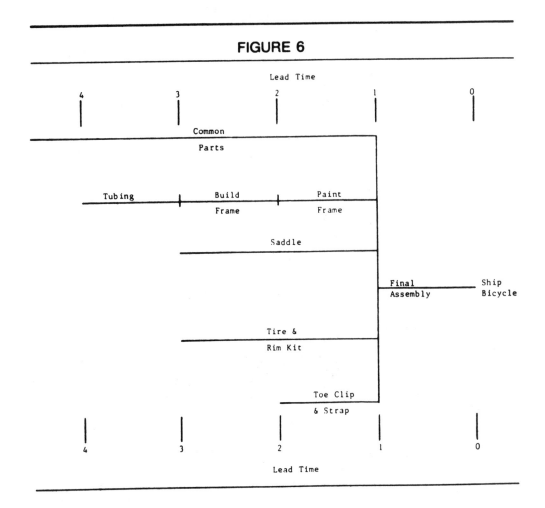

FIGURE 6

where each unique product configuration has a unique part number and structure, marketing will have to furnish a forecast per each part number. Using the super bill of material approach, marketing could furnish a model forecast and their best estimate on the percentage use of options and attachments. A computer program can now be used to generate the option forecast using the model forecast and option percentages. This provides a more realistic forecast from both the marketing and master scheduling perspective.

The super bill of material approach also provides an opportunity to better coordinate the option planning. Some overplanning can be done on the options to compensate for percentage forecast error. Naturally, the major parts in the common parts module can be held to the model forecast provided by marketing since they are required one hundred percent of the time.

Figure 7 is the super bill of material for the bicycle illustrating the percentages on the options. These percentages are used to generate the master schedule forecast from the forecast at the model level. This is the

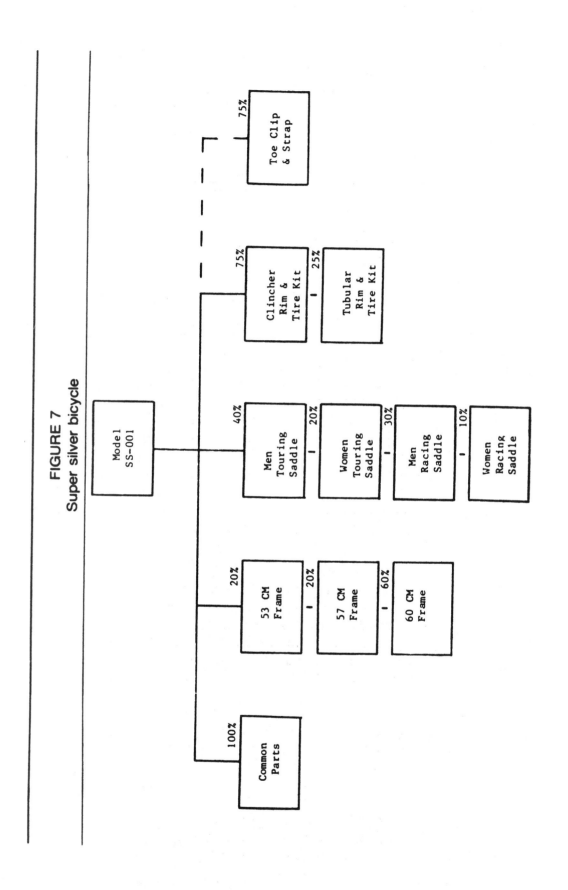

FIGURE 7
Super silver bicycle

initial plan. However, as the master scheduler recognizes that common parts have been sold out in a specific time-frame, he would then modify the plan for the options based on this demand history. In this way, he can accomplish overplanning versus assignment of percentages on options that would be greater than one hundred percent. Assignment of percents that equate to greater than one hundred percent would inflate the overall plan.

The super bill of material approach forms the basis for effective communications internally, as well as with the customer. A specific customer configuration is made through selection of common parts and the required unique options. The delivery promise date can be made through the visibility of availability at the option level. Any reschedules can be coordinated through this visibility and the specific customer order configuration in super bill of material terminology.

Bill of material maintenance is also aided using the super bill of material approach. If a super bill of material contains one common parts bill of material and 32 option bills of material, maintenance of 33 bills of material is required at the master schedule level. The same product family using the unique part number per configuration concept would require 4608 end item part numbers to cover every combination. Thus, bill of material maintenance as well as forecasting would be much larger in scope.

This can be further illustrated using the simple bicycle example. As shown in Figure 8, with only 11 part numbers in the super bill of material, 48 unique bicycles can be built. If a decision is made to offer the bicycle in two additional sizes (5 frames) and colors (5 frames plus 3 colors = 15), the number of unique models would jump to 240, while the master schedule parts would only jump to 23. Under the unique part number per product concept, all planning including forecasting would have to be accomplished on 240 unique part numbers.

MAKING IT HAPPEN SUPPORT REQUIREMENTS

The super bill of material concept up to this point of the article has been discussed in relation to structuring and master scheduling. A manufacturing company is in the business to ship the product on time to the customer, and hopefully at a profit. Therefore, the super bill of material concept must integrate well into some important supporting functions.

Customer order entry must be accomplished using the same terms as the super bill of material. But, more important, the delivery dates promised to the customer must be coordinated through the master scheduling function, using the visibility of planning based on the super bill of material. One company went through the effort to establish the super bill of material concept in planning and customer order entry. However, the policy was then set to quote a six-week delivery date on any configuration of the product. This approach failed to gain the many benefits because no check

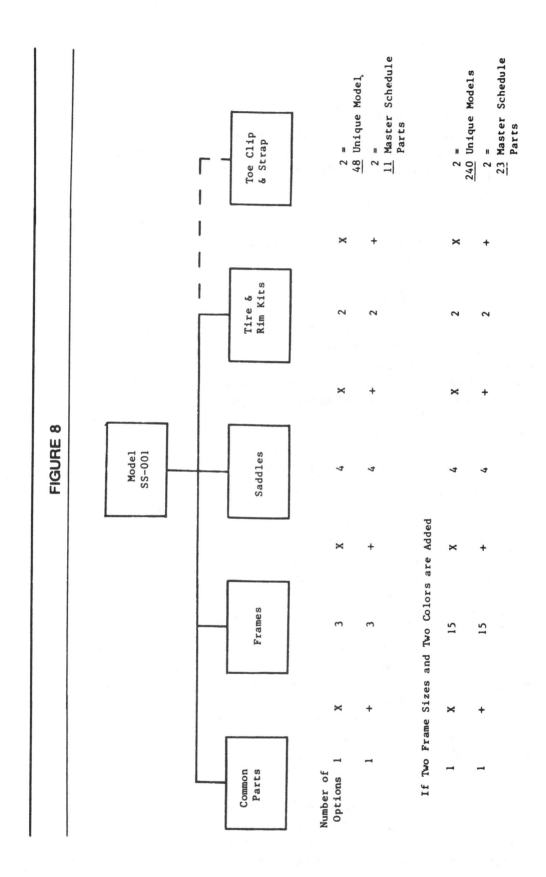

FIGURE 8

was made on option or common parts availability. One of the key elements of the Master Schedule Report is the available-to-promise horizon. It provides available quantities in a time-phased format for common parts, as well as for the options. This is key to a coordinated procedure to develop a realistic customer delivery date. If this method had been used instead of a fixed lead time quote, some products could have been shipped in less than the quoted six weeks.

Figure 9 is a simple example of a customer order form for the bicycle. The master scheduler would use the selected configuration and his master schedule plan to develop availability dates on the selected options. This allows a realistic placement of the customer order into a final assembly schedule. The customer order form is very similar to the catalog excerpt shown in Figure 2. However, the result of Figure 2 was a unique part number for the customer order. Thus, manufacturing lost valuable information as to the configuration of what the customer ordered. The configuration is very important when attempting to resolve a conflict over competition between customers for inventory and capacity.

A second critical supporting function to consider is pricing and product costing. Inherent in the super bill of material is that no unique part number is assigned to the shipment level of the product. Costing can only be accomplished to a structure level, one level below the family model part number. The final product cost cannot be made until a specific product configuration is selected and final assembly costs are incurred. This, as well as pricing, requires cautious analysis in the implementation of the super bill of material concept.

A third area of support function requiring analysis is the shop paper requirements for final building of the product. Inherent in structuring for super bill of material support is the loss of a unique product part number. This part number usually was the key to the documentation by which the product is built: drawing, routing, layout, etc. Thus, a new procedure is required to communicate to the shop personnel the necessary information to build the final product. In some companies, a general assembly drawing and instructions can be used in conjunction with the parts list generated using the customer order. However, where multiple or complex operations are required to integrate the options for a unique product configuration, some creative generation of shop documentation is necessary. Often, a multiple packet approach is used to integrate option parts with their structure. The solution on how to move the planning concept of a super bill of material to the actual effort on the shop floor will differ with each company and product family.

A further illustration of the problem relates back to the super bill of material for the bicycle (Figure 5). For planning purposes, the spokes and hubs were structured under a pseudo part number for common parts. However, the method of building the wheel requires the spokes and hubs,

FIGURE 9

CUSTOMER ORDER FORM

Super Silver Bicycle

Order No. _____

Customer Name _____ No. _____

Date Requested _____ Order Quantity _____

Office Use Only (Dates)

Common Parts ☐

Frames
    53 CM ☐

    57 CM ☐

    60 CM ☐

Saddles
    Men/Racing ☐

    Men/Touring ☐

    Women/Racing ☐

    Women/Touring ☐

Tires
    Clincher ☐

    Tubular ☐

Toe Clip & Strap ☐

Assembly Start Date

Ship Date

as well as rims and tire kits. The shop instructions must communicate this relationship.

One technique is to retain the original bill of material for the wheel, but code it as to be used for engineering and/or assembly instruction only.

It would not participate in the material planning process. At order release time, the bill of material would be included in the shop paper. The components on the common parts structure would be coded with a point of usage to allow a cross relation with the original product structure.

A final critical supporting function is the definition and formalization of roles for the key functional areas within the company. The establishment and maintenance of the super bill of material requires open communication and coordination, as does other master scheduling functions. The master scheduling function is normally responsible for:

- Participation in plan development;
- Maintenance of an attainable Master Schedule;
- Maintenance of Super Bills of Material;
- Participation in establishing and executing to policy;
- Identification and negotiation of conflicts to resolution;
- Maintenance or monitoring the final assembly schedule;
- Communication; and
- Understanding opportunities

The accomplishment of the above responsibilities cannot be done without some key roles performed by top management and marketing. Top management must:

- Understand the role of Master Scheduling;
- Insist on a double Master Schedule;
- Participate in conflict resolution; and
- Insure assignment of responsibility for maintenance.

Marketing must play a key role through:

- Assistance in Super Bill of Material definition;
- Participation in policy-making;
- Participation in plan development, forecasts, option mix;
- Participation in demand management and order-promising integrity; and
- Understanding of constraints.

SUMMARY AND CONCLUSIONS

The master production schedule has been called "The Company Game Plan." It requires company-wide agreement and commitment. The master scheduling concepts have led to a new way of running a company based on some very formal techniques and principles.

The product structure provides the basic planning skeleton on which a master production schedule is based. This requires company-wide agreement to philosophy of the product structure to support master scheduling. The challenge in implementation is to arrive at a product structure philosophy which can be accepted by the various users of bills of material. Often, design engineering, manufacturing engineering, cost accounting, etc. see a restructure of bills of material as a threat to their function. A project to restructure bills of material must consider all functions impacted. It must then provide for their input as well as education on the reasons and benefits of this significant effort.

About the Author

LELAND R. KNEPPELT has over twenty years' experience in the design and implementation of software and information systems. The systems implemented include drafting design automation, numerical control symbolic compilers, compiler-operating software and various commercial applications with recent emphasis on production and inventory control. At NCR, Lee developed the design specifications for Inventory Control and Material Requirements Planning modules of an applied software package, and at Industrial Nucleonics supported the development and installation consultation for the AccuRay 3000 Program. As Vice President Manufacturing Systems R & D, was the key designer of the Generalized Systems Components offered by Arista Manufacturing Systems. Lee has provided consulting and leadership in workshops on Master Scheduling, Materials Management, Capacity Management and Shop Floor Control, and Project Management as Vice President of Arista Education and Consulting. Currently, he works for Management Science America (MSA). Lee attended Ohio State University, is a member of the Association of Computing Machinery, as well as APICS, and has made presentations at the National Computer Conference and National APICS Conferences.

Ling, Richard C., "Demand Management: Let's Put More Emphasis on This Term and Process," 26th Annual Conference Proceedings (1983).

Demand management encompasses detailed item forecasting, spare parts forecasting, customer order entry, branch warehouse replenishment, inter-plant demands, and new product introductions. Many authors have not included new product introductions in demand management. Because a new product will require capacity and it will also be impossible to make a forecast based on past data, some way to include its impact on factory capacity is necessary. Additional candidates might also include special promotions and large contract sales (e.g., a furniture manufacturer taking a large order for a hotel chain).

This article also identifies the proper process for updating fore-casts. The author points out that in many firms forecasts are only offi-cially updated once per quarter. Daily changes, however, are made to requirements. As this takes place, the forecast ceases to be the source of requirements.

The author shows how forecasts should be consumed and updated as one rolls through time. There is a temptation to drop a forecasted requirement for a given week if it does not materialize. The impact on material requirements planning and capacity requirements needs to be assessed carefully. The key to doing this is to focus attention on the aggregate forecast of demand for the company. The key question is when will this overall forecast and the production plan be changed?

The production plan provides the overall signal for master production scheduling. The sum of the parts must be maintained so that it equals the whole. The author suggests adding a forecast adjustment time bucket to time-phased records. Only when this quantity passes some predetermined limits will the forecast be changed.

Abnormal demand is something that all firms face. Detecting abnormal demand on an item basis can be done with statistical filtering. The issue is whether an abnormal demand is simply a different consumption of the forecast than expected, or if it is a one-time event that is an add-on. A more critical question is whether the add-on should be a total or global add-on. In other words, is this demand part of the overall expected demand for the company or does the production plan need to be revised?

The key to making production plan revisions is to have the entire organization, through the executive committee, agree. These revisions typically involve work force changes, overtime, subcontracting, and other major changes that will impact the overall financial performance of the company. It is imperative that production plan changes be made after due consideration, with total organizational commitment, and not in response to random events.

94

DEMAND MANAGEMENT: LET'S PUT MORE EMPHASIS ON THIS TERM AND PROCESS

Richard C. Ling, CPIM*
Richard C. Ling, Inc.

A comedian in one of our Master Schedule classes said quote, "We have an excellent demand management approach in our company. Management demands and somebody trys to do it." A weak attempt at real humor; however, unfortunately an accurate definition for some companies.

The phrase "Demand Management" brings focus to the fact that in most manufacturing companies the demands truly need better understanding and management. What is a demand? The term speaks for itself. Any requirement, real or perceived, for product or capacity of a manufacturing company that creates a need for inventory or replenishment of that product or capacity.

This term first appeared in Master Production Scheduling Principles and Practices, Berry Vollmann Whybark 1979, APICS.

Who is responsible for the demands? What are they for and how should they be expressed? Figure 1 depicts the demand management process. It can be very straightforward or, in some companies, may involve all of the demand streams depicted.

What does a manufacturing company need in order to support demand.

1. An up-to-date statement of demand.

2. Demand broken down to an appropriate level of detail.

3. A demand management process that modifies or consumes forecast as more is known and time passes.

4. An organization which is responsible and accepts accountability for the important demand process.

Manufacturing's role is to be responsive and accountable for the supply.

FIGURE 1

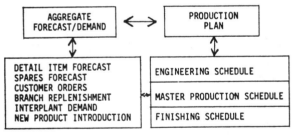

THE PROBLEM

The demand management process is confusing and counterproductive in many manufacturing companies today. Why? The process has not been truly understood. This has led to poor communications. Much of the problem stems from people being defensive over a forecast (just because it's wrong) and not really knowing the use it is put to in manufacturing. When people say that they can only get around to reviewing and updating forecasts quarterly, they obviously do not understand the needs of manufacturing. It is also usually true that when you get to the mechanics of the detail forecasts with these same people, they are making changes to the forecast and don't really know that they are doing it.

Let's examine the root of this problem by using an example to enable us to understand the demand data and how it is used. Another key point to realize is that the problem has become more acute with the advent of computers. We can now examine so much data with such speed that there is the possibility of introducing change too rapidly.

Figure 2 shows some planning and scheduling information.

FIGURE 2

		1	2	3	4	5	6	7	8
PROJECTED GROSS REQUIREMENTS		5	5	5	5	5	5	5	5
SCHEDULED RECEIPTS						30			
PROJECTED AVAILABLE BALANCE	20	15	10	5	0	25	20	15	10
PLANNED ORDER RELEASE									

Now let's say that a week goes by and no demand is received and the balance on hand remains the same. What should the forecast of demand be now in periods 2-8, A or B.

FIGURE 3

	2	3	4	5	6	7	8
A	5	5	5	5	5	5	5
B	10	5	5	5	5	5	5

Before answering the question, answer this one. Which is a change to the forecasted demand A or B. A majority of people say B is the change. It is not, A is the change.

The way we determine what is a change to a forecast is to first understand what a forecast is to be used for.

Its purpose in a manufacturing company is to be a formal request to the manufacturing operation to have either product or capacity available a point in time for a given quantity. The way we evaluate a change to a forecast of demand is to determine which scenario above, A or B, is communicating to manufacturing that a change can be made. Figure 4 shows what happens if the forecast is dropped as the calendar rolls.

FIGURE 4

		1	2	3	4	5	6	7	8
PROJECTED GROSS REQUIREMENTS			5	5	5	5	5	5	5
SCHEDULED RECEIPTS						30			
PROJECTED AVAILABLE BALANCE	20		15	10	5	30	25	20	15
PLANNED ORDER RELEASE									

Exception message -- reschedule out 1 week.

Many companies do this improperly and don't understand it. Most early MRP systems did it wrong. Many of the software systems even today throw away the forecast a week at a time. The paradox is that we see many companies forecasting monthly, spreading the demand so that the MPS and MRP can do proper prioritizing but then taking all deviations to the weekly forecast each week. This, in most cases, is inappropriate forecast or demand management.

A proper approach is to replace or consume the forecast with customer orders as they are received and to carry a $\pm$ forecast adjustment that is managed by a responsible individual in sales and marketing. A rule that you might follow is to consume the forecast within the forecast interval and don't expect the forecast to be accurate in any less of a time period. Many companies forecast monthly spread weekly for scheduling purposes, however, consume quarterly. Figure 5 shows how to calculate a forecast adjustment and carry it as a front-end modifier to the forecasted demand stream.

FIGURE 5

	FORECAST ADJUSTMENT		2	3	4	5	6	7	8
PROJECTED GROSS REQUIREMENTS		+5	5	5	5	5	5	5	5
SCHEDULED RECEIPTS						30			
PROJECTED AVAILABLE BALANCE	20	15	10	5	0	25	20	15	10
PLANNED ORDER RELEASE									

This approach is especially critical for service or spares demand at lower levels of MRP or things get very nervous. This is counterproductive to proper MRP.

AGGREGATE THEN DETAIL

Now that we understand the issue of what is a change to a forecast/demand, it is imperative that we recognize that forecasting is first and foremost an aggregate issue that must be dealt with at the executive level. It is the aggregate forecast/demand (Figure 6) that must interact with the production plan and our inventory/backlog strategy that needs to be resolved before we can then deal with detail forecasts and master schedules. In order to support a proper process we need good aggregating techniques and also must realize that timing can be crucial. Too many times we find the forecast review process taking too long to be effective.

FIGURE 6

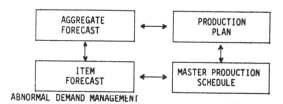

ABNORMAL DEMAND MANAGEMENT

More companies are recognizing the importance of having a procedure that will aid in detecting abnormal demands that are caused by events that are outside the forecast. These could be:

1. Abnormal one-time events that are additive to the forecast,

2. A first indication that the forecast is wrong and needs to be changed,

3. An indication that the seasonal pattern is wrong, and

4. One of those demands that is part of the total but is still a spiked demand, i.e., timing or quantity is wrong.

If you don't have such a procedure in your company, maybe you should give it serious consideration.

CUSTOMER PROMISING

If we are going to handle the demands on our business properly where we have to promise future delivery then it is important to link the Master Production Schedule with the order promising and customer service function. The appropriate data can be provided in the format we see in Figure 5.

FIGURE 5

		PERIOD						
	1	2	3	4	5	6	7	8
FORECAST								
PRODUCTION FORECAST		2	4	5	10	10	10	10
ACTUAL DEMAND	11	7	6	5				
PROJECTED AVAILABLE BALANCE	23	12	3	33	23	13	3	33	23
AVAILABLE-TO-PROMISE		5	5	34	34	34	34	74	74
MPS				40				40	

This could be a printout, a video display or maybe even a computer what-if coming up with a best dates promise. The key is maintaining the (ATP) Available-to-Promise information. This requires accurate stock balances and very doable master production schedules in order to provide the integrity needed for promising customers.

Notice that the actual demand/customer orders has consumed the forecast so that the projected available balance can be used to critique the schedule (MPS). The ATP has been calculated as a time-phased cumulative available so that it can truly be utilized to make a proper evaluation and promise to the next customer. What we owe ourselves and our customers is an approach that helps in making quality promises.

COMING TRENDS

There are a number of things that are evolving in the area of demand management that should get some special attention.

1. Distribution Resource Planning

There is finally a book, DRP Distribution Resource Planning, by André J. Martin, available on this subject which details very well for those companies with branch warehouses for finished goods or spare parts how and why DRP is the system to use. It is the way that distributed demand can be managed for transportation, space, and manpower as well as product replenishment planning.

We are surprised at how slowly DRP has caught on. Lloyd Hager, Group Vice President at Hager Hinge, where DRP has been very successful, has said, "DRP can be implemented easier and more quickly than MRP and the payoff is immediate."

2. Customer Intelligence

We see many companies beginning to work together to link up their planning data for the benefit of both parties. Why forecast when the forecast you seek can be another company's output from its planning systems.

3. The Demand Manager Concept

We believe that more companies will become aware of the criticality of demand management and actually assign a person as a Demand Manager for the company -- not a sales person, nor a manufacturing person, but one whose job it is to apply quality management to the demand streams of the company.

FORECASTING TECHNIQUES VS. A SYSTEM

The issue is not the particular forecasting technique chosen. Statistical approaches are just fine where they apply whether they are simple or sophisticated. A combination of statistical techniques with the computer choosing the one that seems to work best (Focus Forecasting). This, coupled with a good override mechanism where judgment can prevail, seems to get the job done quite nicely.

Most important is an aggregate demand management process which should be the authorization (guidelines) under which the whole organization should be proceeding.

Since forecasts are going to be wrong, both detail and aggregate, we also need to indicate a confidence level in the forecast. What do we think are the upper and lower limits? What could be our contingency plan in support of these limits? Too many managements are talking about what might have been if they had only reviewed and understood the alternatives. Whether you are using a mainframe computer or a micro, the ability to what-if some of these demand alternatives is not only possible but getting more important in the ever-increasing competitive business environment in which we find ourselves.

The issue is not just forecasting, we need an appropriate demand management process where people are accountable. Why not embrace the term and the concept?

ABOUT THE AUTHOR

Dick is President of Richard C. Ling, Inc., a company that provides education and consulting assistance to manufacturing companies.

He is formerly Executive Vice-President of Arista Manufacturing Systems. For a number of years, Dick has conducted the successful "Hands-On" MRP and "Hands-On" Master Production Scheduling courses. Dick's firm currently conducts the MPS course in association with Oliver Wight Education Associates, Inc.

Dick is a frequent speaker at APICS events, local chapter meetings, seminars and the International Conferences. He has been active in APICS as a Program Chairman, Seminar Chairman and as President of the Piedmont Triad Chapter. Dick is an APICS fellow.

Formerly with IBM, Dick is a 1960 graduate of the University of Rochester, and presently resides in Winston-Salem, North Carolina.

Reprinted from 1985 APICS Conference Proceedings.

MAKING QUALITY PROMISES TO CUSTOMERS

Richard C. Ling
Richard C. Ling, Inc.

There is no question in this day and age that the quality of our products has become a more important issue for most manufacturers. Along with this, also, has come an emphasis on delivering on time or in many cases just in time.

Therefore, if we are going to be viable suppliers of products it is imperative that we make quality customer promises; it is as important in most cases as the product itself.

BAD PROMISES REALLY HURT!

As consumers, each of us no doubt has had a bad experience with lousy promising. When the new sofa or car promised in six weeks doesn't arrive for 12, frustration mounts to the point where you may never really enjoy the product once you have it! Did the salesman deliberately mislead you? Maybe, maybe not! If his company has a poor track record on deliveries, he may feel pressure to stretch the truth to get your business. Most of the time, however, his poor promise is caused by a lack of timely information. Regardless of the real cause, you the customer view the poor promise, as you should, as part of the total service and you end up with a bad taste in your mouth for both him and his company.

Frequently, this type of situation is caused by another common business practice -- quoting "standard" delivery lead times. Such quotes often do not work well. Company policy cannot decree that delivery lead time to customers will be X weeks. This concept is naive. A customer service policy ought to state the delivery lead time objective and indicate the range of lead times with which one can successfully operate. Business conditions, however, dictate that customer delivery lead times vary. A rash of customer orders may well create a backlog which realistically will take some period of time to diminish.

There are plenty of companies that consistently do a good job of making intelligent, high quality customer promises and regularly make them happen. These firms have found that the keys to good promises are:
1. Respect for the integrity of a customer promise
2. Defined customer service objectives
3. Accurate records
4. "Doable" master schedules
5. Good promising tools
6. Procedures for managing abnormal demands

Each of these keys requires some discussion.

RESPECT FOR THE INTEGRITY OF A PROMISE

Evolving into a company which makes good promises starts by establishing good promises as an attitude and a basic principle of the way you run your business. True, we need to be able to say "yes" in order to obtain the customer's business; however, our answer should be yes only when it can be accomplished, not just a yes to get the business. This attitude is a cornerstone of good customer promising.

Sometimes this is easier to say than do, because of business pressure both from within the company and from customers who want an answer. Management must take the lead in establishing the importance of valid promises. Unfortunately, top level managers are often the worst violators, especially when their subordinates can't really tell them if and when something can be accomplished. Ollie Wight made an observation many years ago that a manufacturing person without the facts must say yes. It is imperative then that companies determine what information and procedures are required to support a proper promising function.

DEFINED CUSTOMER SERVICE OBJECTIVES

Poorly defined policies and improper techniques, such as the quoting of "standard" delivery lead times noted earlier, often confuse your customer base and breed false expectations. In many companies, all products may not be available "off-the-shelf" even though the majority are. In some cases, stocks of an item are adequate to handle certain size orders but are not adequate for large order quantities. Terms such as "standard" versus "special" products further confuse things since the normal expectation of our customers is that all "standard" products have the same delivery lead time. Often, this is just not the case.

These, and other, poorly defined situations are common. Thus, it takes a real company effort to properly define how product is positioned to meet customer demand. It takes creative and timely communications with sales representatives and customers to clearly communicate the company strategy which, of course, changes over time. Far too often, false customer expectations are a direct result of a failure to set proper policy.

One client company producing industrial products has a well-defined product positioning policy. Each product belongs to one of four delivery lead time categories -- A, D, E, and F. Category A products are available "off-the-shelf" in reasonable quantities. Category D includes minor modifications of basic products with short lead times (two to four weeks). Category E covers OEM product with longer lead time scheduled deliveries (e.g., eight weeks). Category F includes engineered products with even longer lead times because of engineering and/or special manufacturing requirements.

Actual delivery lead times quoted in all cases vary based on current backlog conditions. Customers, however, have very clear expectations initialy based on the product's category. Frequent price lists are distributed to manufacturer representatives and distributors updating product categories as things change. A Category D item, for example, may change to Category A off-the-shelf if sales volume or customer needs dictate.

The other troublesome aspect of good customer service is the need to develop proper performance measurements.

You just can't realistically promise something unless you know what you are able to do. Knowing what you can do starts with measuring what you have been doing. Sounds simple enough but in a surprising number of manufacturing companies, rigorous performance measurements do not exist. Therefore, the management group can't determine what it has been accomplishing in the past relative to plan and therefore does not know what to expect in the future.

There is an interesting measurement of overall customer service which relates to stocking strategies. Type M fast food hamburger stores sell from finished goods inventory. Most of the time, they fill your order from stock in very short order (pun intended). Type W hamburger stores assemble to your order drawing from standard component inventory -- patties, buns, lettuce, onion, etc. Some delivery lead time is always required since assembly commences after receipt of your order.

Have you ever noticed how Type M firms sometimes seem to take forever to recover if you happen to catch them out of stock of the item you ordered? That's usually because they have other stock products tying up critical capacities (the stove). In the meanwhile, you wait. It can take awhile before they're able to replenish inventory to meet your order.

The measurement issue here is that of tracking all of your delivery lead times. A 96% fill rate from stock may sound pretty good. However, if it takes 15 minutes on average to fill a backorder, that may be totally unacceptable to your marketplace. After one or two bad experiences, Type M customers may be going to W where there is less chance of suffering a long wait. We see a correlation with manufacturing firms that must determine how to position themselves to provide the best overall service with the combination of inventory and delivery lead time.

ACCURATE RECORDS

We have long recognized that accurate records are required to support Class A MRP II. It should be no surprise to anyone, therefore, that all of the records used to prepare a customer promise must be very accurate. They must also be monitored to maintain their accuracy. These records include: (1) on-hand balance, (2) bills of material, (3) Master Schedules, and (4) promises from both your suppliers and your own factory. What can be more frustrating than making a promise, only to be done in by sloppy record keeping?

"DOABLE" MASTER PRODUCTION SCHEDULES

MRP Practitioners recognize the extreme importance of realistic, attainable master schedules. 95% MPS performance is necessary for Class A MRP II status. 95% MPS performance, or better, is also a fundamental pre-requisite for good customer promises.

Make-to-order businesses live in a world where they must promise customers based on future build schedules. Some, such as assemble or finish-to-order companies, have planned and produced substantial lower level component materials prior to receipt of the customer order. Others, such as defense contractors, buy or build little without a customer order. They all share a common need -- future schedules reflecting both material and capacity availability must be committed to incoming customer orders in order to make a realistic promise.

Make-to-stock companies delivering from stock normally are not concerned with promising customer orders out into the future. They do develop this concern, however, when backorders develop or customers do request future delivery, e.g., OEM's ordering to a schedule.

The Production Plan states family rates of manufacture, e.g., 500 steel office desks per week. The Master Production Schedule translates the family build rate into an anticipated build schedule stated in terms of specific items, quantities and dates, e.g., pedestals, drawers, top variations, etc. In many firms, the MPS items drive material planning with prerequisite capacity planning accomplished by Rough Cut Capacity Planning and detailed Capacity Requirements Planning. In engineer-to-order firms, the MPS items drive primarily capacity plans initially since most material requirements do not become known until later in the cycle. Either way, the MPS is the specific schedule against which one can promise an incoming customer order.

Attainable schedules, consistently met, are absolutely necessary for good promises. Such schedules are the basis for a fundamental promising tool -- the available to promise.

GOOD PROMISING TOOLS

Many companies labor with antiquated techniques not only to enter and promise orders but also to respond to inquiries such as, "Can we take this order?," "Can we increase the schedule?," or "What will the impact of this action be?" Most companies need to improve their "What if" simulation capabilities to provide management with better tools for decision making. They also need accurate available to promise (ATP) information.

Although it is not my intent to get into a lot of technical detail in this paper, a basic understanding of the ATP tools that are readily available today is a must. ATP is the first level of "what if" and order entry systems without ATP capabilities are totally inadequate today.

ATP information is deceptively simple to put together. For many businesses, it's a matter of comparing time-phased customer commitments to the on-hand balance plus the Master Production Schedule. Figures 1A and 1B illustrate ATP calculations.

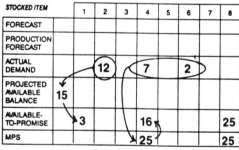

Figure 1A

ATP is calculated by comparing the actual demand to the on-hand and MPS receipts over time. 12 units are committed to customers in week two. Since the 25 due in week four are coming too late to cover this commitment, 12 of the 15 on-hand must be reserved to meet it; thus, three are available to promise in the current week.

In a similar manner, nine of the 25 due in week four are reserved to meet customer commitments of seven in week four and two in week six. Thus, 16 of the 25 are available

to promise since there are no customer demands presently against that receipt. Note that the latest available receipt is used to satisfy a given customer commitment.

Some firms prefer a cumulative display of ATP. In that case, in Figure 1A, the cumulative ATP would be three in weeks one to three, 19 in weeks four to seven, and 44 in week eight.

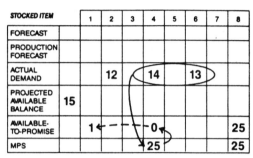

Figure 1B

Figure 1B illustrates the one tricky aspect of ATP logic. Proceeding as in Figure 1A, one would originally expect to see an ATP of three in week one. However, a total of 27 actual customer orders exist in weeks four and six for the 25 due in week four. This creates a negative ATP of minus two which the standard logic handles by reaching back for earlier ATP. This reach back reduces the original three to one in week one.

In many businesses capacity, not materials, is the driver for available to promise. Many capacity-managed businesses, such as foundries, contract machining operations, plastics molding, textiles, process and engineer-to-order businesses fit this mold. In these businesses, customer promises are primarily based on capacity availability, not material availability. Either rough cut capacity profiles or estimating processes are used to convert incoming customer orders to demands on critical capacities such as people, facilities, engineering functions, etc. These demands are then used to make "available to promise" capacity commitments.

Figure 2 illustrates the ATP capacity process for a bank of injection molding machines.

Capacity Booking

	1	2	3	4	5	6
MOLDING HOURS	240	240	240	280	280	280
SOLD	240	240	180	140	70	
AVAILABLE-TO-PROMISE	0	0	60	140	210	280

Figure 2

The ATP mechanism keeps track of all existing commitments. It insures that we account for all existing commitments against our capabilities so that we don't over-promise these resources. Many manufacturing companies have developed responsive, available to promise processes. Many commercial software packages now have these capabilities as a fairly standard feature.

There is also a trend in software to provide more "what if" capabilities for material and capacity availability as on-line interactive tools. For example, the MPS may not provide available to promise sufficient to meet a given customer request. With today's "what if" tools, many companies now routinely check lower level items examining critical component or subassembly availability. Frequently, lot sizing at lower levels will make key materials available. For example, the MPS may call for 25 desk crawer lock options. Critical components, however, such as the purchased lock, may be purchased in quantities of 100 to get a better price.

Rough cut capacity "what-if's" are common. Detailed Material Requirements Planning and Capacity Requirements Planning simulations may be called for under certain conditions. Net-change systems and today's computers now permit more frequent use of these computer-intensive tools.

MANAGING ABNORMAL DEMANDS

Too many companies cause themselves and their customers problems because of their inability to properly identify and manage abnormal demands.

If not properly handled, a significant order from a customer or segment of the marketplace which was not formally forecasted and planned is a real potential problem. Naturally, there is excitement about the opportunity to satisfy the unforecasted demand. Unfortunately, however, a first come, first serve approach to making a promise can leave us without a product that is genuinely needed to service regular ongoing customers. Thus, overall customer service can suffer, since we can often continue to make bad promises in response to the pressure and expectations of these regular customers.

Recently, a client company pursuing MRP II decided to alter its order entry mechanism to determine who should get priority in the event of abnormal demand orders. Their procedure requires that those orders be reviewed by the proper level of management. One specific high impact order got the V.P. of Sales and President involved. They made a decision not to accept the order as requested.

They explained the situation to the customer by telling him that an additional three months' lead time was mandatory for a major portion of the order because of existing customer forecasts (not orders) they were committed to support. The company was convinced that this response would cost them this potentially very large piece of business.

The customer accepted the terms much to the surprise of the client. What a marvelous thing to happen in support of the company's new resolve to improve the quality of their customer promising. The key, of course, was the good procedure and early communication with the customer before a poor commitment was made.

In a different case, we were quite disturbed with a client recently where we discussed the process and the data required to support ATP. We were talking about who owned the data. In this client's view, Sales and Marketing own both the forecast and the customer order data, and Manufacturing owns the master schedule data. Because the company has separate data processing staffs for marketing systems and manufacturing systems, the client asked, "Who owns the system?" (The answer is, THE COMPANY.)

This ridiculous question is very indicative of the massive communications problem that exists in this, and many, manufacturing companies between Sales, Marketing and Manufacturing.

GOOD PROMISES REALLY HELP!

Our customers always will and should expect a proper promise from us. It follows naturally that if we are going to gain the respect and continued business of our customers, then we should all place making good promises very high on our list of corporate objectives.

TEST YOUR COMPANY'S PROMISING ABILITY

	YES	NO
1. Our company rates making good promises very high	___	___
2. Our promises are based on fact not hopes	___	___
3. We have a well defined customer service objective with measurements	___	___
4. Our records are accurate	___	___
5. Our Master Schedule is achieved 95+% of the time	___	___
6. We employ good promising tools such as ATP	___	___
7. We manage abnormal demands well	___	___
8. We perform to promise 95-100%	___	___

If your answer to #8 is no, use your "no" responses to questions 1-7 to focus attention on what needs to be improved. Don't settle for less than a perfect score.

ABOUT THE AUTHOR

Dick is President of Richard C. Ling, Inc., a company that provides education and consulting assistance to manufacturing companies.

He was formerly Executive Vice-President of Arista Manufacturing Systems. For a number of years, Dick has conducted the successful "Hands-On" MRP and "Hands-On" Master Production Scheduling courses. Dick's firm currently conducts the MPS course in association with Oliver Wight Education Associates, Inc.

Dick is a frequent speaker at APICS events, local chapter meetings, seminars and the International Conferences. He has been active in APICS as a Program Chairman, Seminar Chairman and as President of the Piedmont Triad Chapter. Dick is an APICS fellow.

Formerly with IBM, Dick is a 1960 graduate of the University of Rochester, and presently resides in Winston-Salem, North Carolina.

Reprinted from 1980 APICS Conference Proceedings.

MASTER SCHEDULING:

A KEY TO RESULTS

Richard W. Malko, CPIM
V. P. - The Forum, Ltd.

This paper is written in an effort to identify the key elements of Master Scheduling. It will provide the reader with definition, concepts and techniques.

INTRODUCTION

As manufacturing companies become more complex, the job of communicating becomes more difficult.

One of the functions of communication is getting the right information to the right people. This paper is not written as a paper in communication, but it is designed to cover a specific function within a manufacturing company that starts one of the most important communication networks ever created.

The network I am talking about is an effective manufacturing control system which uses Materials Requirements Planning as one of its major sub-systems. An effective manufacturing control system is really an effective communication system. It shuffles data around and presents the data in useable format so that a decision maker can make good sound decisions.

In developing an effective manufacturing control system, it is important to note that the system is only as good as its weakest link. During the last few years the need for manufacturing control systems has been highlighted and many companies have either installed one or are in the process of installization. The success ratio has been poor and I feel the major reason is lack of knowledge as to what makes an effective manufacturing control system and how to implement one.

There are many sub-systems that must be developed, disciplined and constantly maintained. This book is written to cover one of these sub-systems. I consider it one of the key sub-systems, but by no means the only one. This sub-system is called Master Scheduling.

In my opinion, Master Scheduling has been discussed from a mechanical point of view. That is, how does a computer take some raw data and compute demand onto other items that make up the total Master Schedule. There has been very little written about how you get the raw data to begin with and what techniques are used to remain consistent. This paper is written to address this part of Master Scheduling.

DEFINITION

I find that I must define Master Scheduling from two different viewpoints.

The Dictionary viewpoint:

A Master Schedule is a realistic, detailed, manufacturing plan for which all possible demand put upon the manufacturing facilities have been considered.

I have underlined some key words in this definition that I would like to expand upon.

Realistic

One of the most common faults in Master Scheduling is that they are not realistic. There is a tendency to "jam" more into the schedule than is possible to produce.

This is one of the toughest facts to face for top management. If sales are good, no one wants to hear that we can't make the order or we can't deliver on time.

A lot of hard-nosed decisions must be made constantly so that the Master Schedule is realistic. The Master Schedule cannot be a "wish list". Knowing what you really can produce is not easy. Especially if you are in a job shop environment. The product mix plays a key role in what your capability really is. However, the need to be realistic is very important if you want good control over inventory, cost and service.

Detailed

This schedule is not in general terms. We are talking about specific part numbers, quantities and time periods. A Master Schedule must be maintained with a high degree of accuracy. Clerical toughness is a must.

Manufacturing Plan

Another key fault in Master Scheduling is using the sales forecast and transferring it directly into the Master Schedule. You must realize that the Master Schedule represents the way that you want to manufacture the product not sell the product. A sales forecast is a very valuable tool to use to help develop the Master Schedule, but it should not be directly transferable.

There are many things to consider when developing the Master Schedule.

All Possible Demands - Considered

There are many different demands that must be considered in developing a Master Schedule. Let me list the major ones:

A. Sales Forecast

B. Customer Orders

C. Interplant Requirements

D. International Requirements

E. Service Part Demand

F. Plant Capacity

G. Product Lead Time

H. Inventory Planning

Another viewpoint for the definition of Master Scheduling is that it is a major sub-system that has joined the ranks of other major sub-systems such as:

Bill of Material

Part Master

Open Order

Routing

Work Center

I look at MRP as the needle and thread that ties all of these major sub-systems into a dynamic operating network that can maximize results in areas of customer service, inventory levels and manufacturing effectiveness.

Master Scheduling is a key ingredient to that network and from the above definition you can see that it is an art as well as a science. One of the objectives of this paper is to break down the function of Master Scheduling so that you can approach it more objectively and eliminate the unknown.

WHAT TO MASTER SCHEDULE

A very common question is what do I Master Schedule and how do I get the information? Before addressing that question specifically, I feel there is a basic need for understanding a relationship between dependent and independent demand.

Before Master Scheduling was developed, most companies products and inventory control systems did some kind of forecasting on every component part listed in a bill of material.

The key to Master Scheduling is to identify the least number of items that need forecasting (independent demand) and calculate all other demands from these few (dependent demand).

The use of an indented bill of material can help me illustrate the relationship of dependent and independent demand:

In the above structure, let's assume that A is an end product that we sell. In older systems such as order point, minimum-maximum, etc., all parts were treated independently and we forecasted demand for A, B, C, D and E parts.

The concept of dependent/independent demand says that you only have to forecast the independent demand items and calculate the demand for the dependent demand item.

Therefore, in the above example, forecast A and calculate B, C, D and E based on quantity per and bill of material structure.

Therefore, a key to start with is master schedule the independent demand items. A problem that crops up is that the total independent demand items might be too large of a number to really control properly. For instance, if you master schedule your end product and that amounted to tens of thousands of items, you may feel uncomfortable about controlling such a large number.

Therefore, another consideration must be made and that is the bill of material structure. If your product has so many options that by scheduling all end items you have a huge number to control, I suggest that you look at modular bills of material whereby you can group your independent demand items into common bills and end up reducing your master schedule dramatically while achieving excellent results.

I feel that the symbols below help illustrate my point.

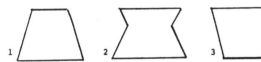

* These symbols represent just about every manufacturing company I can think of. The first symbol represents a company that has a controllable number of end products made from multiple component parts. In this case you master schedule the end product.

The second symbol represents a company whose product has many options and master scheduling the end item is uncontrollable. Therefore, this company uses modular bills and master schedules one level down from the end product.

The third symbol represents a company who has many end products made from few components. Here you master schedule the bottom level.

Therefore, there are two key areas involved in what to master schedule:

1. Independent demand items
2. Bill of Material Structure

I would like to discuss an important technique that I have used very successfully over the past 5 years. I call it Key Component Scheduling.

Key component scheduling comes into play when one of your key components has both independent and dependent demand. Let me explain.

I look at a key component as a part that has a critical effect on my manufacturing cost. For example, in a plant that builds tractors on an assembly line, a key manufacturing cost is line stoppage. So I look at what items will definitely stop the line. Granted, we need all parts to build the unit, but only some of them will actually stop the line. Therefore, I want to watch those parts even closer than the others.

My experience has been that those key components normally have both independent and dependent demand.

* Presented by John Piepgras, V.P., Booz, Allen, Inc., at the APICS National Convention, 1974.

In the case of a tractor line, let's assume that the engine is a key component. When examining the engine assembly line, you will find that engines are built for tractors in one plant and for other vehicles in the other plants. You may even find that engines are built for OEM customers.

A common mistake is made when you master schedule the tractor line and get it level and assume the feeding lines are level automatically. You must evaluate each key area for actual demand and normally you find that other independent demands are occurring and if not watched, will cause a lumpy demand for a line that is manned for a level output.

Therefore, key component scheduling takes a look at one level below the normal master schedule and recognizes bottlenecks and replans the master schedule before actually passing it on to the MRP explosion.

You may have heard this technique expressed as a rough cut capacity analysis, but it is not just that. I look at a rough cut capacity analysis as an exercise to show if we are in the ball park as far as meeting the master schedule. I have not been able to level every work center by manipulating the master schedule. In a job shop environment, you usually will have peaks and valleys in the load on a work center by work center basis. I try to level the key areas and leave the balance up to the individual efforts of the shop scheduler and foremen.

Not only must you level the key component areas, but you must measure the performance. I recommend that these measurement functions be done by the master scheduler so there are no chances of communications problems.

Primarily a good master scheduler measures performance and reports the results. He must include the key components as part of this measurement and reporting. By doing so, you can detect serious problems before your final assembly foreman does and therefore plan a more economic alternative or prevent an uneconomical shutdown.

In summary, keep these fundamental points in mind:

1. Bill of Material Structure - must fit the needs of the company.

2. Dependent/Independent demand relationship.

3. Key component scheduling.

MASTER SCHEDULE CONTENTS

The actual contents of a master schedule record is very important. I am sure that you can dream up all kinds of information that you feel is important. What I would like to do is highlight six (6) important items that I feel are a must to do good master scheduling.

A.   Requirement

Naturally the most obvious is the actual requirement itself. This means the specific part numbers and specific quantity in a specific time frame. The source of your requirement - independent demand - can come from the following areas:

1. Sales

-Forecasts
-Customer orders
-Interplant orders
-International orders

Your manufacturing plant will fall into one of the following areas:

-Make to order
-Make to stock
-Some of both

In the make to stock environment, you rely on a sales forecast as a main source of information along with current backlog of orders.

In the made to order environment, you rely on the customer order. Some companies are experiencing that even though they are made to order; they must forecast and master schedule items ahead of the actual order. This causes another problem of transferring forecast demand into actual order demand. Many companies operate in an environment where they build to stock and build to order. Again, you must recognize what environment you are in and where you get the raw data to work with. Staying on top of the requirements is probably the toughest job of the master scheduler because most people are not planners or at least will not commit. It is his job to force commitments where the schedule is in jeopardy. I will discuss this later.

2. Service and Repair

Probably the toughest area for forecast because of the volume of items and the lack of good marketing information on service parts.

3. Safety Stock

If you use safety stock, I recommend that you enter it in the master schedule for the following reasons:

a. As a manager you can easily measure it.

b. It prevents people in lower levels of management from entering "fudge" in the requirements.

I do not believe in using safety stock except in two areas. One is when I must stock a critical path item in order to cut my product lead time so that it is competitive. The other safety stock is in those super critical items that warrant safety stock from both a space and dollar analysis.

4. Engineering Changes

You can use the master schedule to get those critical path items going when you are waiting for a complete new bill of material from Engineering. If a new product is coming out, identify the long lead time items and get them released first. Master schedule them as an independent demand and when the full BOM is released you can replace the item with the normal master schedule item. The execution areas such as purchasing and production control should not see any change.

5. Miscellaneous Requirements

Probably the only other areas of any volume may be engineering prototypes. If their demands are such that it may interfere with normal production, you must master schedule their demand. If not, you can withdraw material from inventory as a miscellaneous withdrawal.

B. Source Identification

When involved in master scheduling, you will find that the actual number of parts in the master schedule is still quite large - primarily due to service demands. Therefore, I find it necessary to code the record so that I know why I have the requirement in the schedule. In other words, where did the real demand come from in the first place. I feel this is very important in reviewing the need for re-planning requirements.

C. Time Increment

A common question is how long should the time frame be in the master schedule. I suggest that it be one week. You may choose a month as an input document and then let the computer break it down into weeks. I don't feel that longer time frames will be of use in keeping proper priorities. You may be in an environment where days should be the time increment. My experience shows me that weeks are satisfactory, however, you must analyze your own environment and decide.

D. Product Identification Code

When doing an effective job of master scheduling, it is very important to know your product lines. Instead of remembering the various products, it is advantageous to code each item in the schedule so that you can tell by that code if the products are actually similar or different.

For instance, if sales are actually increasing on product A and decreasing on product B, your desire is to increase production on A and reduce B. If the products are similar, you can change the master schedule in the short term; but if they are different, you are forced to change further out in the schedule. By coding the products, you prevent personnel turnover from carrying away valuable information.

E. Time Horizon

Another common question is how far out do you master schedule? My first response to this question is to schedule out as far as the aggregate lead time of the product. This is fine for starters, but I must highlight some exceptions. One is where only a few components are causing long aggregate lead times. Then you may choose to safety stock the critical path items and master schedule the balance in a shorter interval. But probably the best answer I can provide is you must master schedule as far out as is needed for your execution departments, primarily purchasing and production control, to make sound operating decisions. For instance, in purchasing, if the time horizon is short, a buyer is faced with economical buys that may extend beyond the horizon of his plan. Should he buy more or not? Probably his decision would be based on historical facts. I propose that the people involved in the master schedule will know more about the future than purchasing. Therefore, master schedule out far enough to eliminate those kind of purchasing decisions or at least reduce them to an exception. Granted, the farther you schedule, the more chances for change; but at least the change will be planned and not just re-acted upon.

F. Relationship to Sales Plan

Your master schedule which reflects the detail of the production plan must constantly be monitored along with the actual activities of the sales plan. Remember, both the sales and production plans are really forecasts based on knowledge known at the time along with various assumptions. Both must be measured to see if the future is happening as expected. Whenever it is not, you must re-evaluate your plans and perhaps re-plan. The main theme is to be able to identify a serious deviation pattern and re-plan the future accordingly.

PEOPLE INVOLVED IN MASTER SCHEDULING

Another common question is who should do the master scheduling and what are his qualifications? I would like to address myself to this by exploring three (3) areas:

1. Knowledge Required
2. Experience
3. Education

Knowledge Required

I feel there are eight (8) key areas of knowledge involved in master scheduling:

Product Lead Time

Probably one of the major reasons for master schedules being unrealistic is the lack of knowledge to actual product lead times as well as maintaining that knowledge. Take your bill of material structure and explode it by offsetting individual part lead times. What you have is a pert chart showing all items from the lowest level upward in sequence as to time. The aggregate lead time is your product lead time. You can easily identify the critical path items. Now if a customer wants shorter lead time, all you have to do is review those items outside his desired lead time. This reduces the analysis to the real exception. The benefits are as follows:

1. You can acknowledge shipments honestly.
2. If you cannot acknowledge as desired, you can identify when with a high degree of success.
3. If you cannot acknowledge as desired, you can identify the specific parts that cause the problem and perhaps the customer can help you solve this problem.

Anyway you look at it you are servicing the customer in the best manner possible. This technique also helps you in the following situation:

Suppose your sales and marketing people want shorter lead time. You can identify what items must be safety stocked and cost that inventory investment. Now you can not only assure management that you can meet the new lead time request but can be very specific as far as what that decision will cost in terms of inventory investment.

Plant Capacity

Knowledge of plant capacity is also invaluable in master scheduling. Unusual demand may cause temporary capacity restraints such that normal lead time is impossible. Also, recognizing new capacity problems in the future will force top management to either invest in capital equipment or back off in sales demand. The latter is not likely, so it is even more important that capacity limitations be identifiable in specifics. The master scheduler should be deeply involved in the development of any capacity planning activities.

Product Knowledge

As mentioned earlier, product knowledge is very important. By coding the records you can secure this knowledge, but whatever personal knowledge is available is always useful.

Plant Flexibility

Knowing how flexible the plant can actually be. Knowing the type of operation and the kind of people that manage the various areas. This information helps you in being realistic as to what really will happen if we change the schedule.

MRP

The person responsible for Master Scheduling must be at least certified in the MRP module of APICS certification. For those of you not familiar with this, let me explain: APICS stands for American Production and Inventory Control Society. They have developed a series of examinations whereby, if passed, people are certified at one of two levels of expertise. MRP is one of these modules and the master scheduler must thoroughly understand MRP. He is actually driving the MRP system and must understand the mechanics of the system. Not only will this knowledge help him in scheduling, but will help him solve problems thought to originate from the master schedule.

Good Business Sense

The person doing the master scheduling is really one of the most powerful people in the plant. By creating this schedule and exploding it through MRP, he is communicating to people in purchasing, manufacturing and production control and indicating what to do and when to do it. If he makes mistakes, they are multiplied many times over through the system. He is making business decisions every day and, therefore, must have good business sense.

Shortages

To insure a valid schedule, certain shortage information must be fed back to the master scheduler. He then has that magical decision to reschedule or not to reschedule. This is not an easy decision and I suggest that you evaluate your own company and try to develop some basic rules as to when you should or should not reschedule based on various shortage information. Let me point out some problems. First, if you reschedule and do that as a policy, you tend to take the pressure off and slowly find yourself missing shipping dates continuously. Secondly, if you constantly reschedule, you are upsetting the utilization of the manpower in the shop. Third, if you reschedule because of one shortage, you will automatically reschedule all other components not already in stock. This may move them into a bottleneck situation and later you find yourself rescheduling again only for a different part. If you don't reschedule, you create a falsehood in your assembly area and perhaps upset the utilization of that department. If you don't reschedule, you are forcing parts through the plant that will not go out the door as expected. If you don't reschedule, you may build up inventory value not originally anticipated. So, what do you do? First you do everything possible to eliminate the shortage. Spend some time analyzing shortages as to why they occur. Perhaps your master schedule was wrong from day one. Perhaps you have an execution problem. Identify the real cause and then come up with your solution. Assuming everything is planned properly and you do have an isolated execution problem, you must decide on rescheduling or not. You normally will have one of two decisions. Build the product less the shortage. Reschedule to the future and expect no new problems.

Possible Changes

A good master scheduler will keep involved in various meetings throughout the organization. Marketing and Engineering as well as Manufacturing may be discussing new plans not released. This is good to know and may have an earlier input on scheduling than they are aware of. So it pays to keep your ears open for new changes not officially on the drawing boards.

Experience

I highly recommend that the person doing the master scheduling has a manufacturing or production control background. Since the definition highlights master scheduling as a manufacturing plan, the person doing it must have a good understanding of manufacturing. That does not mean that he must know the mechanics of manufacturing the product, but he must know what it takes in terms of effort and managing.

This is not a starting position. It could be if watched very closely and limited to a small amount of items, but I suggest that you use an experienced man in the manufacturing area.

Education

A college education is not necessary, however it is desirable. The person is making business decisions every day; and if he does his job very well, is in a position for future growth. Therefore, having the college education will help, but you can do a good job without it.

UPDATING THE MASTER SCHEDULE

In talking about updating the master schedule, I refer to three (3) processes.

1. Relieving the schedule
2. Changing the schedule
3. Adding to the schedule

Relieving the Schedule

What I mean here is how do you relieve the schedule based on executing the plan. From what I have seen, there are basically two methods:

A. Shipments
B. Production

If you design your master schedule to reflect what will be available for shipments, then your shipping transaction can be used to relieve the master schedule.

If you design your master schedule to reflect what you want to build, then your production transaction will relieve the schedule.

My preference is to design the master schedule to reflect what is available for shipment and allow the shipping transaction to relieve it.

By designing the master schedule this way, I feel you accomplish a number of things:

1. The bottom line is the actual build schedule that reflects down through MRP.
2. The top line reflects what will be available to ship.
3. The computer will automatically apply the finished goods against the first line and create the build line.

Using the same situation but designing the master schedule for production requires the same mathematics as above, but through either manual arithmetic or other sub-systems. Therefore, I recommend the available for shipment design. I feel it is more controllable as well as more information to all parties. From one file you can satisfy production and sales.

Changing the Schedule

The demand for change comes primarily from three (3) areas:

A. Sales Performance
B. Production Performance
C. Purchasing Performance

No matter how well you plan, there will be changes. The better you plan, the less change will incur; but there will always be some performance problems in either sales, manufacturing or purchasing.

Whenever there is a demand to change the schedule, then there are a few simple rules that may apply.

1. In the short term, reschedule the whole quantity. Do not change quantities.
2. In the long term, you can change both time and quantity. The reason I say this is that for many of your "A" components, the quantities coming in are in the exact increment of the master schedule. If you change quantity instead of time, you create quite an execution problem.

Adding to the Schedule

When adding to the schedule, you will normally experience two phases:

A. Routine add to the tail end of the schedule.
B. Unplanned additions prior to the end of the schedule.

Assuming your master schedule is designed for weekly increment, then each week you must be prepared to add new requirements into the schedule on a timely basis so that you always reflect good visibility through MRP to the execution departments.

If your addition is in shorter range, then your analysis of aggregate lead time or critical parts must come into play.

Frozen Period

A decision that is very important but very hard to agree upon is what I call the frozen period. The frozen period is that block of time within which the schedule cannot be changed. There are two good reasons why there must be a frozen period.

A. There is a period of time that manufacturing cannot react to regardless of cost.
B. There is a period of time that manufacturing can react to, but may be extremely costly.

Therefore, as a policy, a frozen period must be agreed upon. I feel the main advantage this gives a company is that they fully recognize the need for firm planning and if the need arises to change within the frozen period, they are fully aware of all costs and consequences.

The actual amount of time periods used in the frozen period will vary from company to company. You must evaluate your own situation and determine what your company can actually do.

ADDITIONAL USES OF A MASTER SCHEDULE

Besides using the master schedule for reflecting production requirements, you can use the schedule for the following:

A. Customer Delivery Promises

By designing the schedule to reflect available for shipment, you will be able to predict customer delivery based on back-orders in house balanced against the master schedule. Sales can get this information from the same file as production control and you have serviced a vital communication link in your company.

B. Order Entry Measurement

As customer orders are received, you can measure them against the master schedule and give you an early warning system when sales are deviating beyond expectations.

C. Inventory Projection

By costing out the master schedule, you can tell how much material and labor you expect to consume. This can contribute towards two measurements.

1. Does this total compare with the production plan.
2. Using this for projected shipments and using the final output of MRP, you have the input and output to inventory, time phased. The result is a very precise inventory projection.

D. Cash Flow Projection

Some of the key ingredients to a cash flow projection include:

Payroll
Material Invoices
Capital Expenditures
Expected Receipts

Each of these ingredients can be projected through a good manufacturing control system that uses Master Scheduling, MRP and capacity planning.

SUMMARY

An effective manufacturing control system requires a number of efficient sub-systems as a team. It really is no different than the management of the company. You need all members of the team to be strong in their areas and they must blend together as a working unit.

The systems are not different. You need all the pieces to work independently and then tie them together to perform as a dynamic network.

These types of systems can be made and are being used in companies today. Master Scheduling is one of those key sub-systems, but it needs the help of other sub-systems to generate final results.

If you have all the pieces together, but the results are not there, I suggest that one of the pieces is very weak. Perhaps it is the Master Schedule.

Remember, Master Scheduling is a key to results.

Richard Malko is Vice President of THE FORUM, LTD, a management education and consulting firm located in Milwaukee, Wisconsin.

Prior to joining THE FORUM, Dick spent almost 20 years in manufacturing and materials management with Dumore Corporation and J. I. Case Company.

As Vice President of Manufacturing and Materials Manager, Dick was responsible for manufacturing, production and inventory control, purchasing and data processing.

Dick is a business management graduate of the University of Wisconsin and a member of the U.W. Production and Material Control advisory committee. He has also served as President and Director of the Milwaukee chapter of APICS and is certified in the field of Production and Inventory Control at the fellow level.

Dick is an active speaker at management conferences throughout the U.S. and is the author of "Master Scheduling: A Key to Results".

Reprinted from the *Production & Inventory Management Review*, May 1982.

Demand Management: A Quantitative Alternative

by James W. Muir

Demand Management is the application of proven scientific techniques to the areas of order processing, sales forecasting, and sales management. It is a formalization of functions already taking place within manufacturing companies. The key intent in Demand Management is to recognize and forecast all of the potential requirements which should be considered in establishing inventory levels: customer orders, branch warehouse requirements, interplant transfers, international requirements, and service parts demand.

Demand Management, used in conjunction with scientific inventory management, is the area which will have the most dramatic effect on return on investment, especially as business becomes more and more complicated.

Most companies have carefully planned and well managed programs for controlling sales activities, costs and receivables. Very little change can be made over the short term to effect the value of physical assets. For most companies, the value of raw material, work-in-process, and finished goods inventory exceeds the value of physical assets, making inventory and extremely important and leverageable element. It is the only element for which a dramatic improvement can be made over the short term. Demand Management encompasses activities which are important in the management and reduction of inventory.

Demand Management is also necessary to support other quantitative planning systems including Manufacturing Resource Planning (MRP), Distribution Requirements Planning (DRP), the Master Production Schedule (MPS), and all facets of scientific inventory management.

Order Processing Considerations

With the exception of the sales effort, the only contact with the customer may be through order processing. Therefore, how we treat this important function within our business creates an image of our company. Order processing is the link between forecasting and the master schedule, and as such is a vital part of Demand Management.

The purpose of order processing is to transform an order, which is entered in the customer's language, into an order we can deal with in our own language. This may include transforming his part number to our part number, his unit of measure to our unit of measure, and generally preparing the order for shipment depending upon the date requested and product availability.

One of the forecasting considerations is what to forecast: orders booked, orders booked by requested ship date, or shipments? When the determination is made as to which of these are important to forecast, the order processing system will have to capture the necessary demand to do the forecasting. Most companies have systems in place to collect the data required to forecast shipments. If the order processing system cannot capture true demand, serious consideration needs to be given to whether or not forecasting demand is truly necessary, as it may be a major undertaking to begin to collect the necessary data.

There are a number of types of orders that must be considered in order processing. The order might be for immediate shipment, or future shipment. The unit of measure of the line item ordered may be different than the unit of measure in which it is packaged and sold. It is the responsibility of order processing to be aware of these conditions.

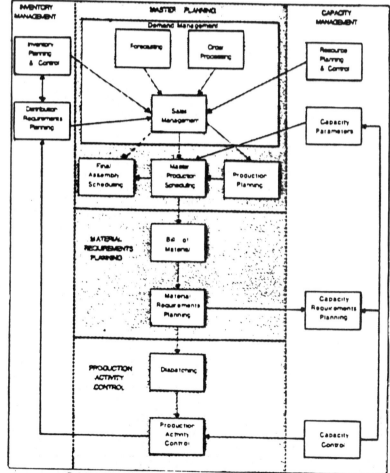

Relationship of Demand Management to Other Activities
Figure 1

Order processing should also edit the order for reasonableness

Once an order has been entered and accepted into a computer-based system, changing the order may not be an easy job. Keep in mind that even if the order is wrong, it will be shipped if inventory is available.

There is probably no single area of the company more important than the Customer Service department, where additional sales may be obtained or lost based upon the customer's experience.

Forecasting Considerations

Forecasting is concerned with predicting the future and is at the heart of all planning and decision making. Sound forecasts are based upon applying statistical techniques and management judgment to high quality, timely, and appropriate data. A variety of techniques have been developed to assist in processing the data to create forecasts. These techniques may be classified as qualitative, statistical, or causal.

Many good forecasting techniques are available, so the need in forecasting today is certainly not better techniques, but rather better utilization of existing ones.

The only family of forecasting techniques that can be considered viable in a typical production and inventory control environment would be the statistical family. This is not to say that there are no good qualitative or causal techniques available. However, using either of these families is absolutely prohibitive in terms of cost and time in this environment in which we must forecast thousands of SKU's—on a repetitive basis.

Since most situations of interest have some random aspect or non-controllable feature, forecasts inherently have some error, and measurement of the error is necessary in order to control it. Any sound error measurement technique, properly applied, will achieve the desired results.

Forecasting does not exist for itself alone. A forecast is meaningful only in relationship to planning and decision-making activities in some other area of the business, such as

Master Scheduling or DRP. A review of Figure 1 shows the relationship of Forecasting to Demand Management, of Demand Management to Master Planning, and of Master Planning to other typical activities performed in a manufacturing business.

Some situations have such a profound effect on sales forecasting, that they warrant special attention. These situations include items with seasonality, items with irregular demand, and items requiring refinements to insure reasonableness.

Management Role

The number one cause for system failure is lack of management review, interface, intervention, and participation. The system will be a success if, and only if, it meets the needs of management, management uses the results, and management can readily see the effect of its input upon the forecasting process.

There are two kinds of conditions which would cause a statistical forecast to be inaccurate:

1. Anything which has either occurred consistently in the past or has occurred in the recent past will influence the forecast. If this condition is not going to recur in the future, the forecasting system will not achieve the desired results.
2. If something is going to happen in the future which has not occured in the past there is no way that a time series based forecast can be aware of it and respond accordingly.

Additionally, statistical forecasting systems do a poor job of predicting turning points. Management not only has an opportunity, but an obligation to assist the statistical forecast with its knowledge of these situations.

Forecasting is an imprecise science in which we try to minimize error. Having done that, we must still deal with the situation where things don't happen according to our prediction. The purpose of sales management is to recognize that there are alternative ways of filling an order and achieving customer satisfaction.

Since risks are very real, and there

is no precise way to calculate the effect of a late shipment on overall sales activity, we must weigh the added cost of an alternative method of satisfying the order with the probable cost of losing some business. Alternatives include: product substitution, product upgrade (upgrade the order to a more desirable product at no additional cost to the customer), order rotation (ship the order from a more distant warehouse), partial shipment, and split shipment (ship that portion of the order now which can be shipped from the preferred warehouse, and rotate the remainder of the order to another warehouse).

Conclusion

As we enter the '80s, there will be even greater emphasis placed upon Demand Management. With the cost of money reaching record levels, methods of reducing inventories must be sought out and implemented.

A significant percentage of inventory can be saved from most companies while maintaining the same level of service. This can be done by a sound order entry system passing improved data to a forecasting system, by passing a more accurate forecast to the next planning system, and by effective sales management when inventory is not available—that is by improved Demand Management. □

An expanded version of this article appears in the series "Computers in Manufacturing Manufacturing Resource Planning," published by Auerbach, Pennsauken, N.J.

About The Author

James W. Muir is Vice President of American Software, and Atlanta-based computer software firm dealing in the full spectrum of Forecasting, Production Planning, Inventory Control, DRP, Purchasing, Manufacturing Management, and MRP.

Jim is a Past President of the NNJ Chapter of APICS, Past Vice President-Region II, and former member of the National Curriculum and Certification Council. He earned a B.S. from the University of Rochester and a Masters Degree in Management Science from Lehigh. He has been honored as a Fellow of APICS including a Fellow Rating in Forecasting. Jim is a frequent speaker at APICS and other professional society meetings.

REDUCING UNCERTAINTIES IN DEMAND

George E. Palmatier

G. E. Palmatier & Associates

INTRODUCTION

This paper presents concepts and techniques for reducing the uncertainties in customer demand within a manufacturing company, as part of the Demand Management process.

As manufacturers have improved their ability to respond to the marketplace with Just-In-Time (JIT), Total Quality Control (TQC), and Manufacturing Resource Planning (MRP II), they have begun to focus their efforts on improving the reliability of forecasts through reducing the uncertainty of customer demand.

Companies that have successfully reduced the uncertainty of demand have: 1) established close relationships with their customers via customer linking techniques, 2) improved their demand planning, and 3) utilize improved and/or innovative forecasting techniques. They have also developed a formal means for communicating demand information to Manufacturing, Sales and Marketing, and Upper Management, as part of their Sales and Operations Planning process. This demand information becomes integral to implementing sales and operations planning and developing forecasts for master scheduling, which leads to improved operations performance and better customer service.

This paper discusses the process of reducing uncertainty in demand through customer linking, improved demand planning, and improved and/or innovative forecasting techniques. The roles of Manufacturing, Sales and Marketing, and Upper Management in the process will be discussed. Guidelines for developing a formal means for reducing uncertainty in demand and improving forecast accuracy also will be presented.

WHAT IS DEMAND MANAGEMENT?

During the past decade, major efforts to improve manufacturing performance have been undertaken by many manufacturers. Efforts have been expended to implement MRP II, JIT/TQC, and automated design and manufacturing processes, which have resulted in a general upgrading of the manufacturing profession. These efforts have focused on the manufacturing, or supply, side of the business.

Surprisingly little effort has been expended to better understand and communicate the demand side of the business. To achieve long-term competitive success, a company cannot simply work the supply side of the issue.

When addressing the demand side of the business, it quickly becomes apparent that the issue is more than just improving the forecast. It encompasses the entire subject of demand management.[1]

The need for demand management was recognized by APICS in 1979 when it first published a definition of demand management:

---

[1]Richard C. Ling and George E. Palmatier, "Demand Management: Integrating Marketing, Manufacturing, and Management," 1987 International APICS Conference, St. Louis, Missouri.

The function of recognizing and managing all of the demands for products to ensure that the master scheduler is aware of them. It encompasses the activities of forecasting, order entry, order promising, branch warehouse requirements, interplant requirements, interplant orders, and service parts requirements.

Another way to describe demand management is to define it as the process of ensuring that the demands and capabilities of the company's manufacturing resources are in sync with each other. Demand Management has four key elements: to predict, communicate, influence, and manage demand.

Manufacturing, Sales and Marketing, and Upper Management participate in the demand management process. Because Sales and Marketing are closest to the customers, they can best determine anticipated demand and communicate that demand to Manufacturing. Manufacturing then develops its production plan in support of the anticipated demand information supplied by Sales and Marketing. Sales and Marketing's participation in demand management helps ensure that customers' needs are satisfied while simultaneously stabilizing demand for the company's manufacturing, engineering, and other support organizations, enabling them to improve their performance.

Demand management, in its fullest sense, is a communications process that involves or is directly related to:

[] Forecasting anticipated customer demand, evaluating internal and external factors that may affect customer demand, and planning the company's response to changes in these factors.

[] Formally analyzing the resources and capabilities of the company to meet anticipated demand.

[] Gaining consensus between Sales and Marketing, Manufacturing, and Upper Management upon a unified course of action to meet anticipated demand through Sales and Operations Planning.

[] Performing necessary Sales and Marketing functions through sales, pricing, and promotion so that anticipated demand results in real customer orders.

[] Actively managing orders as they are received from customers, including identifying abnormal demands.

[] Continuous monitoring to identify potential, out-of-balance situations between supply and demand.

[] Linking customer plans to factory plans and thereby minimizing the need for forecasting.

[] Developing contingency plans to determine the company's action if orders are received differently than forecast.

REDUCING THE UNCERTAINTY OF DEMAND

Demand management has one underlying purpose: To reduce the uncertainty of demand. As one CEO has observed, "We don't have any trouble forecasting. Our forecasts are always 100 percent accurate. The trouble is, our customers don't read our forecasts."

The more certain you are of demand, the

better your company can perform. When demand is uncertain, the manufacturing, engineering, and support organizations in a company are handicapped in their efforts to provide a quality product at a low cost, delivered to the customer on time as promised. Sometimes these organizations simply don't have enough time to truly concentrate on improving quality, cost, and delivery. The more uncertain the demand, the more of their time and energy is devoted to coping with constant, continuous changes caused by unplanned demand.

There must be a continual effort for reducing the uncertainty of demand. The following techniques can be utilized for achieving continual improvement in reducing the uncertainty of demand:

[] Demand stream analysis

[] Distribution Resource Planning (DRP)

[] Total Quality Control (TQC) tools

[] Methods for coping with the uncertainty of demand

[] Customer linking

[] Measurements and feedback

When these techniques are applied, you can improve your company's understanding of the marketplace, better communicate demand information and plans, and improve the execution of sales plans.

DEMAND STREAM ANALYSIS FOR IMPROVED PREDICTIONS

Often in the forecasting process, demand for product is treated as though it came from one homogeneous demand stream. In reality, however, most demands can be separated into independent demand streams. By separating demands into streams, you gain a better understanding of the business and an improved ability to forecast, plan, and manage by individual demand stream.

For example, a plastics manufacturer on the west coast was plagued by inaccurate forecasts. The company's general manager finally requested that the forecasting errors be analyzed. The analysis determined that the software functioned properly, the demand data input into the forecasting program was correct (it considered the timing difference between shipments, bookings, and demand), and the forecaster was aggressively working to improve the forecast. The root cause of the forecasting inaccuracies was that the company did not understand the various demand streams that made up its aggregate demand.

Erratic demand was traced to three product lines and to two large volume customers. These customers routinely increased or decreased their orders with the company on short notice. Also, one of the market segments the company served was experiencing a downturn in business. The company had not analyzed markets by segment in developing sales plans and forecasts. Finally, a new product was more popular than anticipated, and customers were ordering less of an older version of the product and more of the new one. All of these issues were contributing to inaccurate forecasts.

By utilizing a more structured approach for analyzing demand, the types of problems cited in the example above can be avoided. A structured approach to analyzing demand streams involves the following steps:
1. Analysis of aggregate demand history: View the history (in **aggregate**) in graphic format to determine overall trends and seasonality of demand.

2. Segmentation of demand history into demand streams: The purpose of this analysis is to determine the source of demand by individual market, territory, customer, and product.

3. Analysis of segmented demand streams over the same time period: This analysis enables you to identify seasonality and trends by individual demand streams.

DISTRIBUTION RESOURCE PLANNING

Companies with branch warehouses or large distributors can gain better visibility of demand through the use of Distribution Resource Planning (DRP). DRP has proven to be an excellent tool for managing distribution inventories and all its associated resources. It is a particularly valuable tool for companies that ship many products to many warehouses and distributors, and is applicable for any company with distributed inventories.

For our purposes, DRP provides a communication link between warehouses and the factory. It is used by the demand planner, the distribution organization, and the master scheduler. It ensures that distribution demand is included in the demand planning process and provides forward visibility of time phased demand for planning purposes.

TOTAL QUALITY CONTROL TOOLS

Total Quality Control (TQC) techniques can be used to help reduce the uncertainty of demand.[2] TQC is a systematic approach for solving problems. One of the most useful TQC tools for analyzing and solving problems is Pareto's law. Also known as the "80/20 rule," Pareto's Law can be useful for isolating the root cause of problems. First, the potential causes of a problem are identified and the frequency of their occurrences is measured. The causes that contribute most to the problem are further analyzed by applying the same Pareto approach, and this is continued as many times as is needed until the root cause of the problem is determined.

The following example will show how Pareto analysis can be used to reduce the uncertainty of demand. Your company's sales organization has determined there is a customer service problem since actual customer service has fallen below company objectives. At the first level of Pareto analysis, you determine the possible causes of the problem by using another TQC tool, the Ishikawa or "fishbone" diagram (see Figure 1). Next, you begin to make measurements to gather facts about each possible cause identified in the fishbone analysis. As you monitor, measure, and log the causes of the customer service problem, you determine the largest single contributor to the problem to be forecast errors.

To determine the cause of these forecast errors, you follow the same procedure of using the fishbone diagram and measurements. This analysis reveals that the single largest forecast error occurs in one product line. To analyze the cause of forecasting errors in this product line, you again use the fishbone analysis and measurements. At this level of analysis, you determine the error occurs mostly in one sales territory, and then one

---

[2]William Sandras and Roger Brooks, "Just-In-Time and Total Quality Control," Seminar Course Book, The Oliver Wight Companies.

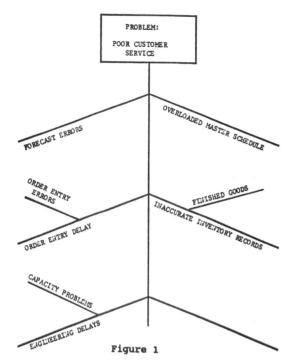

Figure 1

An Ishikawa, or "Fishbone," diagram. The "ribs" list possible causes of the problem.

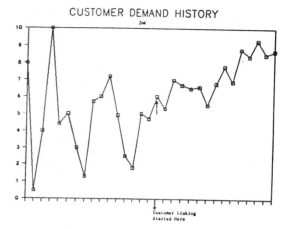

Figure 2

Reductions in fluctuations and uncertainty result after customer linking. (Courtesy The 3M Company.)

---

salesperson, and then one customer. In reviewing the situation with this customer, you learn this is a large volume customer who frequently orders at the last moment with little advance warning. Further, with sales pursuing the issue, you learn this customer is willing to participate in a customer linking program to share its planned purchases with you, which, if implemented, will reduce the problem.

The principle point of this example is to suggest that a wealth of simple, easy-to-implement, TQC "tools" exist to identify and correct the root cause of demand management problems.

CUSTOMER LINKING

As more companies implement MRP II/JIT/TQC, there has been a movement toward direct linking between customers and manufacturers. Those companies who link successfully get so close to their customers that their customers' plans become part of their plans. In essence, with customer linking, the purchaser shares his schedules and forecasts with his supplier.[3]

Some of the benefits to the purchaser include: 1) lower inventories, 2) lower prices through volume purchasing, 3) shorter lead times, 4) less paper work, and 5) a more reliable and committed supplier.

Benefits to the supplier include: 1) the booking of all, or most, of the customer's available business, 2) visibility of the customers' schedules and forecasts, enabling Manufacturing and Purchasing to plan and schedule more productively (see Figure 2), 3) less direct selling time, and 4) less paper work.

---

[3]Steven N. Burns, "Customer Networking: How to Manage Your Customer's Demand," 1987 APICS International Conference, St. Louis,

COPING WITH THE UNCERTAINTY OF DEMAND

After all reasonable efforts have been made to develop and improve demand plans, there will still be inaccuracies in the timing or quantity of demand. So what do you do when confronted with these inaccuracies, despite efforts to reduce the uncertainty of demand?

The objective of your efforts is to develop demand plans and forecasts that are reliable enough to operate the business effectively and provide the level of service your customers expect. With this objective in mind, consider the following issues for coping with the uncertainty of demand:

1. Lead Times: Perhaps the single most effective way to cope with uncertainty of demand is to reduce, or collapse, all the lead times in the company. If the company can quickly respond to changes in demand, then forecasts of anticipated demand can be less accurate, and the company can still maintain the same level of customer service.

2. Safety Stock: Although inventory in itself is wasteful, it is sometimes necessary to maintain customer service objectives. If your demand is unpredictable and the time required to respond to changes in demand is longer than customer requested lead times, inventory can be used to service the customer. When inventory is being used to service the customer, sales and marketing should be responsible for recommending inventory levels. Even when a safety stock strategy is employed, inventory must be kept at levels that are as low as practical.

3. Safety Capacity: For some companies, capacity rather than materials is the primary constraint in meeting demand. These companies use safety capacity as a means of coping with the uncertainty of demand. By allowing some flexibility in their master production schedules, they leave some capacity available to ensure the company provides adequate customer service. As with safety stock, however, safety capacity costs money and presumes that you have extra labor or machinery for various periods of time.

4. Backlog: If the timing of your demand is unpredictable, an effective means of

coping with this uncertainty is to carefully manage the company's backlog of orders. Some companies promise deliveries before the date the customer actually needs the product. When this situation occurs, the company is actually giving away delivery times (material and capacity) that could be used for other customers, who may need the product sooner. Active management of the backlog can assist in coping with the unpredictability of the timing for demand.

5. **Reschedule Another Customer's Order**: When all avenues have been exhausted to meet a customer's requested delivery date, and material or capacity is unavailable because it has been promised to other customers, you still have one more alternative for meeting that customer's needs: Promise the order and move another customer's order. Rescheduling can often be accomplished without sacrificing customer service. Most company backlogs have customer orders scheduled to ship before the customer really needs the products, or there are orders in the backlog where the customers do not need the entire shipments. By managing the backlog and communicating with customers, customer delivery dates may be renegotiated so that all customers are satisfied with your company's performance.

When rescheduling to cope with the uncertainty of demand, the following rule must be followed: Entering an order with a fully committed master production schedule requires that another order or orders be rescheduled out. If this rescheduling is not done, manufacturing quickly has an invalid master production schedule, and the company's priority system disintegrates. That is, the dates in the system become invalid.

6. **Standardize Products or Options**: Often companies have an opportunity to reduce the uncertainties in the mix of products or options through standardization. If the number of products or options can be reduced without significant effect on demand, then forecast accuracy should improve. Not only is this situation statistically improved, but fewer items to forecast require less time and resources.

CUSTOMER SERVICE MEASUREMENTS AND FEEDBACK

To continuously improve, measurements and feedback are required. When you talk about measurements, however, people often become apprehensive, and rightfully so. For in many companies, measurements are used primarily to criticize individual performance rather than improve it.

The purpose of measurements is to improve performance by identifying problem areas that are preventing the company from achieving greater success. The purpose of measurements is not to criticize individual performance. The expected response after measurements are made is to define problem areas, determine the cause(s) of the problems, identify solutions to the problems, and implement the recommended solutions.

Three key measurements are generally made to determine the effectiveness of demand management efforts:

1) **Customer Service Measurements**: These measurements should be structured measurements so they coincide with your customers' expectations. This requires that you determine what your customers view as important. Because customer expectations change, you must also periodically review and update your measurements to reflect changes in the marketplace.

The most important reason for making customer service measurements is to determine how customers are evaluating your performance. Consequently, don't fall into the trap of measuring yourself based upon your own biased beliefs.

2) **Measurement of Sales Performance to Plan**: Commitment to selling the plan is one of the keys to reducing the uncertainty of demand. By measuring how the sales force has performed in meeting demand, you can identify problem areas that are inhibiting the achievement of the plan. Performance to the plan should be measured by product family and should be reviewed at the monthly Sales and Operations Planning meeting. Feedback to the sales organization on how individual sales people are performing to plan is key for continuous improvement.

3) **Measurement of Forecast Accuracy**: Measurement of forecasting accuracy should be used to determine the effectiveness of that process. In determining the effectiveness of the forecasting process, the following are some key questions that should be asked:

a. Does the forecasting process lead to a commitment to manufacture and sell to the plan?

b. Does it lead to an improved understanding of the customers and the marketplace?

c. Does it result in improved communications between all departments in the company that, in turn, enhances the performance of each department?

Answers to these questions should be affirmative, for these are the real measurements of forecasting performance.

Some companies establish forecasting accuracy objectives of 95 percent in the aggregate and 85 percent in the mix or detail. While these are certainly good objectives, it is important to remember there are many variables for determining how the measurements are made, which in turn will affect the actual performance percentage. One of these variables is the timing of the measurements, specifically when should the forecast be frozen for measurement purposes? Since the forecast is updated continuously, which forecast should be used as the reference for accuracy measurements?

Forecast measurements are most effective when linked with the time fences for products. The forecast should be frozen for measurement purposes at each agreed upon time fence, which means saving the forecast as it passes the time fence, then later comparing actual demand to the original forecast.

Since time fences represent points at which manufacturing's flexibility to respond to change are decreased, it is at these points where manufacturing has sufficient time to effectively respond to changes in the forecast. It is not recommended, however, that you freeze the forecast for communications purposes. If you know demand is changing inside a time fence, you have an obligation to communicate that situation to the company by changing the forecast.

CONCLUSION

This paper has discussed how Demand Management requires continuous improvement efforts in reducing the uncertainty of demand. These efforts center on predicting, communicating, influencing, and managing demand—and measuring your performance in managing demand. And while the uncertainty of demand can never be completely eliminated, there are means for coping with the

uncertainty so that your company can still
meet your customers' expectations.

BIOGRAPHY

George E. Palmatier, President, G.E.
Palmatier & Associates, provides consulting
services to manufacturing companies implementing
MRP II, JIT, and TQC programs. He has more than
17 years' experience in sales, marketing, and
management for manufacturing companies.
He has co-authored several articles and
papers. He is the co-author of a book, The
Marketing Edge: The New Leadership Role of Sales
and Marketing in Manufacturing.
Mr. Palmatier is a member of the Oliver
Wight Education Associates and the American
Production and Inventory Control Society. He
teaches the Top Management class and Marketing
and Sales class for The Oliver Wight Companies.

Reprinted from the APICS *1972 Conference Proceedings.*

GETTING THE MOST FROM FORECASTS

George W. Plossl

In all of human history, forecasting, fortune telling, predicting or whatever it's been called has been of tremendous interest. Mankind always has yearned for more knowledge of the future. In the business world this yearning is greatly intensified because of the businessman's dependence on forecasts for planning and control. The heavy penalties of being wrong — giving customers poor service, having too much money tied up in inventory and incurring high costs of recovering from crises — bring the need for better forecasts clearly into focus for businessmen, particularly for production and inventory control practitioners.

Many varied forecasting techniques have been proposed to satisfy these yearnings and needs. The crystal ball is most commonly associated with making forecasts. Many of us have used a modern variation of this, the desk top "Eight Ball" with little floats that come to the glass bottom surface to give short answers to specific questions. (In my own experience these were often better than information I got from more rational approaches.) The seers of old studied chicken entrails, frog brains and other natural phenomena in their attempts to predict the future. We moderns lean heavily on highly sophisticated mathematical techniques and masses of data processed in high-speed computers with about as much success.

The good forecasts in our experience seem to be associated with specific individuals. I have wondered often, as I am sure you have, whether this was a natural gift or an acquired skill. Some colleges seem to think now that it is teachable. In an article in the *Wall Street Journal* on April 18, 1972, entitled "Crystal Balling, 101: Colleges Now Offer Courses on the Future," a new college course called "Futuristics" is discussed. The article says, "Futuristics, or the study of the future, is becoming a big concern of students and teachers across the land." One young student is quoted as saying, "You've got to learn about the future, or you'll be left behind. Futuristics is the way to do it." His opinion is not universal, however. A Stanford economist is quoted as saying, "Sometimes I think they study the future because they can't face the problems of the present." Doesn't this apply also to production control practitioners who always are using poor forecasts as excuses for poor performance? Another educator is quoted as saying, "Futuristics is a lot of bull" and I am sure he was thinking of a two syllable word we all like to use for real emphasis.

Well, skilled individual or amateur, simple technique or sophisticated, the results are always the same. The forecast is wrong and most of us continue to be surprised. My associate, Ernie Theisen, puts us in perspective by looking at the syllables of the word "forecast." "Fore," he says, "is a golf term meaning look out, and cast is a fishing term meaning throw out." I have long felt that forecasting is like sex — we have to have it, can't get along without it; everybody is doing it, one way or another and no one is sure he's doing it the best way!

Forecasting is today one of our major problems in the field of manufacturing control. This field has progressed to the stage where we now know about all the necessary techniques, the tools of the trade. Dr. Joseph A. Orlicky, in his keynote address at the 1972 APICS International Conference in Toronto said, "We have achieved closure." He meant that our minds now can encompass all of the elements of the control system, see how they relate and understand how they work together. It is time we devoted much *more emphasis to finding better ways to make the techniques work rather than seeking better techniques*. In the past, practically all of the emphasis in the literature, in conferences, in formal education and among practitioners in our field has been on making better (meaning more accurate) forecasts. I am much more concerned about making better use of the poor forecasts it appears we will have to live with.

In reviewing my experience over the years with many companies, I have seen six major reasons (Figure 1) why forecasts fail to produce more useful results:

1. **Individual effort** — No individual or small group within a single department and no statistical technique can possibly know enough about all the factors affecting the future to be able to develop an adequate forecast. Such a person or

WHY FORECASTS FAIL
1. INDIVIDUAL EFFORT
2. UNREALISTIC EXPECTATIONS
3. SECOND GUESSING
4. CONFLICTING OBJECTIVES
5. FORECASTING WRONG THINGS
6. NO TIMELY TRACKING

FIGURE 1.

group can, of course, analyze historical data and use some techniques to draw some conclusions about possible future trends, cycles and random variations. *Evaluating how the future will differ from the past, however, is another question*. Internal company activities such as new product designs, product improvements, better customer service and marketing promotions; and external factors like competitors' activities, changing customer preferences, technological developments and the state of the national economy require inputs from many, both within and outside the company. *More important, however, is the need for the forecast users to understand fully the thinking behind the forecast*. To use a forecast intelligently you need more than the numbers written on a sheet of paper. You need to know as much as possible about the factors that were evaluated in arriving at the numbers. Such understanding is too limited when the forecast is an individual effort. Effective forecasting must be a group effort.

2. **Unrealistic expectations** — Hope springs eternal in the human breast for the perfect forecast. This hope always seems to be associated, however, with the idea that someone else will have to make it. *Failure to realize perfection results in rejection of the forecast but not the hope.* I've wondered often what production controllers would use for their number one excuse if they got a really good forecast.

3. **Second guessing** — Faced with the reality of bad forecasts most of us exercise the privilege of making our own guesses. We know why the other fellow's figures were wrong as surely as those market analysts who tell us today why yesterday's stock market went up or down. Unfortunately, we are as able to predict tomorrow's figures accurately as those same market analysts are to tell us what will happen to stock prices tomorrow. In addition second-guessers rarely communicate their knowledge and beliefs so that those responsible for the official forecasts can use them to improve the forecast. *As a result, the whole system degenerates.*

4. **Conflicting objectives** — The major groups within a company's organization view forecasts differently. Sales wants an optimistic figure, a carrot to be held out in front of salesmen to get them to exert themselves to the maximum to achieve top quotas. Top management and financial people, of course, never want to overstate profits. The manufacturing group tries to strike some happy medium between the optimism of sales and the conservatism of finance in estimating what they will be called on to produce. Each of these is a valid objective. Unfortunately in too many cases the various forecasts are inconsistent, with significant differences in product mix as well as total figures. *The result is that the battle for company survival is fought out with different strategies being used by the major forces.* As if competition wasn't enough of a problem!

5. **Forecasting the wrong things** — Figure 2 shows four end products (or finished products) whose sales to customers are forecast at the weekly rates shown on line "D" — demand. Their inventories are replenished in the lot quantities indicated on line "P" — production. Making finished products in lots greater than one week's supply is very common, of course, in some cases to reduce the cost of changing over the lines and in others because some of each product cannot be made every week. *Demand for such products must be forecast;* there is no other way to develop estimates of future requirements. For subassemblies of these so-called independent demand products, however, there is no need to forecast the demand. It can be calculated using the bills of material showing which subassemblies and component parts make up each end product and the lot sizes in which the end products, subassemblies and parts will be produced. *Any company making assembled products, no matter whether screwed, glued, sewed, packaged, welded or chemically joined, can reduce dramatically the number of forecasts it needs by making them only for the end products and calculating requirements for all components of these assemblies.*

END PRODUCTS

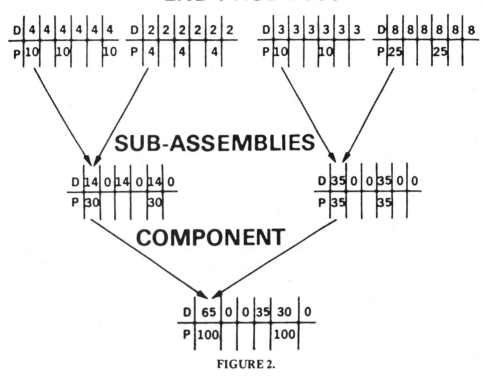

FIGURE 2.

Preoccupation with individual finished products blinds some companies to the right things to forecast. A forging manufacturer saw no way to make a forecast of the products ordered by their customers. Although they got some repeat orders, the bulk of their output was custom-made to suit the customers' drawings. They badly needed information on future requirements, however, to plan capacity, to be sure they had enough people running enough forging hammers on enough shifts. I asked them what they would do with the information if I had a magic slate which would show them specifically all the forgings their customers would order. Obviously they would estimate the standard hours of work on the various sizes of hammers required to produce the specific forgings. *What they really needed, of course, was a forecast of this standard hour work content of their customer's orders and not of the individual piece parts.* Historical data updated by a simple averaging technique furnished them with some very useful capacity requirements planning information. Furthermore they were able to "manage" this forecast. When they saw the load on some sizes of hammers falling off, they had their salesmen contact customers who customarily bought forgings produced on these hammer sizes, offering them immediate delivery or better prices to place orders now.

Many companies' products give their customers a wide variety of options in selecting features, accessories and alternatives in various combinations.

LEVEL

0

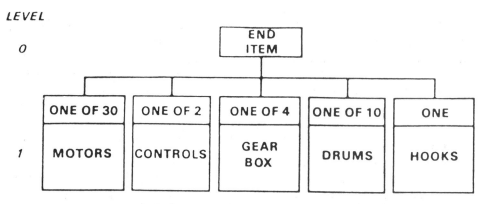

FIGURE 3. Forecasting Options

The outstanding example is the automobile where literally billions of different cars could result from the combinations of options customers might choose. Figure 3 illustrates a fairly simple product, an electric hoist, manufactured in a family of sizes. Each hoist in the family consists of a motor, gear box, drum assembly, set of controls and a hook. The customer now has the number of options indicated on each of these features and the engineering department is working hard to give them more options on the hook. A maximum of 2400 combinations of options is now available to customers; they could order that many different hoists. As soon as Engineering designs another hook assembly this will double to 4800. It is even more evident that *no technique, however sophisticated, and no individual, however much of a genius, could forecast how many of each of the possible combinations customers will order and even come reasonably close* — particularly when total sales of the family are only a few hundred a month. Insisting that a marketing department produce detailed forecasts of finished products like these is as likely to produce useful results as lighting matches in the open on a windy night. I've seen a marketing department go from antagonism to enthusiasm, however, when asked to forecast a total for the family and a percentage of this total for each option instead of individual hoists. Forecasting the right things can produce dramatically better results.

6. **No timely tracking** — Many of those who have to work with forecasts produced by others feel like victims of these numbers. This is completely unnecessary. No one needs to be a victim of not knowing how wrong a forecast is likely to be. Anyone with access to actual sales data can compare these to forecasts and see how wrong they have been in the past. Surprisingly enough, using past deviations as a forecast of future error turns out to be a lot more accurate than using past demand as a forecast of future requirements. And this error holds the key to better use of bad forecasts. *There are two key words in tracking forecast errors* — *do it REGULARLY and do it OFTEN.*

Forecasts have five basic characteristics, often called principles, shown in

Figure 4. A good understanding of these indicates how to make more effective use of forecasts:

```
              FORECASTS
1. ARE ALWAYS WRONG
2. SHOULD BE TWO NUMBERS
3. ARE MORE ACCURATE FOR FAMILIES
4. ARE LESS ACCURATE FAR OUT
5. ARE NO SUBSTITUTE FOR
   CALCULATED DEMAND
```

FIGURE 4. Principles

1. **Forecasts are always wrong** — They always have been and they always will be. Many companies have reached the point of diminishing returns in trying to make their forecasts more accurate. It's time they devoted scarce resources of time and talent to learning how to live with inevitable errors.

2. **Forecasts should be two numbers** — Since they're going to be wrong, we should have estimates of how wrong they are likely to be. The numbers can be expressed as a base forecast plus or minus a percentage error, or minimum and maximum figures establishing a range. A few companies are even using three numbers, a pessimistic, expected and optimistic figure and the expected figure is not always midway between the optimistic and pessimistic. Such approaches are extremely useful — some effort might be expended usefully in making them more accurate; in addition, they are the real key to making effective decisions when putting the forecast to work.

3. **Forecasts are more accurate for families** — Very few companies have errors of more than five percent in their forecasts of total demand for all products, their largest family. Individual product forecasts, we all know, vary from minus 100 percent to plus 300 percent or more. Families of similar products or products sold in similar markets should be forecast as an entity rather than as the sum of their individual members. Making forecasts individually for each product and adding the individual forecasts together will never be as good as forecasting the family as if it were one item and calculating each product's share of this total based on a forecast percentage. When planning manpower, machinery and equipment capacity, raw material requirements, inventory budgets or even a vendor's capacity requirements, it is obvious that families of products are involved. The basic relationships among inventory, production capacity and shipments are shown in Figure 5. The upper equation covers make-to-stock. It simply says that present inventories will be increased by production and reduced by shipments, and future inventories will depend upon the balance between shipments and production. This relationship is used to plan capacity. Even more important it indicates the three vital tools needed to control manufacturing operations. Production (input) consists of both purchased materials and productive labor. Consequently a time-phased plan should be made for both of these to indicate the *rate at which materials should be procured* and the *rate at which direct labor will be added* to meet the forecast cus-

$$\left(\begin{array}{c}\text{INVENTORY}\\\text{NOW}\end{array}\right) + \left(\begin{array}{c}\text{PRODUCTION}\\\overline{}\\\text{PURCH. MAT'L.}\\\text{PROD. LABOR}\end{array}\right) - \left(\text{SHIPMENTS}\right) = \left(\begin{array}{c}\text{INVENTORY}\\\text{GOAL}\end{array}\right)$$

$$\left(\begin{array}{c}\text{BACKLOG}\\\text{NOW}\end{array}\right) + \left(\begin{array}{c}\text{NEW}\\\text{ORDERS}\end{array}\right) - \left(\begin{array}{c}\text{PRODUCTION}\\\overline{}\\\text{PURCH. MAT'L.}\\\text{PROD. LABOR}\end{array}\right) = \left(\begin{array}{c}\text{BACKLOG}\\\text{GOAL}\end{array}\right)$$

FIGURE 5. Basic Relationships

tomer demand and to bring total inventories to the desired level. These plans then should serve as budgets or control reports. Actual rates of procurement of materials can be anticipated through a purchase commitment report and actual direct labor input to inventory can be projected from manload data. The shipment forecast is the independent variable. Actual shipments (output) against plan must be tracked regularly and the input rates of purchased materials and productive labor must be adjusted as shipments vary from forecast if inventory budgets are to be met. The lower equation in Figure 5 covers make-to-order, looking at the order backlog instead of the inventory of finished products. Here the input that will increase present backlogs will come from new orders; the output will be shipments but when making to order these will equal production, again made up of purchased material and productive labor. The prime variable here is the rate new orders are received. This should be tracked regularly to develop the earliest clues to necessary changes in production. These equations should be set up for major families of products and control reports developed with frequent tracking of actual against plan shown for all three variables. Companies that have such control reports meet their inventory budgets and have less drastic swings in production rates.

4. Forecasts are less accurate far out — This is as obvious as the fact that forecasts always will be wrong yet its implications are almost completely ignored. The message should be clear, "Don't commit materials and labor to a specific product until the last possible moment." This really means "Keep the lead time short." Some few companies have good material requirements planning systems which permit them to update priorities on individual work orders. They also have good control of work in the plant and schedules are generally met. This has tempted some to conclude that, under such conditions it is no longer important to keep down the level of work in process (which determines the *average actual lead time*). They argue, "We can always get the jobs we really want through the plant when we need them by exercising the pressure of the priority system." While these people have recognized clearly that adequate capacity is necessary to make this continue to work in the long run, unfortunately they have overlooked this fourth

characteristic of forecasts. The farther out we have to look, as determined by our average lead times, the less we are likely to know what we really need. This is vital if we are to give priority systems the right information. Lead time should be kept to a minimum. The best approach is to use longer range forecasts to GET READY — to be sure to have the proper manload and machine capacity and enough raw materials. Then GET SET — reviewing short range forecasts before firming up specific orders to be released. GO — only at the last minute when you have the best available information on what you really need, using orders in-house plus short-range forecasts.

5. **Forecasts are no substitute for calculated demand.** — I mentioned this earlier when I discussed failures due to forecasting the wrong things. Another way to express this would be, "Never forecast when you can calculate requirements." Since living with forecasts is always pure and unadulterated trouble, live with as few as you can. Explode the few forecasts you must make through bills of material and calculate instead of forecasting demand for many individual components. Significant benefits also can be obtained by the family approach to forecasting which I discussed in connection with the third forecast characteristic. The controls for the hoist in Figure 3 illustrate this point. The two different types of controls could be forecast individually but the total of the two forecasts never would be as good as the forecast for the family of hoists. A much better approach is to forecast what percentage of customers ordering this family of hoists will want the two different types of controls. These percentages will be averages and obviously should equal 100 percent. Instead of these average percentages, however, maximum figures could be used as *forecasts* for the *unique* components of each of the two types of controls. Planning for the components common to *both types* would, of course, be based on the average forecast. This would provide maximum flexibility in meeting customer demands with minimum inventories. Calculating requirements from the bills of material parent/component relationships or from family relationships keeps components in sets and production in balance. It's a way to be wrong consistently, recognizing that you will be consistently wrong.

Forecasting is remarkably like auto safety. It's a serious problem to the people involved — the drivers and pedestrians in the case of automobiles and the sales and inventory control people with forecasts. In both fields we have a few experts whose names are familiar. These men are mounting a massive assault on 5 percent of the problem. We want and need better, safer automobiles and better, more accurate forecasts. Unfortunately, 95 percent of the disasters result from improper use of both. I'm not saying we need less emphasis on safer cars and better forecasts — I am saying we need a lot more emphasis on intelligent use of both.

Defensive driving is based on the principle of expecting the worst and getting ready to react to it. This is exactly what we need to do to get better use of forecasts also. We need more and better early warning systems. Our

FORECAST SHIPMENTS = $ 24 MILLION

T.O. = 2.4   INVENTORY NOW = $ 10 MILLION

T.O. = 3.0   INVENTORY GOAL = $ 8 MILLION

TARGET IS 10 MONTHS

SHIPMENTS = $ 20 MIL   PRODUCTION = $ 18 MIL

FORECAST ERROR = 5 % = $ 1.2 MIL

MONTHS TO GOAL	CHANGE IN PRODUCTION	
	$	%
10	120 M	7
8	150 M	8 1/2
6	200 M	11
3	400 M	22

FIGURE 6.

DEW line should be **DON'T ENJOY WAITING** until your plan is obviously faulty. Expect it to go wrong, make plans now what you will do about it when it does develop significant errors and take action when you are convinced the original forecast is no longer valid.

The penalty for waiting too long can be serious. The necessary corrective action, particularly in adjusting capacity, gets rapidly worse as we delay making a decision. Figure 6 illustrates this point. The forecast of annual shipments is $24,000,000 (at cost). Present turnover rate is 2.4 and inventories total $10,000,000. To increase turnover to the desired level of 3.0 will require an $8,000,000 inventory, and production will have to be $2,000,000 less than forecast shipments over the 10 months targeted to make the change. A forecast error of 5 percent (1.2 million dollars) would not be unexpected in shipments. If the inventory target is to be achieved, production and shipments must be kept in balance. Notice how the required change in production to meet the inventory goal increases dramatically as the time available to make the change is reduced. Failure to detect errors in shipments forecasts early in the game is one of the major causes of failure to meet sales goals and inventory targets, in spite of sharp changes in production.

I've already made the point that making and using forecasting should be a group effort. Regular reviews of actual versus forecast by a group of people in the know about what's happening and about the effect this will have upon operations can be far more productive of good results than more sophisticated forecasting techniques. At one of our recent workshops a West Coast manufacturer of electronic equipment provided a classic illustration of this. Four years earlier they had developed their own weighted-average forecasting technique, which was more complex than exponential smoothing, and had high hopes for this. In the interim I had not heard how effective it was. When I asked at the workshop how it was working, my friend from the company said they no longer bothered with it. They had instituted a series of regular monthly meetings of a key group of marketing, manufacturing control and management people to develop the master schedule when they installed MRP about two years ago. The extra work of using the technique — cleaning up the input data and massaging the calculations to develop and revise forecasts — just wasn't worth the effort compared to the forecasts developed by this small and knowledgeable group. At the same workshop, a Midwest bearing manufacturer also commented that the best thing they had done when installing their program to improve control of manufacturing operations was to have regular forecast review meetings by a small management group. Neither making nor using forecasts can be an individual effort if it is to be effective.

Figure 7 illustrates two tracking signals that can give early warning that forecasts are not performing properly. The first is a simple comparison between the last period's actual sales and long-term average, say six months or a year. This

$$T.S. = \frac{\text{LAST PERIOD ACTUAL}}{\text{LONG TERM AVERAGE}}$$

$$T.S. = \frac{\text{RUNNING SUM ERRORS}}{\text{AVERAGE ERROR}}$$

FIGURE 7. Tracking Signals

is the simplest and crudest approach possible but like many crude tools it can be remarkably effective in the hands of an experienced person. The McGill Bearing Company in Valparaiso, Indiana, uses manually prepared

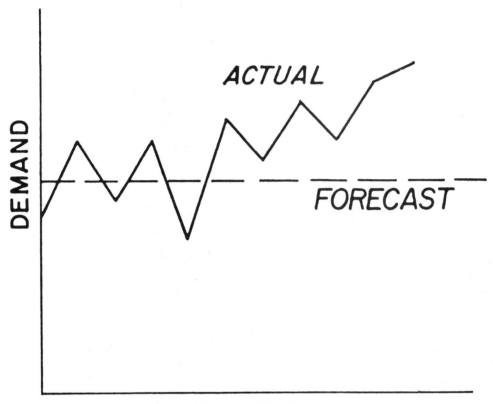

FIGURE 8.

charts similar to Figure 8 for "A" items — their highest selling bearings. They chart actual sales by month compared to forecast. At very little expense these charts provide useful early warnings that major products are not performing the way they expected.

The other tracking signal in Figure 7 develops an index that can be used effectively for many items. For a large number of products a computer will be required to handle the data with this tracking signal. It develops a running sum of the forecast errors, adding the deviations when actual sales are above forecast and subtracting them when they are below, and divides this running sum by the average forecast error. If the forecast is performing properly, plus errors and minus errors will tend to cancel each other out and the tracking signal will stay small. A forecast consistently low or high will develop a steadily increasing running sum; this will cause the tracking signal to grow steadily. Some specific value of the tracking signal (four or five, for example) can be selected so that the system calls attention by exception to those forecasts that are not performing well. Dividing the running sum of the errors by the average error prevents a highly variable demand (which would produce large error sums) from causing false alarms when the

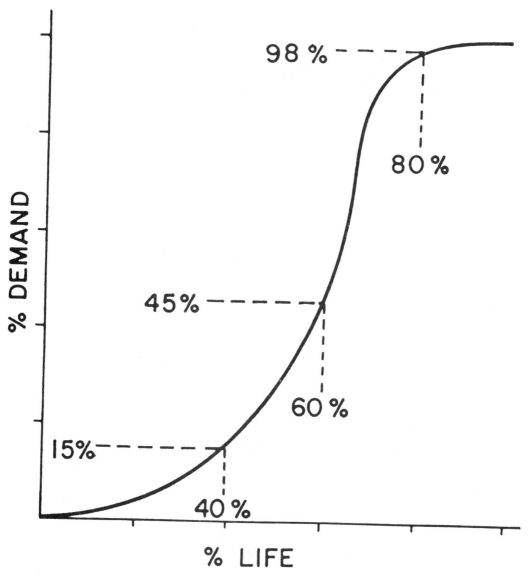

FIGURE 9. Life Curves

forecast is accurately predicting the average.

Probably the most difficult forecasting problems are style items, special promotions or specific marketing programs, all of which have limited life and produce dramatic humps in the demand curve. The Franklin Mint in Franklin Center, Pennsylvania, lives with this problem as a way of life. They are constantly developing new programs — new sets of coins, ingots, precious metal plates, etc. — which they hope will appeal to their customers, the collectors of such items. Practically all of their programs are limited editions with total production limited to those subscribing in the introductory period. Estimating accurately this number of subscribers and the total product they will order is an almost impossible task. By studying previous promotions, however, the Franklin Mint has developed life curves similar to that in Figure 9. The life is the duration of the introductory offer and they have found a consistent percentage of demand is received at each point in the life cycle as illustrated by the curve. Prior to the introductory date they make an attempt to forecast the total demand for each program but they know this will be only a rough approximation. By tracking the incoming demand daily, however, they are able to adjust their estimates of the total program demand *in time to make necessary changes in production.* This obviously requires accurate, sensitive measurement of incoming orders and a production control system and plant geared to short lead times and last-minute changes. In their operation it works remarkably well.

Stock status records also can provide signals to indicate that changes have occurred in demand rates. Using inventory transactions to measure the average rate of usage can provide a quick alert that unplanned transactions have increased significantly. This provides a good supplement to tracking forecasts and production rates; these control only planned transactions. Indicating the time period of supply (how many weeks or months of requirements are covered by remaining stock) or the date of the last transaction also can provide timely information that demand is falling off and some action is necessary. The mark of the professional is that he puts his efforts into developing and using such tools instead of moaning about lousy forecasts.

The real key to using forecasts effectively is to *measure the error.* Errors can be put to work for you instead of working against you. Statistical calculations of safety stocks have been around since 1934 but the great majority of companies still use rules of thumb, basing the amount to be carried on weeks of supply or the ABC distribution. Figure 10 shows the benefits which can result from putting safety stock where it is really needed. For the

ITEM	AVG. WEEKLY DEMAND	REORDER QUANTITY	RULE OF THUMB		STATISTICS	
			1-WEEK S.S.	S.O. PER YR.	CALC. S.S.	S.O. PER YR.
P	500	500	500	2	460	2
Y	500	500	500	9	965	2
Z	500	6500	500	0	0	2
			1500	11	1425	6

FIGURE 10. Safety Stocks, Rule of Thumb vs. Statistics

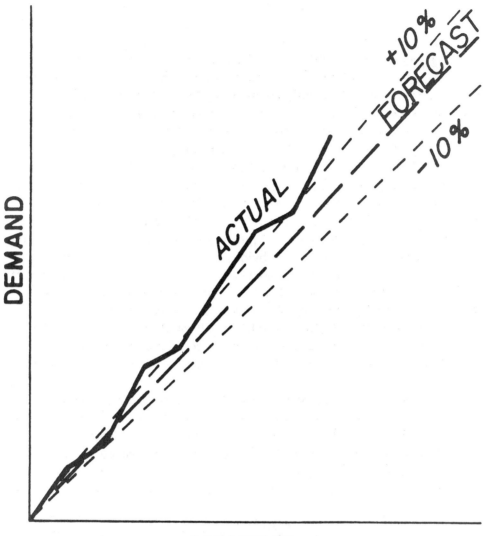

FIGURE 11.

three items total service could be improved dramatically using less inventory if a statistical analysis of the demand error were made. In this example safety stocks were calculated to give equal service on all three items. I've seen companies reduce safety stocks up to 50 percent while holding the same levels of customer service. Others have improved service dramatically with the same amount of inventory. Putting the forecast error to work for you pays dividends.

A more difficult problem is controlling capacity. Only a few companies can enjoy the luxury of safety stock in the form of excess capacity. Following the lead provided by quality control people, however, many companies could benefit from developing and using control charts similar to Figure 11.

Covering a family of products, this shows cumulative forecast totals and a range of errors (plus or minus 10%) from this forecast. As actual total family demand is plotted on the curve, it becomes quite obvious when it is necessary to change capacity. I already have stressed the importance of not waiting too long in making this decision.

Knowing how wrong a forecast is likely to be permits you to hedge your bets in many phases of materials and production planning and control. In planning for production of a new item, which obviously will have wide range of forecast error, consider these approaches. The tooling should be developed for the upper or lower limits, rarely for the expected average. Where the expense of duplicate or high-productivity tooling is high and the lead time to obtain it is long, you obviously must provide for the higher production requirements or risk hamstringing the program. But where you can get additional tooling quickly and inexpensively, why tool up for an optimistic figure? If it develops you always can recover quickly and take advantage of possible economies when the volume to justify the more expensive tooling is real, not forecast. In ordering component parts, if the penalties from excess inventory or obsolescence losses is likely to be high, aim for the low end of the forecast and get ready to recover if the program really takes off. On the other hand, for many inexpensive components such as bolts, nuts, labels and packaging materials, why risk holding up a fast-growing program by ordering these close to the vest? If you've ever been responsible for slowing up a good product's sales rate because you ran out of labels, you'll know exactly what I mean.

In summary, let's return to the five characteristics of forecasts:

FORECASTS

Are Always Wrong . . *Don't Be Surprised — Be Flexible*
Should Be Two Numbers . . *Get Them — Use Them And Not Excuses*
Are More Accurate For Families . . *Group Items That Are Alike*
Are Less Accurate Far Out . . *Keep Lead Times Short*
Are No Substitute For Calculated Demand . . *Forecast Assemblies But Calculate Components*

Forecasts must and will be made. We certainly need more attention to making them more accurate. We must accept the facts of life, however, and not expect too much from techniques — the so-called forecast models. Remember the definition of model — a small imitation of the real thing. It's time we stopped using poor forecasts as excuses, learn to expect and to measure inevitable errors and to use these in planning and reacting for change. This is the real world — the professional will get with it.

© **American Production & Inventory Control Society**

MASTER PLANNING: THE "HOW TO" OF IT
John F. Proud, CFPIM
Proud Enterprises Corporation

What is Master Planning?

In order for a manufacturing company to compete in today's world, it must be able to supply its product when the customer wants it and for a fair price. To do this, the manufacturer needs to address several issues.

First of all, there is a Business Plan that needs to be met. This Business Plan identifies the company's mission, objectives, and goals for some future period of time (usually one or more years). This Business Plan is the driver to the Marketing/Sales and Manufacturing Planning process (see figure 1).

MRPII CLOSED LOOP - TOP PART

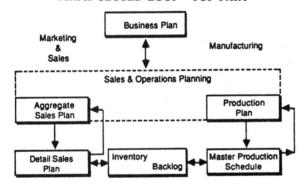

Figure 1

One level below the Business Plan is the Sales and Operations Planning (S&OP) effort. The objectives of S&OP are as follows:
(1) Support the Business Plan.
(2) Insurance that the plans are realistic.
(3) Effectively manage change.
(4) Manage FG Inventory and Backlog.
(5) Measure performance.
(6) Building teamwork.
So, what plans are needed to support the Business Plan. There are several, but the three we are going to concentrate on are the Sales Plan, Production Plan, and the Inventory/Backlog Plans. As we look at figure 1, we see that the aggregate Sales Plan needs to be in balance with the aggregate Production Plan. In addition to the balancing of the aggregate Plans, the detail Sales Plan needs to be in balance with the Master Production Schedule.

Now this is not to say that the Sales Plans will be equal to the Production Plan and Master Schedule. What it says is that there should be balance between the two while taking into account the Finished Good Inventory and the Backlog positions desired. All these Plans are part of Demand Management and Resource Management which are the key elements in Master Planning.

Sales and Operations Planning (S&OP)

How does a company insure that the Sales and Production Plans are realistic? How does a company manage their Finished Goods Inventory and Backlog positions? How does Management communicate its desires to the factory? When change is required, how is that change managed effectively? The best way is to use the S&OP process.

Earlier we defined the objectives of Sales and Operations Planning. As we review these objectives, there are several issues a company must deal with that will lead them to implementing Sales and Operations Planning. To implement this process, the Management Team must be educated on the concepts and how to work the process. Then the first S&OP Meeting needs to be called.

The S&OP Meeting deals with several agenda items. First of all, the key members of Top Management need to be present. The key disciplines such as Marketing, Sales, Manufacturing, Engineering, and Finance must be in attendance.

The agenda for the Meeting requires that Management address any special issues, past performances, assumptions used, vulnerabilities, special projects, as well as conducting a product family by product family review of the Sales Plan, Production Plan, Finished Goods Inventory Plan, and the Backlog Plan. Once these items have been covered, the group reviews the decisions that have been made and critiques the process.

It's at this Meeting that the Executive Management Team determines what rates of Production will be passed onto the Master Scheduler. They need to evaluate the individual plans paying attention to actual performances over the last ninety days. In addition to looking at the Sales Plan, attention is also paid to the Inventory and Backlog positions. Once these Plans are well understood, the Production Plan is developed.

Managing the Demand

Demand Management is defined by APICS as the function of recognizing and managing all demands for products to insure the Master Scheduler is aware of them. This process encompasses forecasting, order entry, order promising, branch warehouse requirements, inter-plant orders, and service parts requirements.

What demand management really needs to do is to recognize and manage all demands for products and services in order to support the customers and facilitate the management and utilization of resources. In order to do this, we need a process that will predict, communicate, influence, and manage the needs of the customer as well as the resources of the manufacturer.

The demand planning process starts by forecasting the anticipated demands by evaluating history, external factors, product plans, marketing plans, promotions, pricing, territory plans, customer plans, marketing channels, incentives, and sales plans. These elements are taken into account in managing the demand and arriving at the Sales Plan that will be used as input to the S&OP Meeting where the production rates will be established.

Preparing the Production Plan

The next step in Master Planning is to prepare the Production Plan. This is done at the S&OP Meeting.

Marketing contributes to the Meeting by identifying the Marketing and Sales Plan; Manufacturing defines its Capabilities and Capacities; Engineering announces new products as well as future product enhancements; Finance informs the group of the profit targets plus the money available to support for the Production Plan.

Two important things should be kept in mind when preparing the Production Plan: (1) Fix the overall rate of production and the approximate model mix so that everyone can prepare in advance, and (2) Within the confines of the overall fixed rate, the model mix can be adjusted, within limits, from which was first planned.

What this means is that Top Management will put together an aggregate plan by Product Family so that everyone in the company can get ready for what is expected to happen. Once the Plan is in place, the individual parties must be ready to react to any changes which may occur. In order to do this, the system must have the capability to display the impact of management decisions prior to these decisions being made.

A level Production Plan is created using the following equations:

Make-to-Stock   Make-to-Order

$$PP = \frac{(EI - BI) + SP}{N} \qquad PP = \frac{(BB - EB) + SP}{N}$$

where
EI = Desired ending inventory level
BI = Beginning inventory level
BB = Beginning backlog*
EB = Ending backlog*
SP = Sales Plan
N = Number of periods in Production Plan
*Orders booked, not shipped.

These are the simplest forms of calculating a Production Plan. In actuality targets and constraints, such as production rate changes, set-up changes, inventory carry costs, ordering costs, overtime requirements, sub-contracting, customer service levels, and productivity targets need to be taken into account.

Once the initial Production Plan has been created, it is loaded into the Production Plan line (Production Forecast line on the MPS format). This Production Plan is translated into discrete part numbers, quantities, and due dates. The process is the creation of the MPS line or the anticipated build schedule

Managing the Master Schedule

Master Production Scheduling (MPS) is a technique supported by a formal system that can improve production and inventory management. However, if the organization is to optimally benefit from the process, there are twelve basic principles that cannot be violated.

(1) The sum of the Master Production Schedule must equal the Production Plan.
(2) Uncouple the Sales Forecast from Material Requirements Planning (MRP).
(3) Initiate Master Production Scheduling at the product level that provides the greatest flexibility and control.
(4) Prepare the Rough-Cut Capacity Plan prior to creating a detail priority plan with MRP.
(5) Establish and formalize the planning and demand time fences.

(6) The Master Scheduler must have control of the MPS line within the planning time fence; no automatic action by the computer system can change this line.
(7) No master schedule lots can be past due.
(8) Consume the MPS with customer orders as they are received and entered as demand on the factory.
(9) Overplanning or safety stock should be done in matched sets of parts during the first unsold period of time.
(10) The MPS should be established as the company game plan and agreed upon by Marketing and Manufacturing.
(11) Responsibilities for the MPS must be assigned, and the Master Scheduler is held responsible for its execution.
(12) All management must understand, support, and commit to the foregoing principles.

The true test of any formal planning and control system such as Manufacturing Resource Planning (MRPII), is how people use and benefit from the information they obtain. The final product in the Master Scheduling process is the Master Schedule report which contains timely and accurate information for the Master Scheduler to use in daily decision making. These reports also provide the information used by key management personnel to set and control the direction of the business. In order for us to fully recognize how very vital the MPS is to successful planning, let's review the role the MPS plays in the manufacturing environment.

Role of Production and Inventory Management

The preceding passage was taken from an article that I wrote explaining the use of the MPS reports. As we look at the planning process, Master Scheduling in conjunction with Sales and Production Planning, are by far the most important activities which need to be accomplished if good communications and success are to be insured.

Business success is measured differently depending on the environment as well as many other factors. The customer is generally interested in three things: (1) delivery schedule, (2) price, and (3) quality. The company's ability to respond to these elements usually determines the amount of interest customers will have doing business with them. To net it out quickly, a successful manufacturing company must be better than its competition in at least one of the above elements. If on the other hand competition succeeds in performing better in all three areas, chances are the company will go out of business.

Besides the customer, other eyes are also looking at the company's performance. The stockholders don't really care directly what price is charged for the product or whether delivery schedules are met in a timely manner. What the stockholder cares about is dividends, return-on-investment, and profit. Sure, the stockholders are interested in pricing if the product is not being sold or the quality of the product has the reputation of being "junk." This is true primarily because it affects profits.

Management is interested in all these measurements as well as others. Inventory turns, shortages, obsolescence, productivity, and customer service levels are key control points which management watches carefully. The interesting point being made here is that each company is measured several ways. The responsibility to perform well against many of these measurements lies squarely on the shoulders of Production and Inventory Management (P&IM).

Looking at this important function we quickly notice that good communications must exist among all the major disciplines in a manufacturing company. The Master Scheduler's job is to see that this communication link does, in fact, exist. It is a difficult (if not impossible) task. Can you imagine trying to communicate with the likes of marketing, manufacturing, finance, engineering and data processing personnel all within the same factory walls. And if this isn't enough, add the problems presented by vendors, suppliers, sub-contractors, stockholders, and general management.

But, wait a minute. All is not lost! Production and Inventory Management has an excellent tool which, if understood and used correctly, can greatly assist the Master Scheduler in getting the job done. The three objectives of P&IM are to optimize customer service, optimize inventory investment, and to optimize facility utilization.

These objectives have been well documented in many papers and books published by APICS. However, how many of us have really looked at the words carefully? Have you ever read the definition of optimize? Well, if you haven't, here it is. Optimize means to make as Perfect, Effective or Functional as possible.

The definition states that the Master Scheduler will balance customer service, inventory investment, and facility utilization in the most perfect way which is effective and functional for the company. By doing this, the Master Schedule can be used as an effective communication tool to get all the company disciplines pulling in the same direction.

Concerns and Issues in Master Scheduling

Now, understanding the role of the Master Scheduler, there are some issues to address. The Master Scheduler has the responsibility to get all departments in the company pulling in the same direction. If we were to ask Material Management personnel what some of their concerns are, they undoubtedly would respond with the following comments:

- Marketing never gives us a good forecast.
- Management doesn't understand our problems.
- Finance only complains about the inventory.
- Engineering continually changes the BOM's.
- Customers are always changing their minds.
- Vendors are quite unreliable.

These concerns are symptoms of manufacturing problems. The real problem is that P&IM is not doing the job. Now, this is not saying that P&IM is not working hard if these symptoms exist in your company. What this saying is that P&IM may not have the proper tools to do the job, or if they do, they may not understand how to use them.

One tool to help P&IM get the job done properly is MRPII. Sometimes referred to as the Closed Loop System, MRPII can provide the Master Scheduler with all the information necessary to make good, sound business decisions.

Management's Entry Point into the Closed Loop

The objective of Master Scheduling is to plan and control the impact of independent demand on material and capacity. What this really says is that the Master Scheduler must prepare a plan which balances the demand for the product with the availability of that product or the resources needed to produce it. By doing this, management can communicate the company's desired direction to the factory.

Master Production Scheduling has five (5) functions which need to be performed in order to balance the supply and demand.

(1) Plan the material requirements.
(2) Plan the capacity requirements.
(3) Keep the priorities valid.
(4) Facilitate order promising.
(5) Strengthen communications between Marketing and Manufacturing.

When reviewing these functions, we need to realize that other segments in the Closed Loop help us to plan material and capacity requirements, but it all starts with Sales & Operations Planning and the Master Schedule. Shop Floor Control is very important in managing priorities, but again it all starts at the MPS level. The same is true for order promising and the communication link between Marketing and Manufacturing.

If we are to have a valid MPS, we must not over load or front-end load the Master Schedule. The build plan must be firm (not frozen) for some period of time. It should have all the information necessary to promise customer deliveries.

Additionally, a good Master Schedule ties to both Material Requirements Planning and Rough-Cut Capacity Planning. This interface provides us with the data necessary to answer "what if" questions as well as projecting financial needs. The key to the whole system is that it balances supply and demand within the constraints placed upon it by the Production Plan.

Preparing the Master Production Schedule

The Master Production Schedule format is a matrix with time periods displayed across the top and requirements, replenishments, and system calculations identified down the side (see figure 2). Each MPS item includes header information that identifies the part number, description, lead time, lot sizing policy, on-hand quantity, and location of the time fences.

MASTER SCHEDULE

PART NUMBER ITEM LEAD TIME LOT SIZE TIME FENCE	PERIODS							
	1	2	3	4	5	6	7	8
SERVICE FORECAST	3	3	3	3	3	3	3	3
PRODUCTION FORECAST	15			15			15	
ACTUAL DEMAND	17			13		6		
PROJECTED AVAILABLE BALANCE 12	14	11	8	10	7	4	-14	-17
AVAILABLE TO PROMISE	15			1				20
MASTER PRODUCTION SCHEDULE	20			20				20

Figure 2

Since the objective of MPS is to balance requirements (demand) with replenishments of material and resources (supply), the matrix displays several types of each. Requirements for a part are made up of service forecasted demand, production forecasted demand (production plan) and actual customer orders. Replenishments consist of manufacturing orders, firm planned orders, and computer planned orders. Once these requirements and replenishments are identified, a projected net available or inventory balance can be calculated....

The projected available balance is calculated by MPS Systems in four different ways. Projected available balance

equals

    (1) (OH + MPS) - (FCST + PFCST)

    (2) (OH + MPS) - (FCST + PFCST + DMD)

    (3) (OH + MPS) - (DMD

    (4) (OH + MPS) - (FCST + PFCST) or (DMD)*

       *Greater of the two

where

    OH = Stock on-hand

    MPS = Schedule receipt lot

    DMD = Customer orders

    FCST = Independent Demand

    PFCST = Dependent Demand

The example in figure 2 starts with an on-hand balance of 12 units. On-hand balance is usually indicated as the first entry on the projected available balance line. Next, the schedule receipt lot of 20 items due in period one is added to the 12 on-hand to identify that 32 units are available in period one. The rquirements total 18 (using calculation 1 which is the total of the forecast lines) in period one. If this 18 is subtracted from the 32 anticipated to be available, the projected inventory balance at the end of period one would be 14. Now, using 14 as the beginning balance going into period 2, the net available for periods two, three, etc. can be calculated throughout the planning horizon.

Customer Orders and Available-to-Promise

With the Production Plan and Master Schedule in place and agreed to by Marketing, Manufacturing, Engineering, and Finance, the individual processes start to take place. Marketing is responsible for the sale of the product. As sales are booked, they are entered into the system as actual demand. These orders should either replace the anticipated build plan or add to it. This is a way of saying what remains is available-to-sell or available-to-promise (ATP) to customers.

ATP is defined as the uncommitted portion of a company's inventory or planned production. It can be calculated and displayed in several different ways. The display of ATP can be cumulative, non-cumulative, or both. In addition it can be calculated for the service business, production business, or both.

When deriving ATP, there are two general equations used. The first takes the on-hand balance, adds to it the MPS for the period, and subtracts the actual demand (customer orders). The second is used for all other periods. Here we take the MPS and subtract the actual demand.

Let's look at figure 2 again. In period one the on-hand balance of 12 is added to the schedule receipt lot of 20 identifying the 32 available. Since forecast is not considered a firm commitment, only actual demand is used in the ATP calculation. Since 17 units have been sold in the first period, they are subtracted from the 32 leaving an ATP of 15 in period one.

Period four can have two different ATP's calculated. The first is known as current period consumption. Using this technique, the actual demand of 13 is subtracted from the scheduled receipt lot of 20 resulting in an ATP of 7 (not shown). If the technique

known as past period consumption is used, the resultant ATP would be 1. This is determined by taking the 7 projected ATP from current period consumption and subtracting the actual demand of 6 booked in period six. As we can see in the figure, no scheduled lot exists to cover the 6 scheduled for shipment in period six until period seven.

Planning Time Fence

The objective of MPS is to balance the demand for material and capacity with the supply of product or resources to make the product within a competitive lead time. As you might expect, time is one of the most important resources a Master Scheduler must deal with.

Due to the importance of time in scheduling and delivering product, time fences are commonly placed in the Master Schedule. Different systems support different time fences and logic. The most common and universal time fence is called the planning time fence (see figure 3).

TIME FENCES

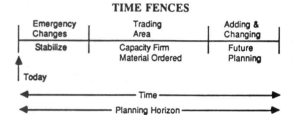

Figure 3

As each figure shows, modifications to the MPS may be difficult in zone one and two. This is true because the material has been ordered for low-level parts. In addition, the capacity at each work center is generally fixed. The planning time fence (PTF) is normally set between zones 2 and 3 (a good starting point is to set the PTF at the cumulative product lead time).

Beyond the PTF, schedule modifications will not impact current material planning. Within the PTF there will be an impact and that impact should be analyzed before making any schedule adjustments. The planning time fence limits the generation of planned orders by the computer (refer to figure 2).

In the example the PTF has been set at the end of period seven. This fence is under the control of the Master Scheduler. Once the PTF is in place, the MPS system will not generate computer planned orders within the first seven periods. Therefore, even though a projected negative balance exists in period seven, the computer planned order has been placed in period eight. The Master Scheduler is informed of the potential problem via the exception or action report....

Multi-Level Master Scheduling

Master Schedule logic can be expanded to cover multi-level Master Schedules. The Production Plan is normally created at a Product Family level. It is also at this level that the Sales Forecast is the most accurate. Service Forecast for lower level parts are input directly against the part being forecasted.

At the Product Family level, the available-to-promise can be calculated by subtracting the actual demand from the Production Plan. This ATP tells us by period how many family configurations are still to be sold. What we do not know is the mix of options that will be ordered.

To forecast this, the available-to-promise for the Product Family is exploded through a planning (ratio) bill. The planning bill is a pseudo bill that shows selected options and the probability with which each option will be ordered (see figure 4). For simplicity let's assume that the finishing lead time is equal to zero. If we explode the ATP through the planning bill, we can see that the Production Forecast for the option in period 1 and 2 is equal to zero since no more configurations are to be sold in these periods (ATP = 0 signifies the Product Family is sold out for those periods).

PRODUCTION PLAN

PART NUMBER MODEL LEAD TIME 2 LOT SIZE 40 TIME FENCE NA	PERIODS							
	1	2	3	4	5	6	7	8
PRODUCTION PLAN			12	28	40	40	40	40
ACTUAL DEMAND	40	40	28	12	0	0	0	0
AVAILABLE TO PROMISE	0	0	12	28	40	40	40	40

MASTER SCHEDULE

PART NUMBER OPTION LEAD TIME 1 LOT SIZE DISCRETE TIME FENCE 1		PERIODS							
		1	2	3	4	5	6	7	8
SERVICE FORECAST		0	0	0	0	0	0	0	0
PRODUCTION FORECAST		0	0	6	14	20	20	20	20
ACTUAL DEMAND		16	18	12	6	0	0	0	0
PROJECTED AVAILABLE BALANCE	0	0	0	4	4	4	4	4	4
AVAILABLE TO PROMISE		0	0	10	14	20	20	20	20
MASTER PRODUCTION SCHEDULE		16	18	22	20	20	20	20	20

Figure 4

Period three shows an ATP of 12 units. Exploding this quantity through a 50% option bill generates a Production Forecast of 6 units. In period four, the ATP of 28 is multiplied by .5 (50%) which result in a Production Forecast of 14.

Once the requirements are known for the options, the anticipated build schedule can be loaded. The matrix can be completed by setting the planning time fence, projecting the net available balance, and calculating the available-to-promise.

Determining the MPS Quantities

It's time for the Master Scheduler to create the MPS lots in response to the projected requirements. The first period we will look at is period one for the option (see figure 4). The Production Plan shows that we are sold out in period one. What should the MPS lot be at this option level? Well, if we are not going to sell anymore, then we need to build what has been ordered (actual demand line). That's 24, no more and no less. The same is true for period two where the quantity should be 22.

In period three we need to evaluate the range of requirements. The least that the Master Scheduler needs to schedule is 16, the booked customer orders for the period. The most that the Master Scheduler would see as a requirement is 28 (16 customer order quantity plus 12 available-to-promise at the family

level). The most likely quantity is 22 or 16 for the customer orders and the 6 still forecasted (50% probably).

If the Master Scheduler stays with the strict guidelines of the Production Plan, 22 units would be scheduled in period three. However, we know that since probabilities (forecasted ratios) are being used, there will be some inaccuracies in the plan. Therefore, management may authorize some overplanning in the first unsold period, which is period three.

In our example, management has authorized a 25% overplan for the entire product family. The Master Scheduler has determined that 6 of the 10 units should be scheduled for the option we are looking at. By doing this, the Master Scheduler has protected the company's ability to ship in matched sets of parts (MPS lots will be used as input into MRP). This overplanning technique is the best way to introduce safety stock into the Master Scheduling process.

The same logic is used to determine what should be scheduled for the rest of the periods. Now, once period three is sold out, the overplanning not required will be shifted to the next unsold period/s. As you can see the overplanning MPS lots continue to be moved as the Master Scheduler believes is necessary. Some people may think this is a lot of work, but it's just Master Scheduling the way it should be done.

Role of Key Functions

The Master Scheduler has a very important role to play. The person or persons assigned to this vital function should participate in the Sales & Operations Planning process. Once the Production Plan is available, it is the Master Scheduler's responsibility to create and maintain the MPS. The maintenance includes the MPS itself, Planning Bills, and Final Assembly or Finishing Schedules. Probably the most important role is to identify, negotiate, and resolve conflicts. The Master Scheduler's job is also to inform and communicate.

Marketing's responsibilities include Sales Planning, Planning Bills, Demand Management, and to understand the targets and objectives placed upon Manufacturing. Manufacturing's responsibilities include Production Planning, providing insight into Factory Capabilities, identifying Material and Capacity constraints, Planning Bills, and understanding the targets and objectives placed upon Marketing.

One key to success is to get Marketing and Manufacturing to agree to the MPS. Another is to get Top Management to understand their role in Sales & Operations Planning as well as Master Scheduling. Top Management should insist that the MPS be achievable, participate in resolving conflicts, and assign the responsibility for MPS maintenance. By doing these things, Master Scheduling will provide more information that you may ever have had.

The final step is to take the MPS into a true MRPII environment. This means the quantities on the MPS need to be converted to financial measurements. When this is done, the forecast and actual demand lines will show potential and realized shipping budgets. The MPS line is the production budget. The net available line projects the inventory levels by part, product family, and company.

In addition to converting the projected quantities to financial plans, actuals can be collected and compared to the plan. Variances can be displayed in both units and money. All this data can be nicely consolidated onto one sheet of paper, a real management tool.

Note:

Proud, John F., Master Production Scheduling: The Contract, World Congress Proceedings, 1985, has been reproduced in part and expanded upon to create this paper.

BIOGRAPHY

John F. Proud, an Oliver Wight Principal, has been involved in MRPII implementations since 1968. He spent several years working in the manufacturing industry at Xerox Corporation, Century Data Systems, and Unisys Corporation. His assignments included Manager, Just-in-Time Manufacturing, National Customer Education Manager, Western Region Manufacturing Consultant, Manager Information Systems, Production Control Specialist, and Material Control Analyst.

Sari, John F., "The Planning Bill of Material -- All It's Cracked Up to Be?" 25th Annual Conference Proceedings (1982).

This article provides detailed examples using different planning bill assumptions. Readers who are contemplating the use of planning bills or those that are experiencing problems in their use should find this article interesting. The author shows how forecast consumption by actual orders influences the demand for lower level components and options.

An important point made early in the article is that two-level master scheduling starts with a process of two-level forecasting. Three basic types of "mechanics" are used to generate second-level production forecasts. Type I mechanics explode the available-to-promise (ATP) quantity of the parent item. Type II mechanics explode the parent item master production schedule (MPS), thereafter reducing (consuming) the amounts by actual customer orders with the particular second-level options. Type III mechanics involve explosion as done in Type II followed by consumption based on actual orders. But now all remainder quantities (plus and minus) are cumulated into the next period for which ATP exists at the parent level.

Type I mechanics, in essence, are based on the belief that every new customer order is an independent event; the probabilities for each option do not change on the basis of what orders have been received, except perhaps in a long-run estimation. Use of Type I mechanics, however, has the potential for producing nervousness at the lower level production forecast. This will surely be the case if no option overplanning (safety stocks) is maintained, and actual results are allowed to generate new plans at the second level. In fact, it is mainly for this reason that two-level master scheduling is done. Stability (though firm planned orders) needs to be managed at the option level.

Type II mechanics will be less nervous than Type I, but there is a concomitant reduction of responsiveness. Adjustments for over and under consumption of the forecast are not made, except that over consumption only brings the forecast to zero, not negative. On the other hand, if the belief is that over the long run the percentages used for the option explosions are correct, Type II may well be a good technique.

Type III mechanics are even more stable (and less responsive) than Type II. The assumption here is more akin to the idea that since one has just tossed a coin with seven heads in a row, the next toss must come up tails.

It is important to note that the author takes care not to confuse the issue by including MPS and ATP quantities for the second level options. This is a separate issue. He concentrates on the inputs to the second-level MPS. That is, the process of setting the MPS to buffer uncertainty and provide stability should be decided after first considering the way in which second-level production forecasts are to be generated.

Reprinted from the APICS *1982 Conference Proceedings*.

THE PLANNING BILL OF MATERIAL—ALL IT'S CRACKED UP TO BE?

F. John Sari, CPIM*
Richard C. Ling, Inc.

The planning bill of material has long been a standard solution to a wide variety of master scheduling problems, especially for make-to-order and assemble-to-order manufacturers. There are many situations in which it works very well. There are also, however, many conditions under which it really does not work well, if at all. The objective of this paper is to identify some of the common pitfalls in the use of planning bills of material.

BILL OF MATERIAL TERMINOLOGY

The terms used to describe various forms and types of bills of material seem, to the author, to be one of the least standard areas of APICS terminology. Paraphrasing the 1980 APICS Dictionary, we have several to understand.

1. Planning bill (of material)

    Artificial grouping of items, in bill of material format, used to facilitate master scheduling and/or material planning.

    (This definition was surely kept very general in order to cover the wide variety of bills of material in use to accomplish planning. We've got to push further to understand the various types.)

2. Super bill (of material)

    . Type of planning bill, located at the top level in the structure, which ties together various modular bills (and possibly a common parts bill) to define an entire product or product family.

    . "Quantity per" relationship of super bill to modules represents forecasted % popularity of each module.

    . Master scheduled quantities of the super bill explode to create requirements for the modules which also are master scheduled.

3. Modular bill (of material)

    . Type of planning bill which is arranged in product modules or options.

    Often used where products have many optional features
    e.g., automobiles.

4. Common parts bill (of material)

    . Type of planning bill which groups all common components for a product or family of products into one bill of material

This paper will focus on proper use of the type of planning bill described above as a "Super Bill." The terms "planning" and "super" will be used interchangeably.

The classic example used in existing literature is the hoist example (See Figure 1) popularized by Messrs. Orlicky, Plossl and Wight. With 2400 possible combinations of modules (options, features, attachments, etc.), planning bills are very useful for forecasting this type of product. One needs to know the forecast of total number of hoists to be produced and the forecasted mix of options. Although frequently discussed as "two-level" master scheduling, the process is really a "two-level" forecasting procedure initially.

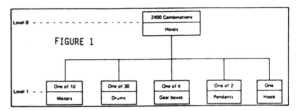

FIGURE 1

PLANNING BILL NERVOUSNESS

One of the significant pitfalls of this planning bill process is the potential for generating nervousness in our formal planning systems, especially the MPS. The actual mechanics of planning bills generate different results.

Figure 2 illustrates the typical 3-zoned master schedule situation of make-and-assemble-to-order companies. The planning process involves setting a Production Plan (40 per month) for hoists which considers marketplace needs, desired backlog levels, staffing required, etc. With a forecasted split of 50/50 between pendants 1 and 2 (P1 & P2) the second level forecast for P1 & P2 becomes 20 per month or 10 every other week as shown. (The examples all assume 4-week months for simplicity.)

Zone 1 covers weeks 1-3 in which we are completely sold out. Second-level forecasts for P1 & P2 are no longer needed since actual backlog fully describes Zone 1. Zone 3 covers weeks 7 and beyond. There is no customer backlog beyond week 6 and we must deal with pure 2-level forecasts. Zone 2 is in the middle, weeks 4-6, where we must plan with a mixture of backlog and actual demand.

FIGURE 2

FORECAST NERVOUSNESS

HOISTS 40 PER MONTH

	PERIOD							
	1	2	3	4	5	6	7	8
PROD. PLAN / MPS		20		20		20		20
ACTUAL DEMAND		20	16		8		0	
AVAILABLE-TO-PROMISE				44				

PENDANT 1 (50%)

	1	2	3	4	5	6	7	8
FORECAST			36					
PRODUCTION FORECAST		10		10		10		10
ACTUAL DEMAND		12	7		5		0	
PROJECTED AVAILABLE BALANCE				24				
AVAILABLE-TO-PROMISE			19					
MPS								

PENDANT 2 (50%)

	1	2	3	4	5	6	7	8
FORECAST								
PRODUCTION FORECAST		10		10		10		10
ACTUAL DEMAND		8	9		3		0	
PROJECTED AVAILABLE BALANCE				20				
AVAILABLE-TO-PROMISE			17					
MPS								

The actual demand in the example indicates the 50/50 forecasted mix isn't bad. Of 36 hoists sold through week 4, 19 went P1, 17 went P2.

Three basic types of mechanics are used to develop second-level forecasts. Type 1 mechanics (See Figure 3) explode the available-to-promise (ATP) of the hoist family. In week 4, (Zone 2) 16 of 20 hoists have sold. Of the 4 ATP, our best estimate is two P1's and two P2's. In week 2 (Zone 1), this approach produces a zero second-level forecast which is desirable. In week 8 (Zone 3), it produces the desired 10. Potential for nervousness exists with each sale in Zone 2. In week 4, the original forecast of 50/50 has now been changed to a 45%/55% split between P1 and P2. The combination of remaining P1 forecast and 7 actual P1 demand totals 9. 9 of 20 is 45%. A responsive MPS tool might be recommending a reschedule or de-expedite of P1 material in week 4 since the original forecast of 10 has been reduced to 9. The opposite is true in week 6 for P1. The original forecast of 10 has been replaced by requirements for 11, 6 remaining forecast and 5 actual demand.

FIGURE 3

MECHANICS
1. EXPLODE AVAIL-TO-PROMISE

HOISTS 40 PER MONTH

PERIOD	1	2	3	4	5	6	7	8
PROD. PLAN / MPS		20		20		20		20
ACTUAL DEMAND		20		16		8		0
AVAILABLE-TO-PROMISE		0		4		12		20

PENDANT 1 (50%)

	1	2	3	4	5	6	7	8
FORECAST								
PRODUCTION FORECAST		0		2		6		10
ACTUAL DEMAND		12		7		5		0
PROJECTED AVAILABLE BALANCE								
AVAILABLE-TO-PROMISE								
MPS								

PENDANT 2 (50%)

	1	2	3	4	5	6	7	8
FORECAST								
PRODUCTION FORECAST		0		2		6		10
ACTUAL DEMAND		8		9		3		0
PROJECTED AVAILABLE BALANCE								
AVAILABLE-TO-PROMISE								
MPS								

People who understand the theory of flipping coins prefer Type 1 planning bills. 16 tosses have been made in week 4 of Figure 3. 4 tosses remain. The best estimate of results in those 4 tosses is a 50/50 split.

Type 2 planning bill mechanics (See Figure 4) consume second-level forecasts week-by-week with actual demand. Originally, all P1 forecasts were 10. As 7 sold in week 4, 7 of the forecast of 10 were consumed, leaving 3. In week 2, all 10 were consumed by 12 actual demand, etc.

FIGURE 4

MECHANICS
2. CURRENT PERIOD FORECAST CONSUMPTION

HOISTS 40 PER MONTH

PERIOD	1	2	3	4	5	6	7	8
PROD. PLAN / MPS		20		20		20		20
ACTUAL DEMAND		20		16		8		0
AVAILABLE-TO-PROMISE								

PENDANT 1 (50%)

	1	2	3	4	5	6	7	8
FORECAST								
PRODUCTION FORECAST		0		3		5		10
ACTUAL DEMAND		12		7		5		0
PROJECTED AVAILABLE BALANCE								
AVAILABLE-TO-PROMISE								
MPS								

PENDANT 2 (50%)

	1	2	3	4	5	6	7	8
FORECAST								
PRODUCTION FORECAST		2*		1		7		10
ACTUAL DEMAND		8		9		3		0
PROJECTED AVAILABLE BALANCE								
AVAILABLE-TO-PROMISE								
MPS								

Type 2 mechanics must deal with the P2 situation in week 2. Even though only 8 sold, the 2 remaining forecast must be eliminated. Otherwise, the MPS would call for 10

sets of P2 material, 2 of which are not required. Type 2's must also deal with situations where forecasts and the actual demands don't fall in the same week.

Type 2 planning bills do a better job of protecting the original 50/50 forecast split than Type 1's. The assumption made is that 20 hoists will sell 50/50 in the end.

Type 3 planning bills extend the thought process of Type 2. (See Figure 5.) Examine P1. Type 3 mechanics recognize that through week 4, 19 of the original 20 forecast for P1 have sold and 1 unconsumed forecast remains in week 4. Through week 6, 24 of 30 have sold and 6 remain -- 1 in week 4 and 5 in week 6. Type 3 tries to hold to the 50/50 split projected on a cumulative basis. It potentially generates less MPS nervousness than either Type 1 or 2. Type 3 is also slowest to respond to a changing mix.

Which type is best? The answer for any given company is a function of several factors:

1. Family rate of sales or volume (hoists).

2. Customer order size relative to family volume.

3. Stability of mix.

4. Percentage of option forecast, i.e., 50% options would prove more stable than 5% options.

Which is least nervous -- Type 3.

FIGURE 5

MECHANICS
3. CUMULATIVE FORECAST CONSUMPTION

HOISTS 40 PER MONTH

PERIOD	1	2	3	4	5	6	7	8
PROD. PLAN / MPS		20		20		20		20
ACTUAL DEMAND		20		16		8		0
AVAILABLE-TO-PROMISE								

PENDANT 1 (50%)

	1	2	3	4	5	6	7	8
FORECAST								
PRODUCTION FORECAST		0		1		5		10
ACTUAL DEMAND		12		7		5		0
PROJECTED AVAILABLE BALANCE					Σ 24 OF 30			
AVAILABLE-TO-PROMISE								
MPS			Σ 19 OF 20					

PENDANT 2 (50%)

	1	2	3	4	5	6	7	8
FORECAST								
PRODUCTION FORECAST		0		3		7		10
ACTUAL DEMAND		8		9		3		0
PROJECTED AVAILABLE BALANCE					Σ 20 OF 30			
AVAILABLE-TO-PROMISE								
MPS			Σ 17 OF 20					

MAJOR CUSTOMER SITUATIONS AND PLANNING BILLS

Major customers frequently impact planning bill forecasting techniques. (See Figure 6.) It describes the situation of a major customer who buys 200 hoists per year with P1 pendants on a 4-week shipment schedule. Including this customer, total hoist sales are 600 per year and the P1/P2 split is forecast at 50/50. The actual demands of 15 in week 4 and 16 in week 8 are the major customer's orders.

FIGURE 6

MAJOR CUSTOMER
1. INCLUDED IN PLANNING BILL

HOISTS 600 PER YEAR

	PERIOD 1	2	3	4	5	6	7	8
PROD. PLAN / MPS	12	12	12	12	12	12	12	12
ACTUAL DEMAND								
AVAILABLE-TO-PROMISE								

PENDANT 1 (50%)

	1	2	3	4	5	6	7	8
FORECAST								
PRODUCTION FORECAST	6	6	6	6	6	6	6	6
ACTUAL DEMAND				15M				16M
PROJECTED AVAILABLE BALANCE								
AVAILABLE-TO-PROMISE								
MPS								

PENDANT 2 (50%)

	1	2	3	4	5	6	7	8
FORECAST								
PRODUCTION FORECAST	6	6	6	6	6	6	6	6
ACTUAL DEMAND								
PROJECTED AVAILABLE BALANCE								
AVAILABLE-TO-PROMISE								
MPS								

M- MAJOR CUSTOMER BUYS 200 PER YEAR,
ALL PENDANT 1 CONFIGURATIONS,
MONTHLY SHIPMENTS

The alternative planning bill approach is to exclude this major customer. (See Figure 7.) The hoists which will be sold (400 per year) to normal, unknown customers split 25/75 between P1 and P2. The major customer for P1 is included through a standalone forecast. The 15 originally forecast in week 4 has been consumed by an order in week 4. The 16 in week 8 remains a forecast in Figure 7. The customer has not yet provided a firm order.

FIGURE 7

MAJOR CUSTOMER
2. EXCLUDED FROM PLANNING BILL

HOISTS *600 PER YEAR

	PERIOD 1	2	3	4	5	6	7	8
PROD. PLAN / MPS	8	8	8	8	8	8	8	8
ACTUAL DEMAND								
AVAILABLE-TO-PROMISE								

PENDANT 1 (25%)

	1	2	3	4	5	6	7	8
*FORECAST (MAJOR CUST)				~~15~~				16
PRODUCTION FORECAST (UNKNOWN CUST)	2	2	2	2	2	2	2	2
ACTUAL DEMAND				15M				
PROJECTED AVAILABLE BALANCE								
AVAILABLE-TO-PROMISE								
MPS								

PENDANT 2 (75%)

	1	2	3	4	5	6	7	8
FORECAST (MAJOR CUST)								
PRODUCTION FORECAST (UNKNOWN CUST)	6	6	6	6	6	6	6	6
ACTUAL DEMAND								
PROJECTED AVAILABLE BALANCE								
AVAILABLE-TO-PROMISE								
MPS								

* 200 HOISTS PER YEAR FOR MAJOR CUSTOMER,
400 PER YEAR FOR NORMAL OR UNKNOWN
CUSTOMERS SPLIT 25/75 PENDANT 1 VS. 2.

The Figure 7 approach does a better job of describing the family forecast. Two separate and distinct demand patterns exist. The planning bill does a good job for the normal customer demand but poorly describes the major customer.

LUMPY DEMAND SITUATIONS AND PLANNING BILLS

Master scheduling to cover lumpy demand patterns is difficult at best. Planning bills probably won't help and may in fact hurt. (See Figure 8.) Even though the warehouse uses P1 and P2 equally, it should be forecast separately rather than included in a planning bill. Although the planning bill forecasts P1 and P2 in aggregate, it assumes a smooth rate of usage of each. Once again, a separate forecast of warehouse replenishment (See Figure 9) does a better job of describing the real situation. Distribution Requirements Planning is useful in projecting warehouse replenishment patterns.

FIGURE 8

LUMPY DEMAND
1. INCLUDED IN PLANNING BILL

HOISTS 600 PER YEAR

	PERIOD 1	2	3	4	5	6	7	8
PROD. PLAN / MPS	12	12	12	12	12	12	12	12
ACTUAL DEMAND	'							
AVAILABLE-TO-PROMISE								

PENDANT 1 (50%)

	1	2	3	4	5	6	7	8
FORECAST								
PRODUCTION FORECAST	6	6	6	6	6	6	6	6
ACTUAL DEMAND				25W				
PROJECTED AVAILABLE BALANCE								
AVAILABLE-TO-PROMISE								
MPS								

PENDANT 2 (50%)

	1	2	3	4	5	6	7	8
FORECAST								
PRODUCTION FORECAST	6	6	6	6	6	6	6	6
ACTUAL DEMAND								25W
PROJECTED AVAILABLE BALANCE								
AVAILABLE-TO-PROMISE								
MPS								

W- REMOTE WAREHOUSE USES 200 PER YEAR,
50/50 SPLIT ON PENDANT 1 VS. 2,
REPLENISHES QUARTERLY

FIGURE 9

LUMPY DEMAND
2. EXCLUDED FROM PLANNING BILL

HOISTS
* 600 PER YEAR

	PERIOD							
	1	2	3	4	5	6	7	8
PROD. PLAN / MPS	8	8	8	8	8	8	8	8
ACTUAL DEMAND								
AVAILABLE-TO-PROMISE								

PENDANT 1 (50%)

	1	2	3	4	5	6	7	8
FORECAST (WHSE)				25̶				
PRODUCTION FORECAST (NORMAL)	4	4	4	4	4	4	4	4
ACTUAL DEMAND				25ʷ				
PROJECTED AVAILABLE BALANCE								
AVAILABLE-TO-PROMISE								
MPS								

PENDANT 2 (50%)

	1	2	3	4	5	6	7	8
FORECAST (WHSE)								25
PRODUCTION FORECAST (NORMAL)	4	4	4	4	4	4	4	4
ACTUAL DEMAND								
PROJECTED AVAILABLE BALANCE								
AVAILABLE-TO-PROMISE								
MPS								

* 200 HOISTS PER YEAR FOR WAREHOUSE REPLENISHMENT (LUMPY DEMAND) - 400 PER YEAR NORMAL (NON-LUMPY) DEMAND VIA PLANNING BILL

SMALL NUMBERS AND PLANNING BILLS

Planning bills can generate a lot of planning nervousness when family (hoists) rates are small or when an option percentage is small. (See Figure 10.) A smooth sales rate of 78 per year equates to 6 units each 40 weeks. The sales of one hoist thus represents 16% of the hoist forecast and 33% of a pendant forecast in any month. Since customer order size is so large relative to either forecast, any variation from expected means a large percentage miss.

FIGURE 10

SMALL NUMBERS

HOISTS
* 78 PER YEAR

	PERIOD							
	1	2	3	4	5	6	7	8
PROD. PLAN / MPS	2	2	1	1	2	2	1	1
ACTUAL DEMAND								
AVAILABLE-TO-PROMISE								

PENDANT 1 (50%)

	1	2	3	4	5	6	7	8
FORECAST								
PRODUCTION FORECAST	1	1	1	0	1	1	1	0
ACTUAL DEMAND								
PROJECTED AVAILABLE BALANCE								
AVAILABLE-TO-PROMISE								
MPS								

PENDANT 2 (50%)

	1	2	3	4	5	6	7	8
FORECAST								
PRODUCTION FORECAST	1	1	1	0	1	1	1	0
ACTUAL DEMAND								
PROJECTED AVAILABLE BALANCE								
AVAILABLE-TO-PROMISE								
MPS								

* 78 PER YEAR = 6 PER 4 WEEKS

The real problem may be that one simply cannot forecast small numbers very well. If that's the case, planning bills won't help. You may be forced to accept some risk inventory maintained by safety stock or firm planned order techniques.

PLANNING BILLS IN PERSPECTIVE

The planning bill of material is a powerful tool when used properly. There are many firms who effectively utilize planning bills for selected products. It has, however, been "a solution in search of a problem" for some.

Planning bills make certain assumptions and apply selectively. One must understand those assumptions as well as the mechanics in use. Foremost, however, make sure the solution fits the problem.

ABOUT THE AUTHOR

F. John Sari is Executive Vice-President of Richard C. Ling, Inc.

Formerly, John was Vice-President, Consulting Services for Arista Manufacturing Systems, A Xerox Company, and was responsible for the consulting and project activities of the firm. In this capacity, he also conducted many training courses for the public as well as Arista clients.

John is a Mathematics graduate of Wayne State University in Detroit. Upon graduation, he joined General Electric Co. and participated in GE's three-year rotational Manufacturing Management Training Program. Mr. Sari accepted a GE position as Supervisor-Production and Inventory Control upon completion of the MMP program.

John is an active speaker at APICS seminars and events. He holds a Fellow certification in inventory management. He is a Past-President of the Piedmont Triad Chapter of APICS.

Stevens, A. L., "The Material Manager's Role in Master Scheduling in a Material Requirements Planning Environment," 20th Annual Conference Proceedings (1977).

Although written in 1977, this article is still a complete and relevant exposition of the role of master scheduling in manufacturing planning and control. Readers will enjoy its complete scope, from production planning (PP) to shop floor control, as well as the insights into the job of materials manager.

The paper begins with an overview of a manufacturing planning and control system, which is made up of planning (PP, master production scheduling [MPS], material requirements planning [MRP], and capacity requirements planning [CRP]), internal control (shop floor control and input/output), and external control (vendor scheduling and purchasing support systems). All of this is supported by an accurate database.

The primary emphasis is on master production scheduling. The materials manager's role of developing the production plan and its impact on the MPS are described. Also detailed is the link between the production plan and the overall running of the business.

Development of the detailed MPS is based primarily on planning bills, both for make-to-stock (MTS) and assemble-to-order (ATO) environments. In the MTS examples, overall production plans for a family of end items are based on demand forecasts and inventory objectives. Using percentages, the overall demand is allocated as requirements to individual items. The master scheduler selects firm planned order values to satisfy the overall inventory objectives as well as to balance the inventories across items. The result of this process is the input to the detailed MRP records.

For make-to-order products (actually ATO), planning bills are again used. Options are either/or in all cases; this is accomplished by having a "none" option for what is typically called an add-on, a true option, or an attachment. ATP values for the top level item are exploded as production forecasts to the items at the secondary level. A two-level MPS is advocated to control (with firm planned orders) stability at both levels.

Available and ATP calculations are explained, as well as their implications in the MPS.

The author concludes the paper with detailed examples of CRP, input/output analyses, and shop floor control. He puts it all together in a closed-loop MPR system diagram and returns to the fact that it is the materials manager's job to make this system more effective.

Reprinted from the APICS *1977 Conference Proceedings.*
THE MATERIALS MANAGER'S ROLE IN
MASTER SCHEDULING IN A MATERIAL
REQUIREMENTS PLANNING ENVIRONMENT
by A. L. Stevens

The Materials Manager in a manufacturing company is the key executive vested with the responsibility for Production and Inventory Management, Purchasing, Warehouse Management, material handling, shipping, receiving, and, in many companies, distribution.

Additionally, he is responsible for establishing and maintaining controls over inventory record accuracy and he plays an important role in assuring that bill of material accuracy is maintained. In this important role, in most manufacturing companies, he controls the majority of the company's assets/inventories, and is responsible for spending an amount approximatly equal to one half of the company's revenue in the purchasing of materials and services.

In order to properly discharge his responsibility, it is essential that the Materials Manager be properly schooled in the techniques necessary to achieve and maintain control over his areas, be familiar with and responsive to the needs and interfaces with the functional areas of Finance, Marketing, Manufacturing, Engineering, and Data Processing. Furthermore, it is essential that he keep abreast of the "state of the art" in the functions that he is managing. As he learns techniques that will enable the company to perform more profitably, achieve improvement in its return on investment, and provide better service to its customers, it is his responsibility to communicate his knowledge to the General Manager and his staff. In this effort, it is necessary that he be sufficiently knowledgeable and prepared to be effective in convincing the General Manager and his staff to fund the necessary money and provide the resources to improve and update any control systems that are inadequate.

The purpose of this paper is to present an overview of the current techniques in master scheduling in a material requirements planning environment and to address the role of the Materials Manager in relation to the Master Schedule.

The Master Schedule is one of eight important areas in a closed loop Material Requirements Planning System. In the system there are four areas that relate to planning, two areas that relate to internal control of the factory and two areas that relate to control of outside vendor support required for manufacturing.

The four major areas related to planning are:

The Production Plan

The Master Production Schedule

The Material Requirements Plan

The Capacity Requirement Plan

The two areas that relate to internal control of the factory are: The input/output control report, the dispatching function.

The two areas that relate to controlling the outside vendor are: The vendor requirements plan and the purchasing support system.

In addition to the above eight major areas, it is absolutely necessary that the factory have good control over inventory record accuracy, bill of material accuracy, and that the bills of material be structured properly to accomodate the system.

Production Plan - The Materials Manager participates in the Production Plan and has responsibility over the other seven areas. The production plan is management's handle on the business. Production planning meetings should be established with a specific agenda and should involve the top managers of the company. That is the general manager, the director of marketing, the director of manufacturing, the director of finance and the Materials Manager. In this meeting these people should review the results of the previous month's performance, that is the performance of sales against forecasts, the performance of manufacturing against the production plan, the inventory level against planned inventories and the requirements for cash against the planned cash flow for operations. Additionally, they should review the sales forecast, production plan, inventory plan and cash requirements for the existing month. Next, they should review and set the criteria in each of those four areas for the next month and for several months into the future to a point beyond the accumulative lead time of all of the items that they purchase and manufacture, and to a point in time where they have the ability to respond to changing needs of capacity. The horizon of this production plan will vary by industry, it could be as short as six months, in some industries, or out beyond two and a half years in some other industries. Additionally, it should extend beyond the horizon of the master production schedule far enough so that the total requirements for the lowest level of manufactured component parts are seen at the material requirements planning level and the capacity requirements planning level when you take into account the effect of the offsetting lead time of those components. An example of this is illustrated in figure 1 below:

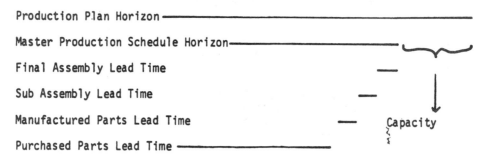

As you can see in the above example, it is necessary to plan the end item requirements far enough out so that the total requirements for the lowest level of manufactured components are seen within the period that represents the total accumulative lead time for those components.

The production plan is management's statement of policy on how the business is to be run with respect to sales volume, production volume, inventory levels and cash requirements for operations. The output of the production plan becomes a constraint to the master production schedule.

An additional purpose of the production plan is that it provides the basis for rough cut capacity planning by key work center. An analysis should be made of each product group to determine what key work centers are affected by each item in a product group. Next, a representative capacity requirement should be determined for that item. Those representative capacities should then be pushed up against the production plan for its entire horizon to determine if any of the key work centers have a capacity requirement that exceeds the capacity available. The purpose of this exercise is to test the validity of the production plan with respect to the existing capacity within the factory.

Master Production Schedule - The next major area in the production planning sequence loop is the master production schedule. The master production schedule has as its input the output from the production plan. The Materials Manager must understand the master scheduling function and be in a position to train, support and supervise the Master Scheduler. The job of the master scheduler is to analyze the feedback that he receives from the material requirements plan and the capacity requirements plan and balance both material

140

and capacity requirements to the requirements of the production plan. In effect, the master production schedule is a master build schedule established by the master scheduler. The sum of the master schedule by individual item within a product group should total back to the production plan. Additional elements of the master production schedule are as follows: It should be reviewed and updated on a weekly basis. The horizon will vary with company, it will be over a period of six to twenty-four or perhaps more than twenty-four months. The total horizon of the master production schedule should be short of the production plan. Essentially, the difference in the horizon is the difference between the accumulative lead time of all the manufactured component parts that make up an end product and the length of the production planning horizon. Essentially, the horizon of the master schedule should be somewhat longer than either the sum of the cumulative lead time of the component parts and assemblies, or the length of time it takes to respond to changes in capacity requirements.

A realistic master schedule will provide the following benefits: One--It provides stability within the material requirements planning system in that the master scheduler establishes the requirements that go down to the material requirements planning system and changes those requirements based on his judgement and the feedback that he gets from the MRP system, the capacity planning system, and the shop floor control system. In this way he is overriding the computer generated planned order release which only responds mathematically to any change in the environment. Two--It balances the internal capacity of the manufacturing facility and the material that is available to meet the plan to the forecast of requirements that come from the production plan. Three--It gives the master scheduler control over planned orders by his utilization of the firm planned order. Four--It maintains the ship date or work order completion date priority throughout the entire system. Five--It furnishes data for order promising on make to order products.

The tool that is used to translate the requirements of the production plan to the master schedule is called the planning bill of material. By definition, the planning bill of material is a non-buildable bill of material for a ficticious assembly that provides a technique to master schedule at a level below the end product level and handle the variety of options that exist at the end level. See the example illustrated below.

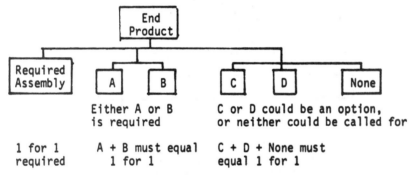

The format of the master production schedule will differ somewhat among make to stock, make to order, and completely engineered products. An example of the different types of master schedules for each type of product are as follows:

Make to stock products master schedule - It is necessary to establish a production plan and through the use of the planning bill of material, translate those requirements to the make to stock master schedule. The formula for the production plan for a make to stock item is: the sales forecast plus the desired ending inventory minus the beginning inventory equals the production plan. To illustrate this, let's use an example for a make to stock product called product group S and look at the input to the master schedule for a two month period as it comes from a production plan. In our example, the input to the master schedule for two months would be a breakdown by each stockkeeping unit within a product group. In our example the sales forecast for a product group for month one has a monthly forecast of 1,000 for product group S. Desired ending inventory is 250, and the beginning inventory is 150. The production plan for group S would be determined as follows: Sales forecast at 1,000 plus desired ending inventory of 250 minus, beginning inventory of 150 would equal a production plan of 1,100. For month two, the sales forecast is 1,050, desired ending inventory is 400 and the beginning inventory is 250. The production plan would then equal the sales forecast of 1,050 plus desired ending inventory of 400, minus the beginning inventory of 250 or the production would be 1,200 units.

To determine the gross requirements input to the master schedule for product group S, let's assume that the product group has four stockkeeping units. S-1 with a popularity ratio of 20%, S-2 with a popularity ratio of 30%, S-3 with a popularity ratio of 40%, and S-4 with a popularity ratio of 10%. Thus, the input to the master production schedule of product group S by using the planning bills and the above mentioned popularity ratios, would be as follows: For month one, where the product group has the requirement of 1,100, S-1 at 20% would have a requirement of 220, S-2 at 30% would have a requirement of 330, S-3 at 40% would have a requirement of 440, and S-4 at 10% would have a requirement of 110. For month two, where the product group has a requirement of 1,200, S-1 would require 240, S-2 would have a requirement of 360, S-3 would have a requirement of 480, and S-4 would require 120.

Product Group S Production Plan	Month 1 1,100	Month 2 1,200
S-1 @ 20%	220	240
S-2 @ 30%	330	360
S-3 @ 40%	440	480
S-4 @ 10%	110	120

Thus, if we follow through on the requirements of stockkeeping unit S-1, we will see a requirement of 220 for month one and 240 in month two. Since the master schedule is updated weekly, it is necessary to break down the monthly forecast into weekly increments. Therefore, we would see a requirement of 55 per week for month one and 60 per week for month two.

An example of how the master schedule would respond to this data appears below. Let's assume that the following information exists on stockkeeping unit S-1. On hand balance, 130 units, lead time 2 weeks, lot size 150, and safety of 15. With this information we can set up the master production schedule for stockkeeping unit S-1.

ITEM S-1		1	2	3	4	5	6	7	8
Prod Forc.		55	55	55	55	60	60	60	60
Act. Cust. Orders									
Available	130	75	20	-35	-90	-150	-210	-270	-330
Available to Promise									
Firm Planned Rec.									

With the above information, the master scheduler would compare the requirements from the production plan to the existing capacity and materials and using his judgement establish firm planned receipts shown by receipt date as follows:

	1	2	3	4	5	6	7	8
Prod Forc.	55	55	55	55	60	60	60	60
Act. Cust. Orders								
Available -130	75	20	115	60	150	90	30	120

	1	2	3	4	5	6	7	8
Available to Promise								
Firm Planned Rec.			150		150			150

The firm planned receipt would then become input to the MRP system shown here by an offset of two weeks lead time from the master schedule. If the product structure of S-1 looked like this:

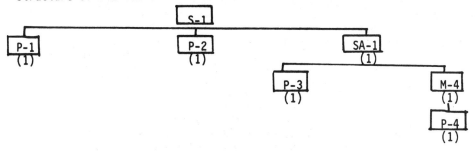

The requirements information on P-1, P-2, and SA-1 to support the schedule of S-1, would be calculated through the MRP system and appear as shown on SA-1 below.

Sub-Assembly SA-1

	1	2	3	4	5	6	7	8
Service Forecast								
Requirements	150		150			150		
Scheduled Receipt								
Available 310								
Planned Order Rel.								

Assume the following status of SA-1. The MRP report for SA-1 would appear as follows: On hand equals 310, lead time equals one week, lot size equals 200, safety stock equals zero.

Sub-Assembly SA-1

	1	2	3	4	5	6	7	8
Service Forecast								
Requirements	150		150			150		
Scheduled Receipt								
Available 310	160	160	10	10	10	-140	-140	-140
Planned Order Rel.					200			

The computer would then generate the requirements of SA-1 to all the component parts used. Those requirements would then be exploded level by level through the bill material to all the parts and sub-assemblies required in the assembly.

   Make to order products master schedule - On make to order items, it is frequently necessary to master schedule at two or more levels. An illustration of this concept will follow. The formula for the production plan is: production plan equals existing backlog plus sales forecast minus the desired ending backlog. As an example, for product group 0 with the following status: existing backlog equals 1,000, sales forecast for month one equals 800, desired ending balance month one equals 900, sales forecast for month two equals 900 and desired ending backlog for month two equals 800. The production plan would be calculated as follows: Month one equals 1,000 ending backlog, plus

800 sales forecast which equals 1,800 minus 900 desired ending backlog which equals a production plan of 900 for month one. Month two equals existing backlog of 900 plus sales forecast of 900 which equals 1,800 minus desired ending backlog of 800 which equals a production plan of 1,000 for month two. The production plan for product group O can then become input to the master production schedule through the use of the planning bill for the make to order products. To illustrate this, assume that product group O is comprised of the following: Common part group A, either sub-assembly B, at 40% popularity or sub-assembly C at 60% popularity and either sub-assembly D at 20% popularity, E at 30% popularity or F at 50% popularity and either option G or product group O could be built without option G. Option G has a popularity of 70%. The planning bill would then appear as follows:

Planning Bill Product Group O

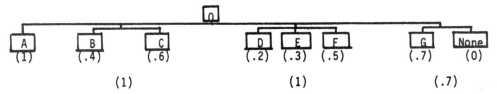

Thus the input to the first level master schedule would appear as follows: Product Group O for month one 900, for month two 1,000. Common part group A, month one, 900, month two, 1,000. Sub-assembly B/C month one 900, month two 1,000. Sub-assembly D/E/F, month one 900, month two 1,000. Sub-assembly G, month one, 630, month two 700.

Production Plan Product Group O

	Month 1	Month 2
Product Group O	900	1,000
Common Part Group A	900	1,000
Sub-Assemblies B & C	900	1,000
Sub-Assemblies D, E, & F	900	1,000
Sub-Assembly G	630	700

To illustrate master scheduling at two levels, it is necessary to follow an optional sub-assembly through both levels. In our example, the production plan for producer Group O is 900 for month 1 and 1,000 for month 2. Sub-assembly B has a popularity of 40% and sub-assembly C has a popularity of 60%. Thus, an example of the master schedules of each of these items could appear as follows (reflecting judgement, and action taken by the master scheduler).

Master Schedule Product Group O

	1	2	3	4	5	6	7	8
Production Plan			125	175	240	230	250	250
Act. Customer Demand	225	225	100	50	10	0	0	0
Available	275	50	325	100	350	100	350	100
*Available to Promise	50		350		490		500	
MPS	500		500		500		500	

Master Schedule Sub-Assembly B (40% Popularity)

	1	2	3	4	5	6	7	8
Service Forecast								

	1	2	3	4	5	6	7	8
Production Forc.	20		140		196		200	
Actual Cust. Demand	90	85	50	15	3	0	0	0
Available	90	5	15	0	3	3	23	23
*Available to Promise	25		135		197		220	
MPS	200		200		200		220	

Master Schedule Sub-Assembly C (60% Popularity)

	1	2	3	4	5	6	7	8
Service Forecast								
Production Forecast	30		210		294		300	
Actual Cust. Demand	135	140	50	35	7	0	0	0
Available	145	5	45	10	9	9	9	9
*Available to Promise	35		215		293		300	
MPS	310		300		300		300	

* Available to promise is non-cumulative.

Let us examine each of these master schedule items, line by line, starting with the first level, Product Group 0.

1. Production Plan - This line reflects the production plan established by management in the production planning meeting. As customer orders are booked, the production plan (forecast) is displaced by the customer orders. The production plan through period G reflects the effect of customer orders.

2. Actual customer demand represents booked customer orders.

3. Available is the result of a calculation based on the formula: Available = (on hand + MPS) - (production plan + actual custom demands). Its purpose is to trigger action messages to the master scheduler if available exceeds requirements by a significant amount or if available is not adequate to meet demand.

4. Available to promise is a non-cumulative figure and calculated as follows: ATP = (on hand + MPS) - The MPS lot is due in. Its purpose is twofold. First, to inform order entry as to the amount of saleable items in a given time period. Second, to provide a basis for determining the production forecast for an option item at the next lower level. i.e. ATP for producer group 0 in period 1 is 50. The production forecast for sub-assembly B for that period is 50 x 40%, or 20.

5. MPS is an amount established by the master scheduler for the item. Its purpose is also twofold. First, to generate requirements to the non-optional parts and assemblies. Second, to provide a basis for rough cut capacity planning.

The master schedule for sub-assemblies B and C are logically identical.

1. Service forecast - Reflects the independent demand forecast for service requirements in the above examples none exists.

2. Production forecast - Determined by applying percentage ratio to the available to promise of the first level master schedule item.

3. Actual customer demand represents booked customer orders.

4. Available is the result of a calculation identical to that in the first level item.

5. Available to promise is also the result of a calculation identical to that in the first level item and used for the same purpose.

6. MPS is a scheduled or planned receipt determined by the master schedule. Its purpose is to generate requirements to the next lower level item in the master schedule or MRP (if the item is non-optional).

The logic displayed in the above examples can be repeated for multiple levels of master scheduling as long as options occur at those levels. When options no longer exist in whole or in part, the MPS quantity becomes input to MRP. Once the input is provided, MRP handles the requirements as described in the make to stock example shown above.

Uniquely engineered product master scheduling - The essential differences between make to order and uniquely engineered products are:

1. Lead time must be included for the engineering and drafting functions in order promising.

2. A representative lead time must be determined by each product type for each manufacturing function, included in the network as a representative router and displaced by actuals as the engineered product emerges.

3. Lead times for unique long lead time purchased materials must be considered in order promising.

In determining the representative lead times, it is not necessary to attempt 100% accuracy, as, in the case of most estimates, the lead time estimate will be excessive in some areas and shorts in others. The idea is to establish bench marks for scheduling purposes to be used for updating priorities until the actual requirements are known. Level by level master scheduling is handled by the make to order concepts described above until the product requirements are defined by engineering. After that, the estimates are displaced by the real requirements as described in the make to stock example above.

Capacity Planning - Capacity requirements are determined as follows:

1. Developing a router file to identify the manufacturing work centers and operations required in processing a part or assembly.

2. Developing standard hours required for each operation.

3. Extending the standard hours per piece by the required lot size.

4. Adding in the set-up time for each operation.

5. Calculating a load factor for each manufacturing work center. The load factor includes time for breaks, down time, lost time, efficiency factors, etc. Its purpose is to provide a method of determining total man hours required at actual to produce a part at standard. For example, through analysis, it could be determined that a specific work center requires 100 actual man hours to produce 70 hours at standard. In that case, the load factor would be 70%. Or, to state it another way, if 70 hours at standard were required through a work center in a specific period, 100 man hours capacity need be available at that work center.

Once the above information has been determined, a capacity plan for each work center can be calculated for released and planned work orders. An example of a capacity plan is:

```
                  Capacity Requirements Plan
                     Work Center VTL 3
                   Planned Capacity 100.0 Hrs.
                   Maximum Capacity 150.0 Hrs.
              Planned    Released    Period    Cumulative
   Period     Hours       Hours      Total       Total

     1           0        110.0      110.0       110.0
     2           0         90.0       90.0       100.0
     3         50.0        60.0      110.0       103.3
     4         80.0        20.0      100.0       102.5
     5        100.0          0       100.0       102.0
   etc.
```

The cumulative total is determined by dividing the running sum of the period total by the number of periods. For example, period three period total is 110.0 + 90.0 + 110.0 = 3100 divided by 3 periods = 103.3. The purpose of the cumulative total is to show long term underloads or overloads. The purpose of the period total is to show underloads and overloads by specific week, so load balancing can take place.

The capacity planning system completes the planning level of the "closed loop material requirements planning system". Next, it is necessary to address the execution phase of the system. The execution phase encompasses both the internal shop floor control system and the control system to support purchasing and communicate with the "outside shop", the suppliers of required materials.

Shop Floor Control - consists of two major areas: Input/output control and dispatching.

The input/output control system provides a method of measuring and monitoring the planned and actual input and output of each work center. Additionally, it provides factory management with a method of identifying responsibility for schedule slippage and exception messages when work throughout is over or under planned levels. An example of an input/output control report is as follows:

```
                      Input/Output Report
                       Work Center VTL 3

week      -4     -3     -2     -1    Cur.    2     3     4     5

Plan In  100.0  100.0  100.0  100.0  100.0  100.0 100.0 100.0 100.0

Act In    90.0   95.0  105.0   85.0

Cum Dev  -10.0  -15.0  -10.0  -25.0
```

                        Tolerence ± 20.0 Hrs.

```
week      -4     -3     -2     -1    Cur.    2     3     4     5

Plan Out 100.0  100.0  100.0  100.0  100.0  100.0 100.0 100.0 100.0

Act Out  110.0  105.0   95.0   95.0

Cum Dev  +10.0  +15.0  +10.0   +5.0
```

                        Tolerence ± 20.0 Hrs.
              Planned backlog 80.0   Actual backlog 85.0

As noted above, the input level is below accepted tolerence of ± 20.0

hrs., which generates the exception message I. U. (input under) and flags a potential problem. Upon investigation, management could discover that the problem lies in production control, if this is a first operation work center, or either in production control or an upstream work center if ATL 3 is not a first operation work center.

If the output is outside of accepted tolerence, the problem is in the work center. The comparison of planned to actual backlog could also indicate a problem. If backlog is too low, the foreman could experience a problem in maintaining efficiency and in machine loading. If backlog is too high, it indicates a real or potential schedule slippage.

Daily Dispatch List - The daily dispatch list is a vital report that, when properly maintained, eliminates the "hot list" and provides the manufacturing foremen with the information and visibility he needs to maintain due dates, and efficiently load his work centers. The format for a typical daily dispatch list appears below:

Daily Dispatch List Date 7/20/77
Department 650
Work Center ATL 3

Daily Capacity 20.0   No. of Men 3   No. of Mach. 2
                             Jobs in work center

S T	W/O	Part #		Desc.	Qty.	Start Date	Opr. Comp. Date	W/O Comp. Date	Opn. No.	Set-up time	Run Time
R	M709	3395	M	Gear	100	7/17/77	7/18/77	8/1/77	20	5.0	10.0
S	M731	3380	J	Gear	20	7/19/77	7/20/77	8/1/77	20	10.0	8.0
Q	M692	3167	T	Spacer	37	7/20/77	7/22/77	8/3/77	30	1.0	16.0
M	M763	3023	J	Ring	150	7/25/77	7/28/77	8/9/77	30	6.0	24.0
										22.0	58.0

Jobs Coming

S T	W/O	Part #		Desc.	Qty.	Start Date	Opr. Comp. Date	W/O Comp. Date	Curr. W/C	Set-up time	Run Time
R	M782	2971	B	Wedge	50	7/19/77	7/20/77	8/2/77	ENL 1	3.0	8.0
R	M785	3018	K	Gear	100	7/21/77	7/22/77	8/4/77	ENL 1	8.0	4.0
Q	M793	3099	O	Spacer	30	7/22/77	7/26/77	8/8/77	GND 3	1.5	12.0
Q	M799	3101	L	Spacer	20	7/25/77	7/28/77	8/15/77	GND 4	6.5	20.0
										19.0	44.0

The information on the daily dispatch list is self-explanatory, except perhaps for ST, which means job status. The codes are R--running, S--In set-up, Q--in backlog and H--on hold. With the information the foreman has a clear idea of the priority of the jobs in his work center, and knowledge of the status and priority of the jobs in work centers immediately prior to his. In order to maintain the proper priority of orders, it is necessary for the foreman to communicate significant delays that he has in meeting the schedule to the master scheduler. If a delay cannot be overcome and the job be back on schedule by the promised completion date, it is necessary to change the completion date. A formal report should be established to communicate the information, called "Anticipated Delay Report". It is a manual report which identifies the work order operation, scheduled start and completion date, reason for the delay and expected completion date.

Additional reports, such as a detailed work order status report, and a work center load report, showing all open work orders that are scheduled to cross a work center by specific week in the future, are found in most shop floor control systems. The key reports, however, are the capacity planning report, input/output control report, and daily dispatch list.

Control of "Outside Shop" - The suppliers. With the information from MRP, showing the time phased requirements for materials, it is possible to use the information to communicate requirements to suppliers. By extending the logic used in the planning bill, a popularity ratio can be applied to the requirements for a part, and a Vendor Requirements Report can be established. An example of this logic is:

Part # 17635

Planned Order Releases by Week

Week	1	2	3	4	5	6	7	8
Total Plan Orders	1,000		1,000		1,500		2,000	
Vendor A 70%	700		700		1,050		1,400	
Vendor B 20%	200		200		300		400	
Vendor C 10%	100		100		150		200	

The requirements can be communicated to the suppliers so he can plan his capacity to meet your requirements. Once this type of communication is routinely established with a supplier, it is possible to negotiate shorter lead times, get him to carry inventory for you, and to negotiate lower prices.

Other reports used in purchasing, other than the purchase order itself, are supplier performance records that track the suppliers delivery and quality performance.

It is purchasing's responsibility to inform the master scheduler, through the use of the "Anticipated Delay Report", of delays. The master scheduler must then analyze the impact of the delay and formally change the completion date of all affected orders. By doing so, he maintains proper priorities throughout the system.

A summary overview of the closed loop MRP system is:

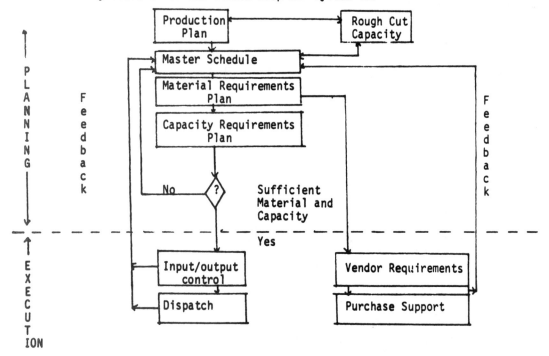

SUMMARY

In the day to day activity of master scheduling many conflicts will arise that require rescheduling of the Master Schedule. The materials manager's role is to oversee the function of master scheduling and to make sure that the manufacturing control system provides effective and timely communications from top management downward, and from the factory floor and purchasing upward. The key points he should participate in are:

1. Production Plan - With other key management members, establish Product Group forecasts, inventory goals and production plan. Also, review previous month's performance against plan.

2. Master Schedule - See that an effective master schedule system is established and maintained in the company. Train the master schedulers and supervise the master scheduling function. Help resolve priority conflicts as they occur and communicate information effecting shipments to marketing.

3. Manufacturing Systems - See that an effective Material Requirements Plan, Capacity Requirements Plan, Shop Floor Control System, and Purchasing Support System exist in the company and that it provides timely and effective feedback to the Master Schedule. If an effective system does not exist, it is the Materials Manager's responsibility to justify the implementation of an effective system to the company's management.

ABOUT THE AUTHOR

Al Stevens is the president of A. L. Stevens, Inc., P.O. Box 2398, Dublin, CA, 94566.

His experience in manufacturing companies includes managerial positions in production and inventory control, data processing, cost accounting, materials management, and the executive level of manufacturing management, in the position of Vice President Manufacturing.

He has been directly responsible for the implementation of Materials Requirements Planning (MRP) in two companies. Additionally he has been an advisor to a number of companies who have made significant improvements in production and inventory control.

An active APICS member, former President of the Golden Gate Chapter and current Vice President for Region X, he has been a frequent speaker at monthly technical sessions, seminars, and the 1973, 1974 and 1975 International Conferences. He is the author of several articles on MRP and Production Inventory Control.

Additionally, he conducts training sessions on Master Scheduling with Walt Goddard of Oliver Wight, Inc.

His education includes a B.A. in Accounting at Golden Gate University in San Francisco, and he has attended The Smaller Company Management Program at Harvard Graduate School of Business.

Sulser, Samuel S., "Advanced Techniques in Master Planning -- A Matter of Systems Design," 27th Annual Conference Proceedings (1984).

This paper provides insights into how master planning can be enchanced. The primary contribution is to show how simulation of alternative production plan scenarios can be evaluated in terms of capacity and materials implications. The paper should be interesting to readers who have well-functioning master planning systems, but wish to make them better.

The definition provided for master planning functions has been around for many years. What is added is the goal of providing management with a clear understanding of the expected implications for materials and capacity if certain programs are adopted. Specifically, the intent is to simulate alternative master production scheduling (MPS) and production planning scenarios to evaluate their feasibility as well as their impact on overall managerial objectives.

The author identifies three capacity management time frames, each of which has concomitant needs, tools, and actions. A load profile can be generated for whatever resource/time frame is of interest. The resources can be anything (e.g., plant, vendor, machine center) that can be extended from the master plan. Routing data are the link from master plan to resource. Included are resource, unit of measure, consumption quantity, lead-time offset, and operation identifiers.

The resource load profile is stated in whatever units of measure are desirable -- labor-hours, dollars, etc. The result is an output similar to capacity requirements planning with percent utilization information.

One resource load profile advocated by the author is for the production plan to determine the sum of the parts continually.

In describing the simulation methodology, a key feature is identified that others call data control. What this means is that a copy of the actual data is input to the simulation of each scenario. Confounding data by previous analysis is avoided and only agreed upon outcomes are allowed to changed the actual database.

Scenarios are, in essence, alternative plans or what-if questions. They may be posed by marketing, manufacturing, top management, or in response to some disturbance (e.g., a vendor strike). What is needed is to analyze alternative scenarios in terms of their impact on material plans, capacity requirements, and strategic objectives.

The approach taken in this paper is similar to research others are conducting in master planning. The objective is to make master planning more responsive to business needs and to better plan and use company resources to that end.

ADVANCED TECHNIQUES IN MASTER PLANNING— A MATTER OF SYSTEMS DESIGN

Samuel S. Sulser, CPIM
Sulser and Associates, Inc.

OBJECTIVE

The purpose of this paper is to identify and discuss Advanced Techniques in Master Planning that are available to the user today, with proper systems design. All of these techniques may have been discussed, presented and explained before but this paper will focus upon the system design aspects required to make them happen. It is important to understand that the author will present the design from an interactive, integrated viewpoint and that the discussion will be limited by time and space constraints.

MASTER PLANNING, A DEFINITION

While Master Planning has not yet been formally defined by APICS, a number of consultants and practitioners are beginning to draft their own definitions. I wil attempt to summarize the activity again and I hope that the definition becomes clearer in the process.

Master Planning is the act of integrating management functions, including Production Planning, Demand Management, Resource Planning, Master Production Scheduling, Rough Cut Capacity Planning and Final Assembly Scheduling, into a comprehensive system providing management with the visibility of the impact of their decisions upon company resources. Figure #1 provides a graphic display of the integrated functions of a Master Planning system. While other definitions have included such management activities as Strategic Planning and Business Planning, I have deliberately begun at a lower level where there is less abstract thinking and moredetailed data available. That is not to say that the results of the Strategic Planning and Business Planning sessions could not be simulated through a Master Planning system. They can be and should be, providing that the output of these sessions can be used as input into Master Planning.

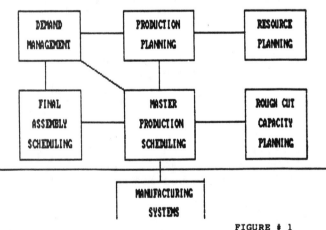

MASTER PLANNING FUNCTIONS

FIGURE # 1

ADVANCED TECHNIQUES

The integration of the functions outlined in Figure # 1 allows for the passing of common data from one functional area to another for planning purposes. This data can be analyzed in order to determine total impact of a decision on the company and not simply upon the originating area of responsibility. The key analysis required include;

1. Capacity Management - to insure the resources are not overloaded in any of the planning time frames.

2. Production Plan = Sum of the MPS - to insure management's plan is being adhered to in the detail of the Master Production Schedule.

3. Simulation - to allow alternative plans to be analyzed prior to the selection of the final management strategy.

Each of the above techniques will be discussed in detail from a design point of view.

CAPACITY MANAGEMENT TIME FRAMES

	SHORT	INTERMEDIATE	LONG
NEED	CONTROL EXECUTE	PLAN MONITOR	PLAN SIMULATE
TOOL	FINAL ASSY SCHEDULE	ROUGH CUT	RESOURCE PLANNING
ACTION	OVERTIME ALT. RTGS. LOT SIZES RESCHEDULE	ADJUST LABOR SUBCONTRACT MAKE VS BUY	FACILITIES CAPITAL EQUIP.

FIGURE # 2

Capacity Management can be broken down into three time frames, each of which have unique requirements, analysis tools, and management action decisions. (see Figure # 2)

- Long Range capacity management is typically referred to as Resource Planning, driven off of a Productio Plan and used to determine load for planning facilities, capital equipment, etc.

- Intermediate Range capacity management is usually referred to as Rough Cut Capacity Planning driven off of the Master Production Schedule and used to determine load for planning subcontract requirements, adjusting the labor force, make vs buy decisions, etc.

- Short Term capacity management, in the case of an assembly or production line, can also be driven off of a Master Production Schedule and used to determine sequence and priority of the Final Assembly orders as they are released from the MPS to the line.

All three time frames can be planned through the use of a load profile technique, where the generated load is compared to the available capacity and the resulting ratio is displayed in a bar chart. The first requirement is a multi-level plannin bill of material capable of maintaining group, family, MPS and other level items. The group level will contain the Production Plan items (units or dollars) or its equivalent. The family level can be used to help spread the Production Plan over a number of product families, or to an MPS model item. The lower level of the bill may be an end item, options of a model or components of an item but will be the level used to drive into the manufacturing system. This planning bill of material will provide for the allocation of the Production Plan to the lower levels, thereby allowing the different level plans to be based on the same source.

The next step is to define the resources to be measured: a plant, a machine center, a vendor, a shipping target, etc. Anything that can be measured through an extension of the Production Plan or the Master Production Schedule should be given consideration. The advice here is to be creative, all you need is a unique identifier and a statement of current and/or future capacity to measure against.

We are now ready to connect the items we are planning (Production Plan and Master Schedule) with the resources to be consumed (plant, vendor) via a routing record. This record can consume multiple units of measure (dollars, pounds) from the resource as long as they are pre-defined to the resource. The routing record can be created at any of the three levels, as long as all items at that level are considered. If the plant resources are to be consumed by the Production Plan of the group level, then all group items must be reviewed for consuming those resources. Key routing data includes;
- unique operation identifier
- resource to be consumed
- resource unit of measure
- consumption quantity for a production unit
- operation lead time offset

We can now begin to tie the Capacity Management pieces together so that a plan at any level will generate the associated load represented by the routing and load analysis can be completed. We do this by simply multiplying the plan quantity of each item times the consumption quantity of each unit of measure for every routing operation required in producing that item. The result of that calculation is a resource unit of measure load quantity. We can then create a load detail record reflecting that quantity, record the associated unit of measure, and date the record using the lead time offset of the routing record subtracted from the due date of the order.

We are now ready to do a resource load profile. This is accomplished by summing all detail records together for a specified resource/unit of measure, sorted by date and comparing that sum to the capacity as specified for the corresponding date. This time phased load/capacity ratio is called a Resource Load Profile and can represent any resource/unit of measure being consumed. (see Figure # 3)

RESOURCE LOAD PROFILE

RESOURCE 12345   U/M LB   CAPACITY 25000

DATE	CAPACITY	LOAD	PCT	PROFILE
10/08/84	25000	32000	128	***********
10/15/84	25000	26000	104	**********
10/22/84	25000	24000	96	*********
10/29/84	30000	24000	80	*******
11/05/84	30000	32000	107	***********

FIGURE # 3

The key to this design approach is that the interactive transactions maintaining the items plan (quantity and date), and the items routing (resource u/m, consumption factor, and offset lead time) must also maintain the generated load detail. This allows the system to access the load detail for any resource, any unit of measure, any plan at any point in time in an interactive mode and display the current load profile for that resource.
System requirements include;
1. Multi-level planning bill of material
2. Resource master file
3. Resource routing
4. Supply plan (production plan or MPS)
5. Interactive maintenance of load detail

PRODUCTION PLAN = SUM OF THE MPS

A key principle in Master Scheduling is that the sum of the MPS must be equal to the Production Plan. (see Figure # 4) This has always been easier said than done. We will review two design approaches that can accomplish this in an on-line interactive mode.

The first approach is the method used in the Capacity Management discussion earlier, only adopted to reflect the consumption of the Production Plan.

Maintain one resource routing record for every MPS item which can be related to a Production Plan. This record would be used to convert the quantity scheduled for the item into the unit of measure stated in the Production Plan.

PRODUCTION PLAN = SUM OF MPS

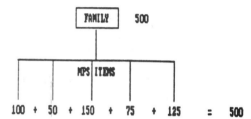

FIGURE # 4

Maintain one resource master to reflect the Production Plan, using the current and planned capacity fields for storing Production Plan quantities.

Modify the inquiry screen to reflect the consumption of the Production Plan instead of a load profile.

Again, maintenance of the MPS will automatically create and maintain the load detail records which now can be summed against the Production PLan at any point in time.

Another approach, which may be more acceptable to the system analysts, is the summarized bill approach expanded to include the quantity of the plan instead of the components. This approach also requires a multi-level planning bill, with where-used capabilities. In this case when we create the Production Plan supply record we include a new field called MPS Summary Quantity. Each maintenance transaction affecting date or quantity of an MPS item is modified to do a where-used search to retrieve the associated parents Production Plan record and the MPS Summary Quantity updated accordingly. Each time we inquire against the Production Plan we also see a sum of the associated MPS quantities.

At first glance, either of the approaches may appear cumbersome. Actually, in an integrated, interactive system they are both processed quickly and easily. This allows management and the Master Scheduler instant warning when the MPS is beginning to vary from the Production Plan. Messages can be generated based on a variance of "n" %, depending on how sophisticated the user wants to get.

SIMULATION

This is not only the most exciting but also the most needed of any of the techniques under discussion. It is also one of the easiest to accomplish with proper system design.

Some software companies tout "simulation capability" but actually only have one set of data that must be changed over and over again in an iterative process in order to change the results. Don't forget where you were before you started though, you may have to change it back manually before you can process in the production mode. While this might be called simulation under a broad definition of the word, it is not the process that I will be referring to in this discussion.

I recommend the use of a Plan Identification Code (Plan I.D.) allowing the generation and separation of multiple plans for the same item. This can be as simple as A-Z added to the item number. (i.e. AB123 A and AB123 B) It could be a group, family or MPS item. Whatever the item, or level, this gives you the flexibility of having up to 26 different versions for the same item. This applies to both supply
- Production Plan
- Master Production Schedule
and demand
- Sales forecast
- Projected actual demand
- Introduction of new line
- Movement of large order delivery date

The multiple plan approach also gives the Master Scheduler the ability to concentrate on one task at a time, while actually accomplishing more than one. He may be asked to simulate a series of marketing scenarios of "what if" situations. He begins by creating Plan A, Plan B, etc If interrupted during the process of simulation, he can stop where he is, access the production data, answer the question or take the required action and then turn back to simulation without fear of mixing the data. You can't do this without the multiple plan ability.

MATERIAL PLANNING

Once we have created multiple supply and demand plans for an item, we can then generate various results by applying supply A against demand A or supply A against demand B and so on. Applying these varying plans can be useful in calculating Projected Available Balance (PAB) in material planning and Available To Promise (ATP) in order promising. The master scheduler now has a powerful tool to be used in answering the "what if" questions concerning PAB and ATP as posed by his management. (see Figure # 5) In the sample illustrated, the question was simply " What happens to our availabilty if we cut the current MPS quantities in half ? "

Another aspect of material simulation is the material planning factors used in the calculation of PAB and ATP. These factors should also be available for simulation including;
- Safety stock
- Actual demand time fence
- Lot size
These are necessary in order for the master scheduler to determine the best planning factors before making the plan a reality.

RESOURCE PLANNING

Once the material plans are in place, the Master Scheduler must determine what impact the plan will have on the resources. Each supply plan can be made to generate load detail records as described in the earlier section on Capacity Management. The Master Scheduler can therefore create the plans required to support the scenarios privide by Marketing, automatically establishing the load detail records and measure the load created by each plan against the available resources. Plan A overloads the resources, Plan B underloads them, Plan C may be the most realistic. All may be analyzed in a matter of minutes. (figure # 6) Again, we are only measuring the plan(s) against the resources and not considering the potential changes in the resource planning factors. In most companies, capacity may change dramatically from one period to another. If that change is planned then we need to reflect it in the system. The factors to monitor include
- current to future capacity
- date of change
- planned increase in efficiency
These types of changes must be included in the resource planning before final approval is given to a material plan.
System requirements include;
1. Inclusion of Plan I.D. for supply and demand
2. Ability to compare plans based on Plan I.D.
3. Ability to modify planned capacity

CONCLUSION

Summarized system design requirements include
- Multi-level planning bill of material
- MPS master file with planning factors
- Resource master with planning factors
- Resource routing with multiple units of measure
- Supply plan variable by Plan I.D.
- Demand plan variable by Plan I.D.
- Automatically updated load detail
- On-line, interactive update of all files

Summarized system functions include;
- Production Planning ability to compare the sum of the Master Schedule to the Production Plan.
- Demand Management ability to measure the impact of a customer order upon both material and resource plans before booking the order. (ATP)
- Resource Planning ability to measure consumption based upon the planning time frame of that consumption. Long range planning consumes facilities, intermediate consumes labor, short range consumes productivity.
- Master Production Scheduling ability to plan for and simulate the impact of various management scenarios without changing the production data.
- Final Assembly Scheduling ability to create and maintain a material plan that is within resources up to the point of releasing to the FAS. Thereby driving the FAS with realistic production data.
These are but a few of the functions supported by the advanced techniques of Master Planning in this discussion.

Two years ago at the Conference in Chicago, a friend of mine stated that a national crusade might be necessary to generate the proper interest in Master Planning. Last year in New Orleans, additional speakers picked up his challenge and spoke on the subject as pertaining to their company. We need to continue this discussion until Master Planning has been defined and implemented in enough places to begin reaping the potential benefits. It is worth the effort.

SIMULATED PAB AND ATP

MASTER PRODUCTION SCHEDULE

ITEM AB123	BOH 0	SFTY STK 500	PLAN T F 4	LOT SIZE 5000		PLAN ID A
DATE		10/08/84	10/15/84	10/22/84	10/29/84	11/05/84
IND FCST						
DEP FCST						
ACT DMD		21000	19000	17000	15000	12000
PAB		10500	17500	24500	33500	53500
ATP		11000	7000	7000	9000	20000
MPS		32000	26000	24000	24000	32000

AB123	0	500	4	5000		B
DATE		10/08/84	10/15/84	10/22/84	10/29/84	11/05/84
IND FCST						
DEP FCST						
ACT DMD		21000	19000	17000	15000	12000
PAB		-5500	-11500	-16500	-19500	-23500
ATP		-5000	-6000	-5000	-3000	-4000
MPS		16000	13000	12000	12000	16000

FIGURE # 5

RESOURCE LOAD PROFILE

RESOURCE 12345   U/M LB   CAPACITY 20000   PLAN ID A

DATE	CAPACITY	LOAD	PCT	PROFILE
10/08/84	20000	32000	160	***************
10/15/84	20000	26000	130	************
10/22/84	20000	24000	120	***********
10/29/84	20000	24000	120	***********
11/05/84	20000	32000	160	***************

RESOURCE LOAD PROFILE

RESOURCE 12345   U/M LB   CAPACITY 30000   PLAN ID B

DATE	CAPACITY	LOAD	PCT	PROFILE
10/08/84	30000	32000	107	***********
10/15/84	30000	26000	87	*********
10/22/84	30000	24000	80	********
10/29/84	30000	24000	80	********
11/05/84	30000	32000	107	***********

RESOURCE LOAD PROFILE

RESOURCE 12345   U/M LB   CAPACITY 30000   PLAN ID C

DATE	CAPACITY	LOAD	PCT	PROFILE
10/08/84	30000	32000	107	***********
10/15/84	28000	26000	93	**********
10/22/84	28000	24000	86	*********
10/29/84	28000	24000	96	*********
11/05/84	28000	32000	114	************

FIGURE # 6

ABOUT THE AUTHOR

Syl Sulser has been involved in the design and implementation of manufacturing systems since 1968 and his experience includes;
- Implementing COPICS in 1974
- Consulting, educational and management responsibilities with Arista Manufacturing Systems from 1975-1982
- Design and implementation of TLA's Master Production Schedule module

He has provided consulting and educational support for client implementations in the U.S., Canada and Europe. Mr. Sulser has spoken at previous conferences and at various chapter meetings. He has recently had an article published on Enhancing the Master Production Schedule.

Reprinted from 1985 APICS Conference Proceedings.

MASTER SCHEDULING AND FINAL ASSEMBLY
SCHEDULING: WHAT'S THE DIFFERENCE?
Michael G. Tincher, CPIM
David W. Buker, Inc.

One of the major tasks a company faces in the definition of their planning and scheduling systems is determining how and at what level a company will Master Schedule.
The definition at what level to Master Schedule will have
implications in terms of the level of detail Sales/Market-
ing will have to provide in their forecasts, the level in
the product structure inventory will be carried, the
leadtime quoted for customer delivery and whether the
Master Schedule and Final Assembly Schedule will be one
and the same document or whether they will be two seperate
and distinct processes.

The Master Production Schedule defines the detailed
product mix to be produced within the production rates of
the Production Plan. It is the What, How Much and When at
the product, model, feature, option or product mix level
for scheduling production in manufacturing to satisy the
Sales Forecast. (Figure 1)

MASTER SCHEDULING

ALLOCATES MONTHLY PRODUCTION RATES INTO WEEKLY PRODUCTION SCHEDULES

BASED ON:
- **PRODUCT MIX**
  - -MODELS, FEATURES, OPTIONS
- **MATERIAL AVAILABILITY**
- **CAPACITY AVAILABILITY**

The Master Production Schedule is normally updated on
a weekly basis and considers material and capacity in the
development of the schedule.

PRODUCTION STRATEGY

The development of the Master Schedule is based upon
the classification of a company's products into the categories of Make-ToStock (MTS), Assemble-To-Order (ATO),
Make-To-Order (MTO), and Engineer-To-Order (ETO). The
first step to classifying products into the various production strategy categories (MTS, ATO, MTO, ETO) is an
understanding of the cumulative leadtime of each product
(Figure 2).

MANUFACTURING RESOURCE PLANNING

DELIVERY LEAD TIME		
INVENTORY	CAPACITY	MAKE TO STOCK

DELIVERY LEAD TIME		
INVENTORY	CAPACITY	ASSEMBLE TO ORDER

DELIVERY LEADTIME		
INVENTORY	CAPACITY	MAKE TO ORDER

DELIVERY LEADTIME		
ENGINEERING TIME	CAPACITY	ENGINEER TO ORDER

CUMULATIVE LEAD TIME			
PURCHASE MATERIAL	MANUFACTURE PARTS	ASSEMBLE PRODUCT	SHIP

"INVENTORY AN CAPACITY MUST BE PLANNED TO MAINTAIN COMPETITIVE DELIVERY LEAD TIME."

The cumulative leadtime of the product is defined as
the time it takes to purchase material, manufacture the
parts, assemble the product and ship the product. This is
the total leadtime required to plan, produce and deliver
the product to the marketplace. The next step is to determine the competitive delivery leadtime required in the
market place. Then Sales/Marketing and Manufacturing can
plan the inventory and production of the product to a state
of completion required to meet this competitive delivery
leadtime. Thus, some products are Make-To-Stock (MTS),
Assemble-To-Order (ATO), Make-To-Order (MTO), or Engineer-
To-Order (ETO). Sales/Marketing and Manufacturing must
come to an agreement to properly plan inventory and capacity to meet competitive delivery leadtimes of the products in the market place.

MAKE-TO-STOCK

The Make-To-Stock (MTS) product is to be produced to
stock and is shipped off the shelf. The delivery leadtime
is very short, usually a day or two. The product must be
planned and produced prior to the receipt of the customer
order. The Production Plan develops the rates of production by product line and the Master Schedule determines the
mix of the various items that are produced to stock. The
Master Schedule is stated in stock-keeping units, end
product items or a saleable configuration. In the Make-To-
Stock environment Sales/Marketing provides a Sales Forecast
or rate of sales by product line and also participates in
determining the product mix forecasts at the stock-keeping
level. (Figure 3)

MASTER SCHEDULE MAKE-TO-STOCK

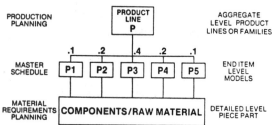

An example would be where Sales/Marketing provides a Sales
Forecast at the product line level (Product line P) and
also provides a mix forecast of the of the individual models
(Products P1-P5). The Master Schedule is developed taking
the Sales Forecast for models P1-P5 along with the beginning finished inventory for models P1-P5 and predetermined
inventory objectives for models P1-P5. The Master Schedule
for products P1-P5 would also be the Final Assembly Schedule in that the Master Schedule is developed at the top
level assembly or finished product. We can therefore
state in a typical Make-To-Stock environment the Master
Schedule and Final Assembly Schedule would be one and the
same.

ASSEMBLE-TO-ORDER

Assemble-To-Order (ATO) product is planned and produced
at the component part or sub-assembly level and is assembled to order after receipt of the customer order. The
Master Schedule defines the sub-assemblies to be produced
in order to be available for assembly in the Final Assembly Schedule.

The Master Schedule becomes a component or sub-
assembly schedule in an environment where a customer may
choose from a multitude of features and options. These
features and options are then assembled into customer
chosen finished product. (Figure 4) One of the main
reasons behind the Master Scheduling of components is that
it may not be feasible to maintain discrete Master Schedule
items (finished products) for every possible finished configuration. For a manufacturer with highly assemble-to-order
or customer configured products the Master Scheduling task
of scheduling finished products (saleable configuration) as
in the Make-TO-Stock environment could become unmanageable
due to the myriad of configurations.
Also Sales/Marketing would be responsible for providing
end item forecasts for each possible configuration. An
example for Assemble-To-Order product would be where the

© **American Production & Inventory Control Society**

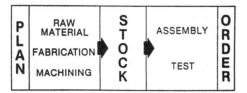

MASTER PRODUCTION SCHEDULING VS. FINAL ASSEMBLY SCHEDULING

| P L A N | RAW MATERIAL FABRICATION MACHINING | S T O C K | ASSEMBLY TEST | O R D E R |

STATEMENT OF THE ANTICIPATED BUILD SCHEDULE IN END ITEMS OR LOWER LEVEL ITEMS

MANAGEMENT COMMITMENT TO DELIVER SPECIFIC END PRODUCTS TO CUSTOMER ORDER OR TO FINISHED INVENTORY

(Figure 4)

finished configurations have been disassembled into their major components or sub-assemblies (figure 5). All of the major components will be grouped under the major heading Product X. This would be the top level Master Schedule item in the two level Master Schedule.

PLANNING BILL STRUCTURE

ASSEMBLE-TO-ORDER

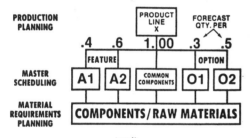

(Figure 5)

This top level Master Schedule item is a non-buildable product whose components are the aggregation of the features and options. Sales/Marketing will need to provide the monthly forecast for the top level Product X. Sales/Marketing will also need to predict the consumption rate of the second level Master Schedule items, in this case features A1 and A2 and Option 01 and 02. This second level forecast is called the mix percentage and is normally provided as a percentage of the Product X. The mix percentage forecasts for Product X components are (.4) A1, (.6) A0, (.3) 01, (.5) 02 and (1.0) for the common components. The mix percentage planning is most easily implemented using a planning bill of material. Using the figure 5 example, if the plan called for 100 of product X the forecasts for A1=40, A2=60, 01=30,02=50 and common components = 100. This mix percentage in the planning bill provides the mix of major components that will be consumed in the Final Assembly Schedule.

Since the defined Product X is not a buildable configuration, but is instead intended to facilitate the proper planning of all the features and options contained in Product X the individual end item (Saleable Configuration) must be recaptured in the order entry process. Therefore, order entry to support the two level Master Schedule must create an end item part number that defines the specific configuration sold. At the time of order entry a temporaty part number is generated. This part number is associated with the specific customer order and would have in the Bill of Material the major components selected by the customer. This part number and Bill of Material would be used by manufacturing for the Final Assembly Scheduling process. This link is easily established using the Product Family Bill as the menu for customer configuration in the order entry process.

In the Assemble-To-Order Master Schedule environment where the major components or sub-assemblies are scheduled the Final Assembly Schedule is used to convey the customer order defined through order entry. The Final Assembly Schedule provides the means to convert a customer configured sales order into a manufacturing order. The manufac-

turing order is based upon the temporary part number that is created. The advantage is that a routing can be created for labor tracking, work order costing and material control can transpire for all final assemblies.

Taking a look at the logic in the typical software sued for Assemble-To-Order products is as follows: Using the example for Product X previously established (Figure 5) the quantity forecasted for Product X is 100 and 100 are Master Scheduled for this top level assembly.

(Figure 6)

Forecast	100
Customer Order	
Actual Production	
Top Level MPS	100
Available to Promise	100

The available to promise at this time is 100. (Figure 6) Taking an order for actual configuration of Product X of 40 would reveal the following new information in the Top Level Master Schedule.

(Figure 7)

Forecast	60
Customer Order	40
Actual Production	40
Top Level MPS	60
Available to Promise	60

The forecast for Product X has been displaced by 40, the quantity of the actual order (shown under customer order). The remaining Top Level MPS of Product X is 60 and the available to promise of 60 is then used in the calculation of the planning bill along with the mix percentages for features A1 (.4), A2 (.6) and options 01 (.3), 02 (.5) to create the second level forecast. Notice that the top level MPS has been reduced to 60 and the column Actual Production now contains 40. The Top Level MPS contains 60 because this is what is left of the original 100 planned. This Top Level MPS has been consumed by the actual manufacturing orders for (40) of Product X. These Final Assembly Orders (manufacturing orders) for the pre-configured assemblies appear on the actual production line. With this type of information the Master Schedule is provided with remaining forecasted quantity, actual customer orders, final assembly orders, unconsumed master schedule of top level item X and the available to promise of Product X.

Contrasting the Assemble-To-Order Master Schedule with the Make-To-Stock Schedule it becomes clear that in the Make-To-Stock environment the Master Schedule and Final Assembly Schedule are one and the same, the Master Schedule and the Final Assembly Schedule for Assemble-To-Order are two seperate or distinct processes.

MAKE-TO-ORDER/ENGINEER-TO-ORDER

Make-To-Order and Engineer-To-Order products are planned and produced based upon customer orders. Make-To-Order and Engineer-To-Order environments Master Schedules and Final Assembly Schedules would be based upon customer end item configurations (backlog), and would therefore be one and the same.

The Master Schedule and the Final Assembly Schedule are not the same at the point where customer order backlog in no longer available. The Final Assembly Schedule as defined is made up of customer orders only. The Master Schedule for periods out beyond customer order backlog would be based upon forecast. In the Master Schedule out beyond customer order backlog there may be instances where some inventory or long leadtime materials are planned in anticipation of the customer order. This will typically transpire when the competitive delivery leadtime is less then the cumulative leadtime of the product. For example if the cumulative leadtime of the product was sixteen weeks, but the competitive leadtime was only eight weeks, it would be necessary to flow material through the Master Schedule for items with leadtimes longer than eight weeks. The method utilized for flowing this material is a planning bill of material in the Master Schedule. For Make-To-Order/Engineer-To-Order products the planning bill is normally developed by product family. The planning bill by product family is based upon a forecast from Sales/Marketing with planning percentages developed for the individual products. This is shown in Figure 8, where the Master Schedule Planning Bill is family P1 with percentages for products P101-P104.

PLANNING BILL - MTO

- BY PRODUCT FAMILY
- DETERMINE PLANNING PERCENTAGE OF EACH MTO
- EXPLODE/SUMMARIZE LONG LEADTIME MATERIALS
- CREATE SINGLE LEVEL PRODUCT FAMILY PLANNING BILL

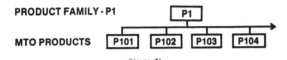

PRODUCT FAMILY · P1

MTO PRODUCTS

(Figure 8)

The long leadtime items for products P101-P104 are summerized resulting in the creation of a single level planning bill in the Master Schedule. This single level Master Schedule planning bill is then consumed when actual customer demand is promised through order entry. At this point in time the Master Schedule for Family P1 is reduced by the actual quantity and the new Master Schedule is created for item P101, P102, P103, P104 or for whichever configuration has been sold. This is again where the Master Schedule and Final Assembly Schedule merge.

CONCLUSION

Most companies that manufacture have products in more than one of the categories of Make-To-Stock, Assemble-To-Order, Make-To-Order or Engineer-To-Order. Many companies have a combination of products in each category. It is important to understand the differences in Master Scheduling and Final Assembly Scheduling for each of these categories, but more important to understand the strategic differences in planning the resources of inventory and capacity to maintain competitive delivery leadtimes. The Master Schedule and the Final Assembly Schedule are only the vehicles to convey these strategic management desisions.

BIBLIOGRAPHY

Tincher, Michael G., "Master Scheduling - The Bridge Between Marketing and Manufacturing" David W. Buker, Inc., Antioch, IL, 1980

Wilkins, Robert, "Master Scheduling anf Final Assembly Shceduling" an unpublished paper. Robert Bosch Video Equipment Division, Salt Lake City, UT, 1984

Michael Tincher is Executive Vice President of David W. Buker, Inc., a Manufacturing Management Education and Consulting firm. Prior to joining this firm, he participated in the development and conduct of Manufacturing Industry Client Education for the Professional Education Division of Arthur Anderson & Company.

Mr. Tincher has served in a number of production and material control positions for Galion Manufacturing Division of Dresser Industries. He has had responsibilities for Production Planning and Master Scheduling and for top management planning and coordination.

Mr. Tincher has a B.A. in Economics from Bowling Green State University and is currently working on an MBA in Marketing at Roosevelt University. He has done consulting for companies in the areas of Production Planning and Master Scheduling, Material Requirements Planning, Capacity Planning and Shop Floor Control. He was the consultant at the Balderson Inc. "Class A" installation. He is a CPIM and a frequent speaker at APICS Chapter meetings and Seminars.

Wemmerlov, Urban, "Assemble-to-Order Manufacturing: Implications for Materials Management," Journal of Operations Management (August 1984).

The assemble-to-order (ATO) firm faces a complex set of issues in the design of its manufacturing planning and control systems. This paper does a good job of identifying critical differences between make-to-stock, ATO, and make-to-order firms. The resultant set of issues for ATO is described, and detailed numerical and actual case examples are presented. The paper will be of interest to readers considering ATO methods for their manufacturing planning/control systems. The issues raised need resolution for a particular firm and will influence both system design and system operation.

The author includes a section on choosing the master production schedule (MPS) unit. This is a basic design question involving the issues of minimizing the number of MPS items as well as providing the necessary stability in manufacturing by using firm planned order techniques.

Bill of material structuring is another basic design question that cannot be separated from the choice of MPS unit. Resolving this issue again involves minimization of MPS units and manufacturing stability. It also involves understanding how the product is sold, that is, how do the customers perceive the option choices?

The author describes order entry and order promise based on available-to-promise (ATP) methods. The time-phased records use the ATP data for first-level items as the driver for explosions to production forecasts for the second-level items. The problem of how to handle the fractional problem is also addressed.

A major section of the paper deals with alternative methods for buffering in ATO firms. This section is one that should be studied carefully by ATO companies so that the best alternatives are selected for the firm.

The case examples are also worth studying in detail. Methods used in actual companies show how the number of MPS items can be reduced, give alternatives to planning bills of materials, illustrate use of firm planned ordering (MPS) at various levels to stabilize production, detail coordination of MPS items produced in different factories, and demonstrate the use of time-phased buffering methods. Again, each of these should be assessed for its potential use in a particular firm.

The paper concludes with a list of areas for future research. It is hoped that some of these problems will be addressed by both academics and practitioners. The ATO approach represents an important way for many firms to respond to market demands. However, as this article points out, there are many ways to design an ATO system, and improvements are always possible.

Reprinted from the *Journal of Operations Management*, Vol. 4, No. 4 (1984).

Assemble-to-Order Manufacturing: Implications For Materials Management

URBAN WEMMERLÖV*

EXECUTIVE SUMMARY

A company's manufacturing is often characterized as either make-to-stock (MTS), make-to-order (MTO), or assemble-to-order (ATO). This classification relates to the degree of interaction between the technological core and the market, with MTS involving the least amount of interaction and MTO the highest degree of contact. ATO represents a hybrid manufacturing strategy for which parts and subassemblies are made according to forecasts while the final assembly of the products is delayed until customer orders have been received. It is evident that each manufacturing philosophy has strategic as well as operational implications.

This paper focuses on ATO manufacturing and, in particular, on the design and operation of the manufacturing planning and control system. The relative differences between MTO, ATO, and MTS strategies, and the reasons why a company may decide to be an ATO manufacturer, are discussed first. Several problem areas, which must be addressed by a company that chooses this form of manufacturing, are then identified. It is found that the ATO philosophy requires special system design considerations, particularly in the areas of master scheduling, bills -of material structuring, order entry/order promising, final assembly scheduling, and buffering against demand uncertainty. Examples of important issues discussed are the selection of appropriate master schedule units and the associated consequences for the structuring of the bills of material; the choice of efficient procedures for reliable order booking using the combined information from forecasts, confirmed orders, and the master schedule; the relationship between the final assembly schedule and the master schedule; and various techniques that can be used to counter the effects of forecast errors related to the demand for customer options.

Following the discussion of all the issues raised above and the presentation of some common solutions, actual industry applications taken from several companies are used to illustrate various aspects of ATO manufacturing. These case illustrations complement the other material since many of them were chosen to reflect alternative procedural approaches to some ATO-related problems. Finally, areas for future research into the design and operation of ATO manufacturing systems are suggested. It is particularly noted that few normative models for systems design exist in this area.

INTRODUCTION

A manufacturing company's operation can be classified as make-to-stock (MTS), assemble-to-order (ATO), or make-to-order (MTO). It is not uncommon, however, that a company belongs to more than one category, producing some products to stock and others to order. The classification is based on the degree of interaction between the firm's

---

* University of Wisconsin-Madison, Madison, Wisconsin.

production function and the customers of the firm, with this interaction growing stronger when moving from an MTS to an MTO situation. Deciding on whether a company should produce to stock, make to order, or assemble products to order can be considered a choice of strategic importance [12, 18]. It is also a decision that strongly affects the way a company carries out its manufacturing planning and control activities [3].

This paper focuses on ATO manufacturing and its managerial implications. It discusses reasons for selecting this manufacturing policy, identifies several problem areas specifically related to manufacturing planning and control, discusses ways to solve these problems, and illustrates some of the decision areas with actual industry applications. Finally, the needs for future research in the area are identified.

ASSEMBLE-TO-ORDER MANUFACTURING

ATO manufacturing is a strategy for which standard parts, components, and subassemblies are acquired or manufactured according to forecasts, while schedules for remaining components, subassemblies, and final assembly are not executed until detailed product specifications have been derived from booked customer orders. The strategy can, thus, be located between MTS manufacturing, where products are sold "off the shelf," and MTO manufacturing, where the products are designed and produced under close collaboration between manufacturer and customer. Several essential relative characteristics of the three strategies are listed in Table 1.

MTS and MTO represent two "pure" manufacturing strategies, while ATO is a hybrid strategy. It is likely that most companies originate as either MTS or MTO firms and later, if ever, "graduate" into the ATO stage. A company starting out as an MTO firm may choose to get into ATO manufacturing because of an expanding volume and a strong similarity between some of its products. The move to ATO, thus, is done in order to capitalize on an increased demand and the possibility of reducing customer delivery times for a subset of its products.

Alternatively, an ATO firm may previously have been producing to stock. Pressured by market considerations it might have steadily broadened its product lines. A wider variety of products offered to the market, however, leads to some serious problems related to materials management:

1. The ability to forecast the sales of each individual product diminishes due to the decreasing sales per product whenever the product lines expand.
2. The inventory of finished goods, as a result, will tend to be unbalanced, with overstocking of some products and the inability to satisfy demand for others.
3. The increasing number of end items makes the master schedule difficult to manage.
4. The number of unique bills of material grows, leading to problems with maintenance and data storage.

These problems, which will aggravate the commonly existing conflict between the marketing and the manufacturing functions [17], sooner or later may become so severe that the strategy of ATO is chosen. By pushing the location of inventory back in the production process and only assembling products according to customer orders (Figure 1), demand uncertainty and, thus, finished goods inventory can be reduced. In order to achieve these benefits, however, the master scheduling system must be changed, the bills

TABLE 1
Relative Characteristics of MTS, ATO, and MTO Firms

Aspect	Make-To-Stock	Assemble-To-Order	Make-To-Order
Interface between production function and customer.	Low	Medium	High
Customer delivery time.	Short	Medium	Long
Production volume of each sales unit.	High	Medium	Low
Width of product line.	Medium	High	Low
Basis for production planning and scheduling.	Forecast	Forecast and backlog	Backlog
Order Promising.	Based on available finished goods inventory	Based on availability of major subassemblies and components	Based on available capacity for manufacturing and engineering
Handling of demand uncertainty.	Safety stocks of sales units	Overplanning of components and subassemblies	Little uncertainty exists
Master Scheduling unit.	Sales unit	Major components and subassemblies	End products, major subassemblies, or stocked fabricated parts
Final Assembly Schedule.	Close correspondence to the Master Schedule	Determined by customer orders received by Order Entry	Covers most of the assembly operations
Bill of Material Structuring.	Standard B/Ms (one B/M for each sales item)	Planning B/Ms are used	B/Ms are unique and created for each customer order

of material restructured, the order entry procedures revised, and a new system for final assembly scheduling devised. Thus, the "front end" of the manufacturing planning and control system needs to be redesigned. There is also another important trade-off that a company has to make if it previously was an MTS manufacturer: in order to reduce its demand uncertainty for finished products, it must increase its customer delivery times. Whether this is acceptable or not depends upon to what extent speed of delivery is a competitive weapon and what type of customer service other companies are offering to the market. Even if delivery times will increase under ATO, the reliability of promised shipping dates are likely to increase as well and this can counter or dominate the previous effect.

FIGURE 1
A Materials Flow Diagram for an ATO Company

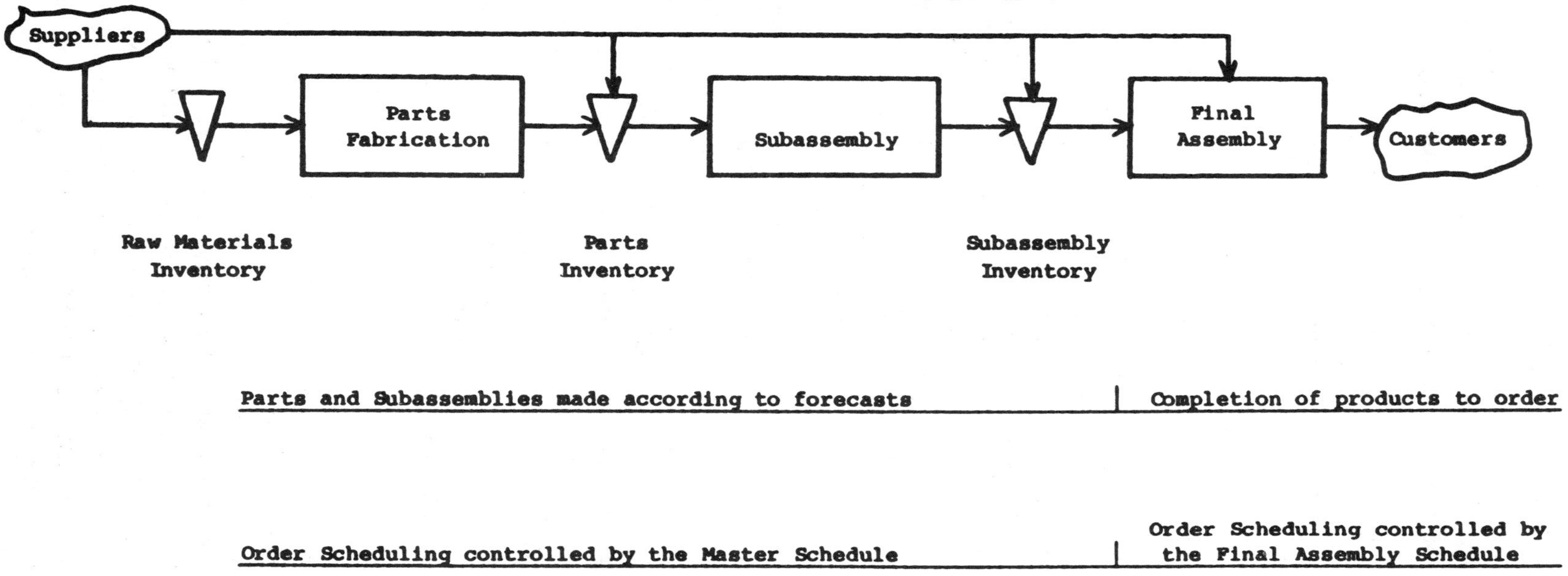

The basic philosophy behind ATO manufacturing is to defer "as long as possible" the commitment of material and capacity to any product, and thereby increase the flexibility of combining components and subassemblies to meet each customer order specification. The study of ATO manufacturing can conveniently be grouped into four areas—one covering the acquisition of material and the production of parts and subassemblies, another covering the interaction between the production system and the market, a third covering the assembly of the sales products, and the fourth covering the demand uncertainty aspect. Of particular interest in the first area are the design of the master scheduling system, the structuring of the bills of material, and the concomitant redefinition of the items to be forecast. The second area encompasses the order entry/order promising procedures, and the interface between the order entry, master scheduling, final assembly scheduling, and the forecasting systems. The third area deals with the design of the final assembly scheduling system. Lastly, ways to mitigate the effects of forecast errors related to customer options are treated in the fourth area.

Each of these critical areas will be further analyzed below. Due to the way the material is presented, some overlapping of the areas is unavoidable.

MASTER SCHEDULING AND BILLS OF MATERIAL STRUCTURING FOR THE ATO FIRM

One of the distinctive features of ATO manufacturing is the existence of two kinds of production schedules: the master schedule (that controls the availability of components and subassemblies, most of which are not committed to specific customers), and the final assembly schedule (that mainly relies on available components and subassemblies and controls the completion of the products, most of which are already sold). By definition, the master scheduling units for the ATO firm are located between the two extreme points represented by the raw materials/purchased components on the one hand and the final products on the other.

There are two major issues related to the design and operation of planning systems for materials (and capacity) that must be addressed by an ATO company:

1. What is the appropriate level, in a product structure sense, at which to forecast demand and to master schedule? That is, where should the "break-point" between the master schedule and the final assembly schedule be located?
2. How should the bills of material be structured in order to be compatible with the selected master schedule items and the final assembly process?

Each of these issues will be discussed in turn.

Choice of Master Scheduling Units

The master schedule represents one of the major information inputs to the material requirements planning (MRP) explosion in which requirements for lower level items are determined. Theoretically, there is a wide variety of choices for the master scheduling unit, ranging from each individual part in the inventory file to each completed sales unit. The selection depends upon many factors, such as the design of the products and how they are assembled, the extent to which common parts and subassemblies exist between various sales items, the number of master scheduling units considered to be manageable, and the ability to adequately forecast the demand for the master scheduling units. Market considerations will also have an influence, since the choice of master scheduling units will determine final assembly lead times and, therefore, customer delivery times. The primary principle used in the design of master scheduling systems is to reduce the number of scheduled units as much as possible [2, 13]. Companies in MTS, MTO and ATO situations will, therefore, position their master schedules at different levels relative to the product structures of the sales items.

Proliferation of marketable products is, for any firm, often based upon the ability to combine major components and subassemblies to generate a multitude of products. Major subassemblies are ideal as master scheduling units for ATO purposes since (a) there are only a few of them in every finished product (thus, if commonality of components and subassemblies exists between end items, the forecasting and the master scheduling effort can be reduced) and (b) they are close to the finished product, i.e., the assembly lead time and, therefore, the delivery time can be held short.

Structuring the Bills of Material

The term "bill of material structuring" usually refers to the restructuring of bills, from standard bills of material, unique to each sales item, to a situation where the modular concept of structuring is used. Modularization of bills of material entails the breaking down of products into "options," or "modules," which, in various combinations, determine the final products [4, 8, 13]. Each module consists of stand-alone subassemblies, or of kits of parts that cannot be put together until final assembly. Choosing the appropriate master scheduling unit affects the way the bills of material are structured, and vice versa (as indicated by the title of Mather's article, "Which Comes First—the Bill of Material or the Master Production Schedule?" [9]), since each master scheduling unit is also the highest level item in a bill of material.

For illustrative purposes, a simplified example (which will be used throughout the article) is shown in Table 2. The product in question is a bicycle. A customer can choose the number of gears, the kind of frame and rims, and the type of saddle. All other parts are common to all models. With three types of gears available, and two options in each of the other option groups, the possible number of different bicycles that can be manufactured is $3 \times 2 \times 2 \times 2$, or 24. Using standard bills of materials, then, 24 of these must be maintained, 24 different forecasts must be derived, and 24 different master schedules must be used.

A planning bill of material for the bike production can be devised, as illustrated in Table 3 [9, 13]. A planning bill is used for materials (and capacity) planning only, and does not represent a buildable end item. The umbrella unit can be thought of as an aggregate, or basic, bicycle, i.e., the manufactured product with no distinguishing traits assigned to it. If this unit is master scheduled, the schedule would tell only the number of bicycles that are planned to be produced per period over the planning horizon, and not the specific models. Each option group is represented on the next lower level of the bill and each choice has a percentage figure associated with it (the bills of material for each option are not shown). For example, the planning bill in Table 3 indicates that 15% of all products sold are expected to be 3-speed bikes, etc. It should be noted that not all modules are buildable. The gear module, for example, consists of individual parts that are mounted on the bicycle during final assembly. Also note that parts which are included

TABLE 2
Customer Options for a Bicycle

Gears	Frames	Saddles	Rims	Common Parts
—3 speed	—steel	—standard	—steel	—tires
—5 speed	—aluminum	—racing model	—aluminum	—brakes
—10 speed				—etc.
	2 choices	2 choices	2 choices	
3 choices				No choice

in all bicycles, irrespective of optional choices, have been put together in a common parts module.

With this kind of setup, the 24 different master scheduling units have been reduced to one. The advantage of this approach becomes clear if the following example is considered. Assume the company wants to offer tires as an option group. There would be two choices: standard tires and racing tires. With standard bills of material the total number of distinct bills would increase from 24 to 48. Under the planning bill approach, there would still only be one. Even if each option were individually master scheduled, the number of distinct bills would only increase from 10 to 12. For a realistic problem the savings in terms of forecasting effort, master scheduling, and bills of material maintenance could be substantial. Garwood cites an example where modularization reduced the number of bills of material from a possible 138,000 standard bills down to 40 modular bills for a specific product model [4].

Disentangling the Bills of Material

The most common problem related to bill of material structuring, and, therefore, to master scheduling, is probably the problem of "disentangling." When trying to separate standard bills into modular bills, there exist lower level items in the standard bills that are common to two or more of the options that the customers will be able to select, once the bills have been restructured. As an example, assume three end item configurations: A, B, and C (Table 4). End item A uses option 1 of option group 1 while end item B uses option 2 of option group 4. End item C, on the other hand, is made up from both

TABLE 3
A Planning Bill for Bicycle Production

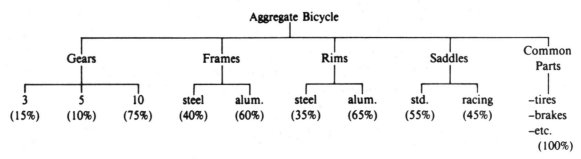

TABLE 4
An Illustration of the "Disentangling" Problem

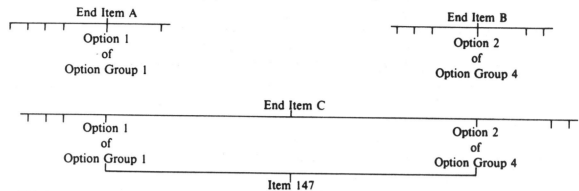

EXAMPLE: 60% of all end items consist of Option 1 and 60% of Option 2. This could mean that 40% of the end items are of type A, 40% of type B, and 20% of type C. That is, item 147 is needed in only 20% of the units sold.

these options, and, in addition, item 147 is needed in order to complete the assembly. The problem, then, is the following: even if p% of the products sold contain option 1 of group 1 and s% contain option 2 of group 4, the percentage that contains the combination is obviously not more than the minimum of p and s, and can actually be much lower. Connections between options must be broken when creating modularized planning bills, and this must be done with consideration to the materials ordering function of the bill of material.

One solution to the example presented above is to include item 147 in the bill of material for one of the options and, therefore, overplan the usage of this item. If the item is a fabricated part, it might be redesigned to achieve a wider usage or perhaps be eliminated by redesigning the parent parts. If item 147 is an assembled item, it could be split into its next lower level parts of which some might always be used with the first option and the others with the second. The disadvantage with this approach, besides the overplanning of material that still would occur, is that it is not possible to completely assemble item 147 that is called out by the planning bill. This is an effect that is not desirable too far down in the structure since the result eventually could be just a set of individual parts. Finally, the alternative to elevate this part to a master scheduling unit status obviously exists [13].

ORDER ENTRY/ORDER PROMISING

The order entry function serves as the link between the market and the productive system. The information it receives dictates the content of the final assembly schedule, the consumption of the finished goods inventory (if any), and the revisions of the master schedule. One pertinent managerial issue in this area for an ATO firm is the following:

What procedures are needed in order to be able to book and guarantee a customer order delivery? That is, how is order promising related to the material and capacity planning systems?

Procedures for Order Booking

Delivery performance can be measured along several dimensions. Two of the most important ones are speed and dependability. That is, how fast can the company ship an order, and how reliable is the promised shipping date? The latter variable will be discussed first.

A number of steps must be taken to ensure that a promised delivery date can be upheld:

1. Components and subassemblies that make up the customer specified product must be available in time for the final assembly operation.
2. If the components and subassemblies needed are not available at the time of booking, it must be ensured that needed capacity for fabrication and subassembly is created and that, if necessary, raw materials and component parts are acquired from outside sources.
3. Enough capacity must be available in the assembly and the testing/final inspection areas to ensure the on-time delivery.

In short, the prerequisite for reliable order promising is a reliable production planning and control system. Put more succinctly, an ATO company's delivery performance depends to a large extent on an executable master schedule and on a final assembly capacity that is in balance with the fabrication/subassembly process. To this end, the MRP system and various capacity management techniques can be used, coupled with a production activity control system for retrieving feedback information for the planning process [13, 22]. Of course, external disturbances, such as late vendor deliveries or changes in customer order specifications, will complicate an already difficult task.

If capacity planning has been satisfactorily performed, so that there is a high likelihood that the master schedule can be executed and sufficient capacity is available in the final assembly area, then order booking can be done solely against the master schedule. If a finished goods inventory or an uncommitted portion of the final assembly schedule should exist, these are, of course, consulted first.

When a sales order has been received, it has to be translated into specifications suitable for manufacturing [4, 13]. The options that the customers select are not always options that appear in the bills of material (even if this has been the case in the bicycle example discussed earlier). Rather, a combination of customer options are often needed to call out the correct material needed for assembly. Commonly, the customer will have fewer options to select than the number of master schedule modules needed to build the product.

Continuing with the bicycle example from Tables 2 and 3, a customer order for 100 racing bicycles would at order entry be translated into the need for 100 kits of common parts, 100 sets of racing saddles, 100 sets of 10-speed gears, and 100 sets each of aluminum frames and rims. The availability of the options would then, manually or by computer, be checked against the master schedule records. Parts that are controlled by the final assembly schedule (paint and decals, for example) are omitted at this time. In order to speed up the order booking procedure, components and subassemblies not considered "key" items can also be disregarded at this point. The earliest delivery date that can be quoted depends on the availability of material of all major options specified in the customer order. After each has been checked, the delivery date is set by the restricting option.

Customer service in terms of speed, i.e., how fast a shipment can be promised, is directly related to the ability to forecast the demand of various options and to have the needed material available. (There is also a type of speed related to how fast a company can respond to a customer order inquiry. This response time depends largely on the efficiency of the order booking procedures discussed above.) Another factor is the company's policy with respect to order backlogs. A long backlog of customer orders is desirable since it reduces the need to estimate the demand. The length of the backlog will, however, affect the delivery time and is therefore an important element in the customer service decision. To guard against forecast errors, buffering techniques can be employed as discussed later.

Order Entry and Time-Phased Master Schedule Records

If booking of customer orders takes place against master schedule quantities, it is natural to display both the master schedule and the actual orders in the same document. A clear identification of the uncommitted part of the master schedule undoubtedly facilitates order promising. Separate master schedule documents for aggregate units, options, and common parts kits are, furthermore, helpful to both master scheduling and order promising. Table 5 illustrates a set of time-phased records useful for this kind of two-level master scheduling [7, 15].

The top record shows the master schedule for the basic product, in this case a bicycle. Also displayed is the actual number of sold bicycles to be shipped in each period, as well as the number of units that are available to promise (ATP). The ATP-variable measures the uncommitted portion of each master schedule quantity. ATP calculations can be performed in different ways. One way is to start from the back end of the time-phased record by subtracting the actual demand for each period from the master schedule quantity that will cover them. If the difference is negative, as for period 2, ATP is set to zero and the net difference is made up from production in earlier periods (for more detail on ATP calculations, see [6, 15]).

The bottom record contains information related to one of the bicycle options, in this case the aluminum frame. This option has a forecast usage of 60%, i.e., out of 100 bicycles sold 60 are expected to have aluminum frames (also see [14]). The master schedule for frames is, in this example, set to 60% of the master schedule for the aggregate unit. The Production Forecast row shows the forecast demand for options. This data changes with the number of booked orders. In period 5, for example, there are only 27 units left to sell if the first-level master schedule is kept firm. With 60% of these expected to have aluminum frames, the production forecast for this option in period 5 is 0.60 × 27, or 17 units (for simplicity, all lead times are zero in this example and all numbers are rounded up to the nearest integer). The Projected Available Balance row is filled out just as in a standard MRP record, with the gross requirement per period being the sum of the actual demand and the production forecast (independent demand for spare parts can, of course, also be entered into these records [15]). The ATP quantities are found as earlier outlined. One difference in this second-level record is that a small inventory exists. This quantity is added to the ATP quantity for the first period.

The booking of a customer order can, with these records, take place in the following

TABLE 5
Time-Phased Records for Two-Level Master Scheduling

Aggregate Unit: the Bicycle	Period				
	1	2	3	4	5
Master Schedule	60	60	50	50	50
Actual Demand	54	63	36	38	23
Available to Promise	3	0	14	12	27

Option: Aluminum Frame, 60%		Period				
		1	2	3	4	5
Production Forecast		2	0	9	8	17
Actual Demand		30	39	24	20	12
Proj. Avail. Bal.	2	6	3	0	2	3
Available to Promise		5	0	6	10	18
Master Schedule		36	36	30	30	30

way: Assume a customer places an order for ten bicycles, of which seven come with aluminum frames. The master schedule record for bicycles indicates that an order of this magnitude cannot be shipped until period 3, although a partial delivery of three bicycles could be made immediately. Assuming that a split shipment is not desirable, the master scheduler proceeds to check the common parts record as well as each of the option records for material availability in period 3. The ATP row for the frame option in Table 5 shows that six frames can be shipped in that period. There are also, however, five uncommitted units in period 1. Thus, a total of 11 frames are available at the time of booking for shipment in period 3. (Clearly, a cumulative ATP row can facilitate order promising.) If the remaining options are available in sufficient quantity in this period, the order for ten bicycles can be booked.

The result of recording the customer order consisting of ten bicycles with seven aluminum frames is shown in Table 6. The Actual Demand row has been changed in both records, by entering ten units for the basic bicycle in period 3, and by entering seven units for the frames in the same period. With firm master schedule quantities, the number of units open for sale must be reduced accordingly. This change is reflected in the ATP rows of both records. Further, with only four more bicycles available in period 3, the production forecast for aluminum frames for this period is reduced to 4 × 0.60, or three units. Finally, the projected on-hand inventory balance for frames indicates a shortage in period 3, should the production forecast be realized. This will make the

TABLE 6
Revised MS Records Due to Order Booking

Aggregate Unit: the Bicycle	Period				
	1	2	3	4	5
Master schedule	60	60	50	50	50
Actual demand	54	63	46	38	23
Available to promise	3	0	4	12	27

Option: Aluminum Frame, 60%		Period				
		1	2	3	4	5
Production forecast		2	0	3	8	17
Actual demand		30	39	31	20	12
Proj. Avail. Bal.	2	6	3	−1	1	2
Available to promise		4	0	0	10	18
Master schedule		36	36	30	30	30

master scheduler aware that a change in the master schedule for this option might be necessary.

Fractional Requirements

One problem that is directly tied to the usage of percentage factors in the disaggregation process is the question of how to handle fractional requirements. For example, all values in the Production Forecast rows in Tables 5 and 6 have individually been rounded up to the nearest integer before they were entered. This procedure can largely overstate the requirements for options and lower level parts, especially if the fractional requirements are small to begin with. One way to solve this problem is to consider the exact cumulative production forecast and make sure that it is covered by an integer schedule at all times. This approach is illustrated in Table 7.

FINAL ASSEMBLY SCHEDULING

The final assembly schedule is the ultimate production schedule by which each end product's configuration is determined. The schedule has a shorter planning horizon, a shorter planning period, and a higher revision frequency than the master schedule. Thus, the final assembly schedule directs, commonly per hour or per day, the assembly of finished products over a one or two-week period. Also, it often initiates the ordering of materials not included in the master schedule. For example, high cost or bulky items

TABLE 7
A Method for Handling Fractional Requirements in Time-Phased MS Records

	Period				
	1	2	3	4	5
Exact production forecast	1.2	3.9	3.3	6.1	2.4
Cumulative exact production forecast	1.2	5.1	8.4	14.5	16.9
Cumulative integer production forecast	2	6[a]	9	15	17
Production forecast entered in the MS record	2	4[b]	3	6	2
Excess cumulative quantity	0.8	0.9[c]	0.6	0.5	0.1

Key:
[a] 6 = smallest integer larger, or equal to, 5.1
[b] 4 = 6 − 2 = difference between two consecutive cumulative integer forecasts
[c] 0.9 = 6 − 5.1 = difference between the cumulative integer forecast and the cumulative exact forecast, i.e., the overplanned quantity

with short lead times can be called out by the assembly schedule. Two issues are of particular interest to ATO manufacturers:

1. How is the final assembly schedule created and what is its relationship to the master schedule and order entry?
2. There comes a time when the likelihood of selling the uncommitted part of the master schedule is very small. What impact will this have on the final assembly schedule?

Creating the Final Assembly Schedule

The preparation of the final assembly schedule should be performed by the master schedulers, who have the best knowledge of the status of the master schedule. Often, the making of the assembly schedule simply consists of transferring the booked orders from the master schedule and sequencing them. Unique bills of material for the final operations, based on the customer order specifications, are then needed to create pick lists for the components and subassemblies of each final product. The same manufacturing bills of material are, of course, also needed to describe the final product for assembly instruction purposes. Orders for which material is missing are usually not entered into the final schedule.

The Dynamics of Master Scheduling in an ATO Firm

As the master schedule rolls through time, it will, in succession, lead to the ordering of purchased material, initiate fabrication and the subassembling of parts, and finally reach the point where the schedule must be closed and replaced by the final assembly schedule. One interesting management problem relates to the explicit or implicit time-fence set by the assembly lead time. If not all of the aggregate units in the first-level master schedule have been committed to customer orders at this stage, a decision must be made whether to drop the uncommitted portion from the schedule or build units to stock. If the latter alternative is chosen, someone must decide (usually marketing) which units to produce out of all the variants possible. These decisions are especially significant for firms whose products are too costly to rework once they have been completed.

BUFFERING TECHNIQUES FOR ATO FIRMS

Protection against demand uncertainty logically takes place where the demand is forecast. Thus, for an ATO company, buffers should exist at the option level in the planning bills of material. By keeping buffer stocks of optional components and subassemblies but not of common parts, the flexibility to meet various customer order specifications increases, while the maximum production volume of finished products is unchanged.

Several alternative buffering techniques are possible in connection with planning bills of material. The buffers that are introduced affect the second-level master schedule either directly or indirectly, depending on how this master schedule is determined. Three different ways of creating the master schedule are proposed here:

1. The master schedule on the option level is found as a percentage factor multiplied by the master schedule for the aggregate unit.
2. The master schedule quantities on the option level are found for each period as the sum of the production forecast and the actual demand.
3. The master schedule on the option level is a set of firm planned orders determined by a master scheduler. The information in the Project Available Balance row will play an instrumental role in determining the master schedule.

Given these approaches to master scheduling, a number of ways to buffer against uncertainty can be suggested:

1. Increase the master schedule for the aggregate unit.
2. Increase the percentage factor that determines the master schedule for the option from the aggregate master schedule.
3. Increase the lower level master schedule directly.
4. Increase the percentage factor that determines the production forecast for the option.
5. Increase the production forecast directly.
6. Maintain a safety stock of options that is subtracted from the current on-hand inventory when the Projected Available Balance row is determined.
7. Create buffer stocks by the use of a hedging technique.

The first technique is clearly not recommended since it leads to an unintentional overstatement of the total production volume. Even if the actual aggregate output level is, in fact, kept at its original level, this approach will overplan for all options, as well as for common parts. A disadvantage with the second and the third techniques is that they do not automatically recognize the decreased uncertainty every time an order is booked and the forecast is consumed. Thus, if the master schedule for the aggregate unit is fully booked, there is obviously no need to overplan at the option level [8, 10].

The fourth alternative will automatically account for the reduction in uncertainty by the way the production forecasts are calculated. In the bicycle example presented earlier (Tables 5 and 6), the master schedule for the frames was initially found as the percentage factor multiplied by the master schedule for the basic unit. As time goes by and orders are booked, the discrepancy between the original forecast and the actual outcome will become evident from the Projected Available Balance row. Positive numbers in this row can be viewed as buffers against demand exceeding the production forecast. Thus, if overplanning using the percentage factors does not take place, the Projected Available Balance row will make any unplanned inventory clearly visible. On the other hand, if overplanning through the percentage factors is taking place, the buffer should be reflected in a positive projected on-hand inventory (also see Hyster in [2]). The fifth method is similar to the previous one, except that it requires manual intervention from the master scheduler.

The sixth technique is straightforward. It simply adjusts the on-hand inventory balance so that the safety stock quantity is preserved. The method is only viable if the master schedule is determined from the Projected Available Balance information. Further, to use the technique it should be desirable to physically store the material that constitutes the option in question.

The seventh and last method can most adequately be described as a "buffering philosophy" and can as such be used in conjunction with all techniques mentioned above, except number six. Normally, forecast accuracy diminishes the further out in the future one tries to forecast. For the near future, on the other hand, companies can many times rely on backlogs, making forecast information unnecessary. This indicates that buffers, if entered into the master schedule, should vary over the planning horizon and be positively correlated with the distance to the period being forecast. Also, the further out in the master schedule the buffer appears, the less expensive is it to maintain the resulting safety stock. This is due to the way in which value is added to the products during the manufacturing process. If a buffer quantity is added to the master schedule just inside the total cumulative production lead time, and kept in the same relative position over time, the effect is restricted to a build-up of purchased material. If the buffer is moved closer in, the production of parts and subassemblies is instigated [10].

Hedging as a buffering technique, then, means that varying buffer levels are kept over the planning horizon. The technique can obviously be practiced in various ways, one of the simplest being the approach of maintaining a constant buffer outside a certain time fence, and no buffer inside the fence. It should be observed that the technique is self-purging. If, for example, a hedge is maintained in the same relative position in the master schedule and the material that has been ordered as a result of the hedge is not consumed, the material build-up will disappear during the next MRP explosion (see Miller [11] for a closer discussion of the consequences of hedging).

CASE ILLUSTRATIONS

The discussion related to the design aspects of ATO manufacturing planning and control systems can be enriched by also illustrating alternative solutions taken from industrial firms. The cited examples touch upon all areas discussed earlier. They do not intend to illustrate either good or bad management practices—just alternative management practices.

Illustration 1

ATO manufacturing can lead to an excessive number of master schedule units if too many options are controlled directly by the master schedule. One company's solution to this problem is presented below [19].

The Volvo Truck Division in Sweden had experienced a rapid and almost exponential growth in master scheduling units over a number of years. In some cases, up to four different options selectable by the customer had to be combined before the complete material requirements were determined. For example, in order to know the material specifications for brakes, it was necessary to know not only the brake type option, but also the wheel dimension and whether left hand or right hand drive had been selected. Another example: to call out the material needed for the rear lights of the truck, the rear light option and the wheel base option were needed. These two options in combination would specify the contents of a third module, consisting of fasteners and cables of varying lengths. In order to reduce the ever increasing number of such master scheduled "combination options," an ABC analysis was performed on all inventory items. It turned out that 50% of the items accounted for only 2.4% of the annual usage and 70% of the items accounted for 7.5% of the annual usage, etc. It was further found that eliminating 70% of the low usage parts from the MRP system reduced the number of master scheduling units by 50% (at the time, the number of items in the master schedule was well over 6,000). The removed parts were put on reorder point systems and the change has led not only to simplified master scheduling but also to an increased availability of the parts that previously were master scheduled.

Illustration 2

It is possible to combine the demand forecasting of options with standard bills of materials, as is illustrated by this case. It is also shown, however, that this interesting approach, in general, produces a less favorable customer service level than does the planning bill approach.

Creating modular bills of material is necessary in order to reduce the number of master scheduling units. An obvious trade-off is the effort involved in the restructuring of the bills of material. Further, since planning bills are simply umbrella units that hold together numerous modules, another set of bills of material is needed to direct the assembly of these modules and thus the completion of the products. In order to avoid the bill of material restructuring problem, one electric company developed what they call a "product characteristic forecasting" procedure for their low volume items that involves the use of standard bills of material [1]. The method will be illustrated here by using the bicycle example from Table 3. Assume that the aggregate forecast calls for a production of 100 bicycles per week. Assume further that the forecast for options shows that 15% of the sales represent 3-speed bikes, 10% are 5-speed bikes, and 75% are 10-speed bikes, etc. The complete option forecast is shown in the bottom row of Table 8. Also assume that each of the 24 possible bicycles that can be built has a unique catalogue model number associated with it (for simplicity, these numbers run consecutively from 1 through 24 in Table 8). It can be shown, using a fairly simple allocation procedure [1], that it is enough to master schedule only six of the 24 different bicycles, with quantities given in the rightmost column of Table 8, in order to ensure the availability of the material needed to meet the forecasts (the procedure does not always generate unique solutions).

TABLE 8
An Illustration of the "Production Characteristics" Forecasting Procedure

Catalogue Model Number	Gears			Frame		Rims		Saddle		Quantity needed/week
	3	5	10	Steel	Alum	Steel	Alum	Std	Racing	
1	×			×		×		×		15
2		×			×	×		×		10
3	×				×		×		×	
4			×	×		×			×	10
⋮										
10		×			×	×		×		
11			×	×			×		×	15
⋮										
20			×		×		×		×	20
21	×			×			×		×	
⋮										
24			×		×		×	×		30
	15%	10%	75%	40%	60%	35%	65%	55%	45%	100 units/week

Check: 40 steel frames are needed per week. They will be ordered as follows:

    15 through catalogue model # 1
    10 through catalogue model # 4
    <u>15 through catalogue model #11</u>
    40 steel frames

The advantages of this procedure for the company are the following: the firm can keep its standard bills of material, one for each of the 24 bicycles, and the restructuring effort is avoided; and, there is no need to forecast sales of each individual catalogue model. Instead, only the product characteristics (the options) and the total number of units sold are forecast. Since forecasting takes place at a higher level of aggregation, it is likely that the forecast accuracy will increase. It should be noted that the intention is not to build the units that are entered into the master schedule. The reason for scheduling these units is only to order lower level material. The method, thus, does not eliminate the final assembly schedule based on acccepted customer orders.

King, who calls this procedure "the covering set" approach (since the standard bills chosen to be master scheduled completely cover the total material requirements), has investigated its mechanics in his dissertation and also compared the method to the planning bill approach described earlier [6]. His hypothesis is that since common parts can be planned separately and do not require any safety stock when ordered through planning bills, this method leads to higher customer service (i.e., shorter delivery lead time) for the same safety stock investment than does the covering set approach. The reason for this is that common parts are overplanned with the latter method since they are represented in each product. As a matter of fact, all options in a product will be overplanned if its master schedule quantity is increased. For example, assume that in order to buffer against forecast errors related to 3-speed gears, 5 more bikes of catalogue model number 1 are master scheduled per week. The result of this will be more protection for steel frames, steel rims, and standard saddles, as well as for 3-speed gears (see Table 8), but it will also increase the inventory of common parts. This inventory is redundant if the aggregate output is fixed to 100 units per week. King's simulation study confirms that, for the same amount of buffer inventory, the planning bill approach outperforms the covering set approach in a variety of environments [6].

Illustrations 3 and 4

The following case examples show the ways two ATO firms have resolved some design issues in the areas of master scheduling, order promising, and final assembly scheduling [21].

The Trane Company

The Trane Company is a large manufacturer of heating and cooling equipment. It master schedules 471 models, each with its own two-level percentage bill of material. (A two-level percentage bill is a planning bill of material that addresses the option-within-option problem. Thus, the master schedules for options appearing at levels 1 and 2 in the product structure are determined by percentage factors multiplied by the respective parent master schedules.) The company has dedicated production lines to ensure the availability of key parts and subassemblies. These 450 key items, which appear as lower level items in the planning bills of material, are master scheduled by using the firm planned order capability of the MRP program. This means that the MRP explosion will not change the timing and sizing of the manually determined planned order releases for these items. In effect, then, master scheduling takes place at several levels in the bills of material. This achieves smoothed production rates for the key items, with accompanied high rates of schedule completions and high levels of capacity utilization.

A customer that orders a unit that is not stocked by Trane must normally choose a configuration based on 23 classes of options. A unique bill of material is created for each customer order. This bill is exploded into its parts and the parts list is given to the master schedulers. It is their task to check the availability of critical components (by consulting the master schedules) before a shipping date for the order can be set. All critical items checked in this way are scheduled using the firm planned order technique referred to earlier.

The company operates with a 12 week time fence. Outside this time fence the master schedule consists of a mixture of confirmed orders and forecasts. Explosion of this part of the master schedule takes place through the planning bills of material. However, once inside the 12 week time fence only booked customer orders exist on the master schedule. Thus, all uncommitted units are eliminated from the schedule at this time and the remaining booked orders are exploded through their exact bills of material.

The making of the final assembly schedule at Trane is the responsibility of the master schedulers. The schedule extends for one month, is made up monthly, and is mostly very close to the master schedule on which it is based. The execution of the final assembly schedule is monitored daily with progress reports. Minor revisions to the schedule take place continuously due to problems in manufacturing, insufficient material or capacity, or due to customer generated changes in shipping dates.

Steelcase, Inc.

Steelcase, Inc. is a multi-plant office furniture manufacturer operating in a repetitive manufacturing mode. Unlike Trane, it uses a two-level master scheduling system. This system, however, differs from the one described in Tables 5 and 6 in that ATP information is not used in connection with the schedule that represents the input to the MRP system. Instead, the second-level master schedule is dynamically adjusted by letting the master schedule quantities per period equal the sum of the actual demand and the production forecast. That is, if this approach was used in Table 5, the resulting master schedule for the frame over the planning horizon would be 32, 39, 33, 28, and 29 units, respectively.

The company has a sophisticated computerized order scheduling system that ties together different product lines produced at a number of local plants. If a customer order consists of products from several plants, the order scheduling system checks the first availability date for all products in the order before a shipping date is set. The complete customer order is later consolidated and shipped from a central warehouse.

For each plant, customer orders are booked against the overall production plan and against master schedules for product groups (first-level master schedules). These plans and schedules are stated in an aggregate unit of capacity. Over and under bookings at the production plan level are accepted within a +5% to a −2% range while a ±10% deviation is allowed at the product group level. No check of available material takes place before order acceptance.

Steelcase uses a cyclic scheduling system for final assembly operations. This means that a fixed schedule, covering the day the scheduling procedure starts (last day in each week for new order entries) and until the orders are shipped 15 working days later, is repeated every week. Five of these days are used for detailed order preparation and order scheduling, and the rest are used for subassembly of parts, finishing operations, and packing. Daily computerized production schedules are created for each department, outlining the operations to be performed and the quantities needed. These schedules are tied together in a cyclical fashion so that parts that are welded one day can be painted the next day and assembled the third day, etc. Since the high volume production involves relatively simple products, based on standard parts with high commonality, parts and subassemblies are not tied to particular customer orders until the very end of the assembly process. Manufacturing for stock usually takes place if the production plan and the product group master schedules are booked short of their lower target levels, comes the cut-off time for the final assembly schedule generation.

Illustration 5

Buffering against demand uncertainty at the master schedule level can obviously be done in many different ways—including using no buffers at all. At the Trane Company and Steelcase, Inc., for example, overplanning of options do not take place. The company discussed below, on the other hand, is an interesting example of how one ATO manufacturer manages its buffers.

The Tennant Company, a manufacturer of industrial floor maintenance equipment, is a company that practices hedging, has visible buffers, and lets the master schedulers manage the allocation of these buffers [2]. A buffer quantity is first determined as a percentage of the sum of the master schedule quantities falling between two time fences. The buffer is manually entered into the records by the master schedulers and distributed over the same time period. The buffer is printed on a separate row in the master schedule document, making it highly visible. The computer further prints an exception message should the hedge quantity between the time fences fall short of the planned quantity. If there is no need for the buffered material, the hedges will disappear once they roll inside the closest time fence.

AREAS FOR FUTURE RESEARCH

Several fertile areas open to ATO-connected research can be identified. These areas deal with both the strategic and the operational aspects of ATO manufacturing.

1. There are potential advantages, as well as disadvantages, associated with ATO manufacturing. One major issue relates to the question of when benefits resulting from this strategy exceed the costs. That is, under what circumstances should a company start out as an ATO manufacturer, or, if already in an MTS or MTO situation, switch to this philosophy? Can the strategic consequences of increasing the customer lead time while, at the same time, offering a wider variety of products, be quantified? Can the cost of restructuring the bills of material, changing the procedures for master scheduling, order entry, and final assembly scheduling be estimated and weighted against a reduced total inventory investment (also see the research issues related to buffering)? Are there other trade-offs involved that need to be identified and evaluated?

2. The issue of bills of material structuring is crucial to ATO manufacturing. Yet very little research have been done in this area to date. For example, how should modules be defined to achieve the most versatile use (for an analytical approach to this problem, see [16]) and how is this versatility traded off against an increased number of master scheduling units? How do different approaches to structuring affect various performance measures, (see [6])? What is the impact on product proliferation from parts commonality resulting from standardizing parts and designing new products around existing modules? That is, will the solution to the problem of product proliferation create an even larger product variety? What effect will the higher production volumes made possible through an emphasis on commonality and modularization have on the manufacturing process [20]?

3. The issue of safety stocks in multi-level inventory systems is not a well researched

area. Particularly for ATO firms, two questions are of interest: What procedures should be used to dimension the buffers for various options, considering that the demands for options are not independent? Further, what is the impact of commonality on the investment in buffer stocks? It is clear that the fewer the number of stocking points, the less buffer inventory is needed for the same protection. Can this in itself be an argument for adopting the ATO strategy?

4. Final assembly scheduling is a topic that has received little attention in the literature. There seem to be, however, a few interesting issues related to the making of the assembly schedule: How to maximize the use of available material at the time the schedule is prepared? Also, how should orders be sequenced with respect to customer preference and material/manufacturing considerations?

5. A final area relates to forecasting and the consumption of forecasts in an ATO setting. The procedure for determining the production forecasts discussed earlier, a common industry approach, is clearly "memoryless." The fraction of future orders requiring a certain option is constant, irrespective of the number of units already booked. Are there other procedures for short-term forecast revisions that are more appropriate?

The scarcity of research related to the important areas outlined above indicates that despite the fact that there exists a general body of knowledge related to manufacturing planning and control systems, little research effort has been devoted to the development of normative models for systems design. This type of research is clearly needed in order to be able to determine an appropriate manufacturing strategy and in order to design planning and control systems that fit the tasks specified by the chosen strategy [12].

REFERENCES

1. Berry, W. L., R. A. Mohrman, and T. Callarman, *Master Scheduling and Capacity Planning: A Case Study,* Manufacturing Productivity Education Committee, Purdue University, 1977.

2. Berry, W. L., D. C. Whybark, and T. E. Vollmann, *Master Production Scheduling: Principles and Practice.* American Production & Inventory Control Society, 1979.

3. Collins, R. S. and T. E. Vollmann, "Manufacturing Planning and Control (MPC) Systems as Tools in Implementing Corporate Strategy," *AIDS Conference Proceedings,* 1981, 2, pp. 128–130.

4. Garwood, R. D., "Stop: Before You Use the Bill Processor," *Production and Inventory Management,* Vol. 11, No. 2, (1970), pp. 73–79.

5. Garwood, R. D., "Customer Delivery Date Promises: Fact or Fiction," *Hot List,* R. D. Garwood, Inc., 1981, 2.

6. King, B. E., *Master Production Scheduling In The Assemble To Order Environment: A Comparison Of Two Techniques,* Unpublished DBA dissertation, Graduate School of Business, Indiana University, 1979.

7. Ling, R. C., "Master Scheduling in a Make-To-Order Environment," *Inventories & Production Magazine,* July–August, 1981, pp. 17–21.

8. Ling, R. C. and K. Widmer, "Master Scheduling in a Make-To-Order Plant," *APICS Conference Proceedings,* 1974, pp. 320–334.

9. Mather, H. F., "Which Comes First, The Bill of Material or the Master Production Schedule?" *APICS Conference Proceedings,* 1980, pp. 404–407.

10. Mather, H. F. and G. W. Plossl, *The Master Production Schedule—Managements Handle On Business,* Mather & Plossl, Inc., Atlanta, 2nd ed., 1977.

11. Miller, J. G., *Hedging The Master Schedule,* Working Paper, Division of Research, Graduate School of Business Administration, Harvard University, March, 1977.

12. Miller, J. G., "Fit Production Systems to the Task," *Harvard Business Review,* January–February, 1981, pp. 145–154.

13. Orlicky, J., *Material Requirements Planning,* McGraw-Hill, Inc., New York, 1975.

14. Pinto, P. A., "Exponentially Smoothed Percentage Forecasting For MRP Systems Using Modular Bill of Materials," *AIDS Conference Proceedings,* 1979, pp. 380–382.

15. Proud, J. F., "Master Scheduling Requires Time Fences," *APICS Conference Proceedings,* 1981, pp. 61–65.

16. Rutenberg, D. P. and T. L. Shaftel, "Product Design: Subassemblies for Multiple Markets," *Management Science,* Vol. 18, No. 4, (1971), B220–B231.

17. Shapiro, B., "Can Marketing and Manufacturing Coexist?," *Harvard Business Review,* September–October, 1977, pp. 104–114.

18. Skinner, W., "Manufacturing—Missing Link for Corporate Strategy," *Harvard Business Review,* May–June, 1969, pp. 136–145.

19. Sodahl, L. O., "How Do You Master Schedule Half A Million Product Variants?," *APICS Conference Proceedings,* 1981, pp. 70–72.

20. Starr, M. K., *Operations Management,* Prentice-Hall, Inc., Englewood Cliffs, 1978.

21. Wemmerlöv, U., *Case Studies In Capacity Management,* American Production and Inventory, Society, 1984.

22. Wemmerlöv, U., *Capacity Management Techniques for Manufacturing Companies with MRP Systems,* American Production and Inventory Control Society, 1984.

CPIM Reprints

Evaluation Form

APICS is interested in your comments so that we can provide you with an educational tool from which to prepare for the CPIM certification examinations. As APICS keeps the material up-to-date, we ask for your comments regarding this material. Please respond by completing this form and sending it to:

CPIM Reprints Evaluation
APICS
500 West Annandale Road
Falls Church, VA 22046-4274

Please circle reprint: Inventory Management
Just-in-Time
Master Planning
Material and Capacity Requirements Planning
Production Activity Control
Systems and Technologies

If you have questions concerning the selection of articles or have suggestions for the inclusion of material in future editions, please provide below.

_____
_____
_____
_____
_____
_____
_____
_____
_____
_____
_____

Thank you for participating in the quality improvement process that will help APICS ensure we are providing our customers with complete educational material.